Beyond Testing:
Towards a Theory of Educational Assessment

Caroline V Gipps

 The Falmer Press
(A member of the Taylor & Francis Group)
London · Washington, D.C.

UK   The Falmer Press, 11 New Fetter Lane, London EC4P 4EE
USA   The Falmer Press, Taylor & Francis Inc., 325 Chestnut Street,
8th Floor, Philadelphia, PA19106

First published 1994
Reprinted 1995, 1998 and 2000

A catalogue record for this book is available from the British Library

Library of Congress Cataloging-in-Publication Data are available on request

ISBN 0 7507 0328 8 cased
ISBN 0 7507 0329 6 paper

Jacket design by Caroline Archer

Typeset in 11/13pt Bembo by
Graphicraft Typesetters Ltd., Hong Kong

*Printed and bound in Great Britain by
Biddles Ltd, Guildford and King's Lynn*

Contents

Acknowledgments

I should like to thank the Nuffield Foundation for the fellowship which gave me the time to write this book. As a result I was able to visit Royce Sadler, Bob Linn and Lorrie Shepard with whom I had some very formative conversations. My thanks also go to Harvey Goldstein, Peter Mortimore, Patricia Murphy and Denis Lawton for their helpful comments on the draft. I am most grateful to Louise Jordan and Amanda Claremont who have typed and edited some truly awful copy with typical cheerfulness.

Finally my thanks to Jo, Marcus and Alexander for their unfailing commitment to my work despite the absences which it involves.

Glossary

Assessment:

a wide range of methods for evaluating pupil performance and attainment including formal testing and examinations, practical and oral assessment, classroom based assessment carried out by teachers and portfolios.

Reliability:

the extent to which an assessment would produce the same, or similar, score on two occasions or if given by two assessors. This is the 'accuracy' with which an assessment measures the skill or attainment it is designed to measure.

Validity:

the extent to which an assessment measures what it purports to measure. If an assessment does not measure what it is designed it measure then its use is misleading.

Formative assessment:

takes place during the course of teaching and is used essentially to feed back into the teaching/learning process.

Summative assessment:

takes place at the end of a term or a course and is used to provide information about how much students have learned and how well a course has worked.

Ipsative assessment:

in which the pupil evaluates his/her performance against his/her previous performance.

Chapter 1

Assessment Paradigms

Introduction

Assessment is undergoing a paradigm shift, from psychometrics to a broader model of educational assessment, from a testing and examination culture to an assessment culture. There is a wider range of assessment in use now than there was twenty-five years ago: teacher assessment, standard tasks, coursework, records of achievement as well as practical and oral assessment, written examinations and standardized tests. There is criterion-referenced assessment, formative assessment and performance-based assessment, as well as norm-referenced testing. In addition, assessment has taken on a high profile and is required to achieve a wide range of purposes: it has to support teaching and learning, provide information about pupils, teachers and schools, act as a selection and certificating device, as an accountability procedure, and drive curriculum and teaching. These new forms and range of purposes for assessment mean that the major traditional model underpinning assessment theory, the psychometric model, is no longer adequate, hence the paradigm shift.

A paradigm is a set of interrelated concepts which provide the framework within which we see and understand a particular problem or activity. The paradigm within which we work determines what we look for, the way in which we construe what we observe, and how we solve emerging problems. A paradigm shift or 'scientific revolution' occurs when the old paradigm is unable to deal with an outstanding problem (Kuhn, 1970). This book is written as part of the attempt to reconceptualize assessment in education in the 1990s. There has been over the last decade an explosion of developments in assessment and a number of key actors have been reconceptualizing the issues. The aim of this book is to bring together much of this work to discuss and synthesize it in an attempt to further our understandings and practice in educational assessment: to develop the theory of educational assessment.

We need to develop a new way of thinking about assessment to deal with the issues that are emerging as assessment takes on this broader definition and purpose. For example, one outstanding problem which we have in assessment is how to reconceptualize traditional reliability (the 'accuracy' of a score) in terms of assuring quality, or warranting assessment-based conclusions, when the type of assessment being used is not designed according to psychometric principles and for which highly standardized procedures are not appropriate.

I use the term theory to refer to a vehicle for explanation and prediction, a framework that will allow us to understand, explain and predict. Theories, as devices for organizing and giving meaning to facts, are built up through the process of analytical work: abstract, conceptual analysis is the vehicle for isolating crucial dimensions and constituents. My aim is that through this analysis we will come to have a better understanding of the design, functioning, impact, as well as inappropriate uses, of assessment within the new paradigm.

It is important too, given the much wider and more significant role given to assessment, that these issues are made clear to a wider audience. This book is therefore aimed at all those who work in and around education and are interested in assessment: teachers and administrators, advisors, lecturers, policy makers and other educational researchers.[1]

In the chapters that follow I shall look at the technical issues, though at a conceptual rather than technical level, how assessment impacts on curriculum and teaching as well as its relationship with learning, criterion-referenced assessment, teacher assessment and performance assessment (and evaluate what they have to offer within the new paradigm), and questions of ethics and equity, before drawing together the analyses to put forward a framework for educational assessment. But first this chapter sets the scene by looking at purpose and fitness for purpose in assessment, the traditional psychometric paradigm and what we see as the new educational assessment paradigm.

Fitness for Purpose

I have already referred to reliability of assessment (by this we mean the extent to which an assessment would produce the same, or similar, score if it was given by two different assessors, or given a second time to the same pupil using the same assessor) which goes alongside validity (by this is meant the extent to which an assessment measures what it purports to measure) but there is more to testing and assessment than technical issues of reliability and validity. Assessments (which I use here to include tests, examinations, practicals, coursework, teacher observations and assessment) come not only in a range of forms but with different purposes and underlying philosophies; these determine the range of appropriate use for an assessment. The first question to be asked then when considering the form of assessment to be used is 'what is the assessment for?' For example assessment to support learning, offering detailed feedback to the teacher and pupil, is necessarily different from assessment for monitoring or accountability purposes (for a start it is much more detailed). We must first ask the question *'assessment for what?'* and then design the assessment programme to fit.

I take the view that the prime purpose of assessment is professional: that is assessment to support the teaching/learning process. But, government, taxpayers and parents also want to know how the education system and individual schools are performing and they must have access to such information. A major, though not the only, element of this information is pupil performance as measured by tests and examinations. Assessment carried out for these purposes is likely to be more superficial since it needs to be relatively quick and manageable and needs to be more reliable than that to support learning. One can picture it as a form of survey (using postal questionnaires) as opposed to an in-depth study (using detailed interviews). Somewhere in between these two extremes of testing to support learning or for accountability purposes lies assessment for certification purposes, as with our public exams at 16 and 18: this assessment has to be both detailed (to provide comprehensive coverage) and reasonably reliable (so that we may have confidence that the results are comparable from one school to another and from one part of the country to another) though in other countries, for example Germany, this is not seen as an issue.

The problem that we have to confront is that tests designed for purposes other than to support learning — the huge quantities of multiple choice standardized tests in the USA, and the formal written exam in the UK — have had, we now realize, unwanted and negative effects on teaching and the curriculum. The stultifying effect of public exams on the secondary system in England has been pointed out by the HMI (1979 and 1988), and was a prime mover in the shift towards GCSE with its emphasis on a broader range of skills assessed, a lessening of emphasis on the timed exam and an opening up of the exam to a broader section of the age cohort. (All of this was brought in and supported by the same government which is now retrenching to a formal, exclusive, written exam, but that is another story). The limiting and damaging effect of standardized multiple-choice tests in the USA has also been well documented and analyzed in recent years (for example, Resnick and Resnick, 1992). But assessment for monitoring and accountability purposes will not go away; on the contrary, a number of countries in the developing world are using assessment even more to gear up their education systems: in the USA, in New Zealand, in Australia as in Great Britain governments have linked economic growth with educational performance and are using assessment to help determine curriculum, to impose high 'standards' of performance and, in New Zealand and Britain, countries which have taken on board the New Right marketplace model, as a market signal to aid parental choice and competition between schools (Murphy, 1990; Willis, 1992a).

Mindful of the distorting effects of assessment for these purposes, the task assessment specialists must address is how best to design accountability assessment which will provide good quality information about pupils' performance without distorting good teaching (and therefore learning) practice. We must also explore other forms of assessment which can be used alongside accountability assessment to support learning, and criteria by which we can evaluate them. This is not to say that traditional standardized tests and examinations have no role to play in assessment policy, but that we need to design assessment programmes that will do what is required of them and have a positive impact on teaching and learning.

This brings us to the second question which should be asked, but almost never is: *what kind of learning do we wish to achieve?*' for we know now that different forms of assessment encourage, via their effect on teaching, different styles of learning. If we wish to foster higher order skills including application of knowledge, investigation, analyzing, reasoning and interpretation for *all our pupils*, not just the élite, then we need our assessment system to reflect that.

But a failure to articulate the relationship between learning and assessment has resulted 'in a mismatch between the high quality learning described in policy documents as desirable and the poor quality learning that seems likely to result from associated assessment procedures' (Willis, 1992b, p. 1).

We need to put on to the assessment agenda issues of learning style and depth. We must articulate the model of learning on which we are to base new developments in assessment over the next decade if we are to develop a sound model and one which will achieve the results we wish for it. After all, the original psychometrics was based on a theory of intelligence, while multiple choice standardized tests were based on a behaviourist model of learning: educational assessment for the next century must be based on our best current understanding of theories of learning.

In considering assessment paradigms I shall look first at the traditional psychometric model, which is where testing in education began, and then look at what has come to be called educational assessment and how it differs from the psychometric model.

Psychometrics

The science of psychometrics developed from work on intelligence and intelligence testing. The underlying notion was that intelligence was innate and fixed in the way that other inherited characteristics such as skin colour are. Intelligence could therefore be measured (since it was observable like other characteristics) and on the basis of the outcome individuals could be assigned to streams, groups or schools which were appropriate to their intelligence (or 'ability' as it came to be seen). Thus the traditional psychometric testing model was essentially one of limitation: measuring attributes which are a property of the individual and which were thought to be fixed. This notion of limitation is seen now to be a major disadvantage of the psychometric approach. Assessment to support learning, by contrast, aims to help the individual to develop and further his/her learning: it is enabling rather than limiting. Another feature of psychometrics is the interpretation of scores in relation to norms: norm-referencing grades an individual's performance in relation to that of his/her peers, that is in terms of relative performance rather than their absolute performance. Norm-referenced tests are designed to produce familiar proportions of high, medium and low scorers. Since students cannot control the performance of other students they cannot control their own grades; this is now widely considered to be an unfair approach for looking at pupils' educational performance.

With the psychometric model comes an assumption of the primacy of technical issues, notably standardization, reliability and limited dimensionality. If individuals are to be compared with one another then we need to be certain that the test or assessment was carried out in the same way for all individuals, scored in the same way and the scores interpreted in the same way. Standardization is thus vital as is the technical reliability of the test within this model. These requirements can have a negative effect on the construct validity and curricular impact of the test since only some material and certain tasks are amenable to this type of testing.

Along with psychometric theory and its formulae and quantification comes an aura of objectivity; such testing is scientific and therefore the figures it produces must be accurate and meaningful. The measurements which individuals amass via such testing: IQ scores, reading ages, rankings etc. thus come to have a powerful labelling potential.

But the psychometric paradigm has two other problematic assumptions which have been articulated more recently (Berlak *et al.*, 1992; Goldstein, 1992 and 1993).

The first is the *assumption of universality*, which means that a test score has essentially the same meaning for all individuals; this implies that a score on a standardized reading test represents the individual's ability to read (the performance is extrapolated from the test to reading in the general sense) and that what this means is universally accepted and understood.

A key factor in this argument is the 'construct'; a construct is a term used in psychology to label underlying skills or attributes. A construct is an explanatory device, so-called because it is a theoretical construction about the nature of human behaviour. In test development the construct being assessed is defined before the test is developed: this is to make sure that the test assesses the attribute that it is supposed to, that it is 'valid'. In the case of reading a detailed definition of the construct 'reading' would include accuracy and fluency in reading both aloud and silently, comprehension of material, interest in reading etc. Thus a test which had high construct validity (i.e. which actually assesses reading adequately) should address each of these aspects of the skill. In fact, standardized tests of reading tend to assess only one aspect of the reading skill, for example, comprehension of simple sentences. This means that such a standardized reading test score does not represent the individual's ability to read in the widest sense, and therefore that the meaning of the score cannot be universally understood (since the user of the score would need to know which aspect of reading had been tested).

The second assumption is that of *unidimensionality* which relates to the conceptualization of constructs and impacts on the techniques used for analyzing test items. The assumption (within psychometric theory) is that the items in a test should be measuring a single underlying attribute. Thus when items are designed for a test they are first screened for obvious biases in terms of stereotypes either in the language or the pictures. The 'pilot' test is then given to a sample of students (which should be similar in characteristics to the intended sample). Item analysis is then carried out to get rid of items which are 'discrepant' i.e. items which do not correlate highly with the total score, because the test is meant to assess only one attribute. Items which have a high correlation with the total score are said to have high 'discrimination' while those which have low correlations are poor discriminators and are usually either dropped or modified. This approach comes from factor analysis techniques and the aim with a 'good' test would be to produce one which had only one underlying factor. This practice has two effects: first it implies an artificial simplicity of measured constructs since many attributes are in fact multi-dimensional as in the example of reading given above. Second, if the original group of items chosen actually measures more than one attribute and only a few items relate to one of these attributes these few items will inevitably have low correlation with the final score and therefore be eliminated from the final test. Thus they will be excluded from the test because they are different from the rest, the majority, of the items. The result will be a test measuring a single attribute, but the interpretations made from the score to a broader conceptualization of the construct will be invalid (and the measured construct will be determined by the original choice of items which might have been balanced in the direction of the second attribute which would then become the main attribute).

Since many of the attributes or skills which we measure in tests are multi rather than unidimensional we can see that forcing tests into a unidimensional structure is illogical (Goldstein, 1993) based as it is on the unproved assumption of unidimensionality. Item response models of item analysis, including the Rasch model, are predicated on the factor analysis model assuming a single underlying factor and this is the basis of critiques of these models (see Goldstein, 1992; Goldstein and Wood, 1989).

Around the 1950s the benefits of the application of psychological measurement in educational settings producing tests such as intelligence tests (including group tests used in the 11+) aptitude tests and the like began to be questioned. This criticism of the psychometric approach had two main foci. First the notion of limitation and the belief that tests are measuring a property of the individual; its focus was, critics argued, on the degree of ineducability of the child which arises from defects in the child or his/her home and parents rather than considering problems in teaching, curriculum, etc. (Meredith, 1974, quoted in Wood, 1986; Walkerdine, 1984).

The second was that the key feature of reliability requires the standardization of administration and tasks as well as scoring. Tests based on psychometric theory have as a prime requirement measurement properties amenable to statistical analysis: reliability and norm-referencing are the prime concerns. This has profound implications for the style of task assessed, the limited ways in which tasks can be explained to pupils and the required non-interaction of the tester. As a result of having to meet these requirements, issues of validity and usefulness to teachers have sometimes been overridden or ignored.

Around the time of the publication of Bloom's *Taxonomy of*

Educational Objectives in the late 1950 educators began to articulate a need for assessment which was specifically for educational purposes and could be used in the cycle of planning, instruction, learning and evaluation. This was termed educational measurement.

Educational Measurement

Wood (1986) cites Glaser's 1963 paper on criterion-referenced testing as a watershed in the development of educational measurement i.e. the separation of educational assessment from classical psychometrics. Glaser's paper made the point that the emphasis on norm-referenced testing stemmed from the preoccupation of test theory with aptitude, selection and prediction. Wood maintains that every development in educational assessment since Glaser's criterion-referenced testing paper is based on the criterion-referenced model. As the chapter on criterion-referenced assessment will show, there are enormous problems in the development of this kind of assessment, that results from criterion-referenced assessment can also be used for norm-referenced type purposes, and indeed norms are often used to set and interpret criteria of performance. But nevertheless, the point is well made, that in order to move away from a *norm* referenced approach the only other reference we have come up with is that of criteria or standards, whether the result is described as criterion-referenced assessment, graded assessment, or standards-referenced assessment. There are different philosophies and techniques underlying these approaches but what they all have in common is that they do not interpret performance in relation to norms.

Educational measurement, by contrast with psychometrics, aims to devise tests which look at the individual as an individual rather than in relation to other individuals and to use measurement constructively to identify strengths and weaknesses individuals might have so as to aid their educational progress.

To find out 'How well' rather then 'How many' requires a quite different approach to test construction. Wood's definition of educational measurement therefore is that it:

1 deals with the individual's achievement relative to himself rather than to others;
2 seeks to test for competence rather than for intelligence;
3 takes place in relatively uncontrolled conditions and so does not produce 'well-behaved' data;
4 looks for 'best' rather than 'typical' performances;

5   is most effective when rules a[n...]
    standardized testing are relaxed;
6   embodies a constructive outlook on a[...]
    is to help rather than sentence the indi[...]

and is happy to accept that this is 'thinking not of ho[w...]
but rather of how they might or even ought to be . . . [...]
p. 194).

Where Wood uses the term competence (rather than in[t...]
he is referring to the product of education, training or other exp[...]
rather than being an inborn or natural characteristic, as intellige[...]
We could more comfortably now use 'attainment' or 'achievement[...]
He argues that a powerful reason why educational measurement should
not be based on psychometric theory is that the performances or traits
being assessed have different properties: 'achievement data arise as a
direct result of instruction and are therefore crucially affected by teaching
and teachers' (p. 190). Aptitude and intelligence, by contrast, are traits
which are unaffected by such factors, he claims. Achievement data is
therefore 'dirty' compared with aptitude data and should not/cannot be
analyzed using models which do not allow for some sort of teaching
effect.

Looking for best rather than typical performance (the fourth
principle on Wood's list) relates to Vygotsky's *zone of proximal development*. In educational assessment tester and pupil would collaborate to
produce the best performance of which the pupil is capable, given help
from an adult, rather than withholding such help to produce typical
performance.

This also relates to the competence/performance distinction: competence refers to what a person can do under ideal circumstances, while
performance refers to what is actually done under existing circumstances, competence thus includes the ability to access and utilize knowledge structures, as well as motivational, affective and cognitive factors
that influence the response. 'Thus, a student's competence might not
be revealed in either classroom performance or test performance because
of personal or circumstantial factors that affect behaviour' (Messick,
1984). Elaborative procedures are therefore required to elicit competence; examination procedures tend to produce non-elaborated performance, i.e. they test at the lower rather than upper thresholds of
performance (a profoundly non-Vygotskyian notion). This competence/
performance distinction is a useful one to make in the consideration
of educational assessment, but so that we do not get drawn into the
question of whether we can infer competence from performance (i.e.

ce) we should think instead
les his paper with a plea for
as saying something about
il; he cites their reluctance
so little use of test results
persuade teachers to trust

genda has changed in only
ajor development in edu-
ers' own classroom based
mance' or 'authentic' as-
acher is centrally involved.
centre stage as an actor in
dministrator of 'better' tests
ood was writing. Because of
educational measurement has now become called
more generally educational assessment; this is largely because 'measurement' implies a precise quantification, which is not what the educational assessment paradigm is concerned with. I shall now look at
some of the key authors who have elaborated and defined educational
assessment.

Educational Assessment

Glaser (1990) makes the case that assessment must be used in support
of learning rather than just to indicate current or past achievement.
Glaser's own work in the area of novice/expert performance indicates
that there are characteristics of learners which differentiate experts from
novices across a range of domains. 'As competence in a domain grows,
evidence of a knowledge base that is increasingly *coherent, principled,
useful* and *goal-oriented* is displayed. Assessment can be designed to
capture such evidence' (*ibid*, p. 477). 'Assessment should display to the
learner models of performance that can be emulated and also indicate
the assistance, experiences and forms of practise required by learners as
they move towards more competent performance' (*ibid*, p. 480).

The sort of assessment that Glaser has in mind here are: portfolios
of accomplishments; situations which elicit problem-solving behaviour
which can be observed and analyzed; dynamic tests that assess respon-
siveness of students to various kinds of instruction; and 'scoring
procedures for the procedures and products of reasoning'. In other
words we need a much wider range of assessment strategies to assess
a broader body of cognitive aspects than mere subject-matter acquisition

and retention (for a more detailed discussion of the nature of assessment to reflect deep learning, higher order thinking and meta-cognitive strategies, see chapter 2).

Glaser's point is that assessment must offer 'executable advice' to both students and teachers; knowledge must be assessed in terms of its constructive use for further action. 'Once mastered, the skills and knowledge of a domain should be viewed as enabling competencies for the future' (*ibid*); in other words the assessments must themselves be useful and must focus on the student's ability to use the knowledge and skills learnt.

Raven on the other hand (Berlak *et al.*, 1992) argues that we must develop assessments which assess performance in relation to valued goals, rather than separating cognitive, affective and conative factors (and indeed failing to assess the latter two). He also argues that we need approaches which assess them in a unified way, since people do not become competent in activities which they do not value. Raven's general argument, that we should move outside the cognitive, is to be welcomed and resonates with some of the ideas from cognitive science and learning theory in relation to the importance of metacognitive processes in performance.

Goldstein (1992) argues that we need to stop seeing testing as a static activity which has no effect on the pupil. On the contrary, the pupil is participating in a learning procedure, he argues, and his/her state will be altered at the end of it. For example, successfully completing early items in a test might boost confidence and result in a higher overall performance than failing, or being unable to complete, early items. Thus we should have a more interactive model of assessment which does not assume that an individual's ability to respond to items remains constant during the test. The more 'authentic' the assessment becomes, Goldstein argues, the more important it is to question the assumption that nothing happens to the student during the process of assessment.

'Authentic assessment' is a term used largely in the USA where the intention is to design assessment which moves away from the standardized, multiple-choice type test towards approaches where the assessment task closely matches the desired performance and takes place in an authentic, or classroom, context. Performance-based assessment, more commonly called performance assessment, aims to model the real learning activities that we wish pupils to engage with, for example, written communication skills and problem-solving activities, so that assessment does not distort instruction. Chapter 6 deals in detail with performance assessment, but briefly the intention in performance assessment is to capture in the test task the same demands for critical thinking and knowledge integration as required by the desired criterion performance. The Standard Assessment Tasks outlined in the blueprint for the National Curriculum assessment programme in England and Wales (DES, 1988) are good examples of performance assessment. Performance assessments demand that the assessment tasks themselves are real examples of the skill or learning goals, rather than proxies. They support good teaching by not requiring teachers to move away from concepts, higher order skills, in depth projects etc to prepare for the tests. The focus is more likely to be on thinking to produce an answer than on eliminating wrong answers as in multiple choice tests. '. . . insights about how to develop and evaluate such tasks come not from the psychometric literature . . . but from research on learning in subject matter fields' (Shepard, 1991). However, when such tasks are required to support psychometric principles such as reliability and standardization, in order to be used in accountability settings, they fall short since that is not the purpose for which they have been designed.

The issue for performance assessment, as some see it, is how can tasks developed from, for example, diagnostic interviews be adapted for large scale administration and offer some level of confidence in comparability of results (which is necessary for accountability purposes). An alternative view is that we cannot force performance assessment into a psychometric model and that what we need is a range of approaches: more formal testing on a psychometric model for monitoring and accountability purposes and teacher-based approaches on an educational assessment model for assessment to support learning. This still leaves us with the question of whether assessment for certification and selection purposes can be more broadly conceived (as for example, the GCSE) to offer both beneficial impact on teaching *and* sufficient reliability for public credibility.

The dilemma that we face is that there are increased demands for testing at national level which must offer comparability, at the same time as our understanding of cognition and learning is telling us that we need assessment to map more directly on to the processes we wish to develop, including higher order skills, which makes achieving such comparability more difficult. Attempting to resolve this dilemma is part of the purpose of this book. There is no doubt we are faced with a paradigm clash, and the question is whether educational assessment can offer high quality assessments for a range of purposes.

In relation to our first question 'assessment for what?' Stiggins (1992) is one of those who take the view that assessment for accountability purposes and classroom-based assessment are so fundamentally different that we should not seek to merge or blend the two, for example, by making standardized tests more 'performance based' or by making classroom based assessment more standardized. While the test developer is looking to isolate traits that are common to all, to extract single elements from complex reality and to assess parts, the teacher seeks to understand and describe the 'complex reality of the individual child, attending to what is unique and changeful' (*ibid*, p. 1). Stiggins refers to these as 'trickle down' and 'trickle up' testing systems: in the first, data are gathered for use at the local or national level and eventually filters down to the teacher, while in the latter, data is gathered in the classroom and is aggregated upward to other levels of decision-making.

Trickle down testing is characterized by standardization first and foremost and may be paper and pencil or performance assessment; a good test is one that has high reliability, validity and efficiency and whose assessor remains a neutral observer; the results are largely used for accountability purposes (and in the UK we would add certification); the need for efficient scoring means that the 'fidelity' of results may be sacrificed; testing occurs at most once a year; the content represents a shallow sample from a broad domain; tests are timed; results are reported summatively, often with norm-referencing and involve considerable delay. (Validity is dealt with in detail in chapter 4, but essentially it relates to the extent to which a test measures what it was designed to measure. If it does not measure what it purports to measure then its use is misleading.)

Trickle up testing, on the other hand, is essentially non-standardized and involves a wide range of activity but its purpose is to gather information for use in decision-making in the classroom; a sound assessment is one that allows understanding of the teaching/learning process for the student and the teacher is assessor, user and interpreter of results i.e. s/he has an interactive role. The results are used by teachers to identify students' needs, assign them to teaching groups and to evaluate their teaching and courses; by students for feedback on their learning which in turn helps to determine their academic self-esteem and attitude to school; by parents to monitor progress and shape their view of the child's academic potential. This assessment takes place almost continuously; the content represents a deep sample from narrowly defined domains with a broad array of achievement targets being assessed; whilst they may be standardized *within* the class and may be timed, the criterion of comparability is likely to give way to the criterion of maximizing students' demonstrated level of competence in order to maximize motivation. Results will be used formatively and summatively and may not always be represented as scores or grades; feedback will be speedy.

Stiggins' paper takes us beyond the commonly used formative/ summative[2] distinction, but he is making the same point that others do (Harlen *et al.*, 1992): assessment for formative purposes has quite different properties and qualities from that used summatively for accountability purposes. Any attempt to use formative assessment for summative purposes will impair its formative role. Not everyone takes this position of course and throughout this book I shall be exploring issues which are central to this problem: the relationship between formative and summative assessment, 'trickle up' and 'trickle down' testing, assessment for accountability purposes and that to support learning.

The Legacy of Psychometrics

The impact of psychometrics goes beyond the specifics of item design and test construction to a broader range of implications: the emphasis on relative ranking, rather than actual accomplishment; the privileging of easily quantifiable displays of skills and knowledge; the assumption that individual performances, rather than collaborative forms of cognition, are the most powerful indicators of educational progress; the notion that evaluating educational progress is a matter of scientific measurement (Wolf *et al.*, 1991). Thus we have tests that rank student performances rather than describe their level of learning in a meaningful way; the most useful form of information is taken to be comparison between individuals or groups, hence items are chosen to distinguish between students rather than because they represent the construct being assessed; and the presentation of performance in a normal curve has led to the belief that because the group of students at the bottom are well below average they cannot learn as much as others. These are all legacies of the psychometric model of testing which developed from the theory of intelligence.

Although American writers refer to the need to change the culture of teachers if we are to move them away from a reliance on norms, and to change their belief that formal exams and tests are necessary in order to make students work hard, the situation in the UK is different. We have not had the same reliance on standardized tests as in the USA: our public exams sit firmly within the performance assessment model while authentic assessment in the guise of RoA and pupil portfolios have been widely accepted as good assessment techniques. In addition, the early experience of having to do SATs at age 7 and 14 together with the teacher assessment element of National Curriculum assessment in England and Wales suggests that our teachers are no newcomers to the wide variety of assessment methods, so that a different culture of assessment clearly exists in the UK. But the problem that we have in the UK is that these developments, and this culture, are being eroded as a strongly right wing government puts assessment for market place and accountability purposes on a traditional, examination model at the top of the agenda and downgrades other approaches.

The particular problem for the USA is that currently new forms of assessment are being held up as *the way* of changing the system and reforming education. Not that this is new: 'Nearly every large educational reform effort of the last few years has either mandated a new form of testing or expanded uses of existing testing' (Pipho, 1985). But, as Haney and Madaus (1989) point out technologies of educational assessment will not of themselves cure the ills in the education system that have been associated with standardized testing (see also Miller and Seraphine, 1992; Shepard, 1991). The same promise was also held for Measurement Driven Instruction (Mehrens, 1992). Various authors (for example, Mehrens, 1992; Wiggins, 1989a; Miller and Seraphine, 1992) point out that the problem for performance assessment in changing the system is that (as already pointed out) it is not particularly amenable to use for large-scale accountability purposes; there are also serious concerns about equity issues in relation to performance assessment in the USA (Baker and O'Neil, 1994). Furthermore, the same teaching-to-the-test problems may occur with teachers focusing on the particular part of the skill that is being assessed, rather than the wider domain. Also, that assessment alone will not develop higher-order skills in the absence of clearly delineated teaching strategies that foster the development of higher order thinking in pupils.

An Agenda for Educational Assessment

What we need is a more measured, analytical, approach to assessment in education. We need to resist the tendency to think in simplistic terms about one particular form of assessment being better than another: consideration of form without consideration of purpose is wasted effort. We must develop and propagate a wider understanding of the effect of assessment on teaching and learning for assessment does not stand outside teaching and learning but stands in dynamic interaction with it. We need also to foster a system which supports multiple methods of assessment while at the same time making sure that each one is used appropriately.

In the shift from the limiting, psychometric model with its emphasis on ranking and statistically derived distributions to a new model we need to focus on pupil achievement. This involves a shift away from a norm-referenced approach towards one in which what pupils can and cannot do is stated. This requires the production of descriptions of performance as in the English National Curriculum. However, this in itself is problematic, since such descriptions will tend to be hierarchical or developmental and, as the research on learning and cognition makes clear, individual learning is idiosyncratic rather than ordered and the 'building-block' model of learning is inappropriate.

There are also implications for how we report performance: the use of a single overall figure as a test result does not fit with current notions of describing pupils' performance in terms of what they can do, or indeed with the complexity of the domains being assessed. It is the legacy of psychometrics that compels us to want data from assessment that we can use to add up, make averages and standard deviations. The integrity of educational assessment requires that we look at profiles of pupils' performance across and within domains. This requires a rethinking of the ways in which information is presented at group level for evaluation or accountability purposes: we must devise alternative ways of presenting results that do not do violence to the domain and the rich judgments made. Details of what pupils have achieved across the broad range of the domain can be provided by 'qualitative' descriptors, or by denoting the level or grade attained within different strands or themes of the subjects and skills assessed. At the back of this argument is a belief that assessment on which so many resources are used should be not only to measure, but also to inform the educational process. To collapse or aggregate these levels or grades to provide a single figure for reporting is to lose detailed information. When scores must be aggregated for reporting then we need to use models which result in the least loss of information and to make the rules explicit.

But the most difficult part of the agenda is in relation to technical issues. Previous notions about the importance of high-agreement reliability have to be reconsidered, both because of the changing nature of the assessments and because we are assessing more complex tasks in a range of contexts. Traditional internal consistency approaches cannot be used with many of the newer developments in assessment so we need to generate other ways of ensuring consistency and comparability where these are important. Considerable effort has gone in to a reconceptualizing of validity over the last five years (Messick, 1989a and 1989b; Linn *et al.*, 1991; Shepard, 1993) but we need to evaluate this development and to see whether the reconceptualization is entirely helpful. Finally, we need to consider ethical issues in the framework which will guide our development and use of assessment, bearing in mind the enormous influence that assessment has on pupils' lives.

In the next chapter I shall start on this agenda by looking at some theories of learning and what these imply for assessment.

Notes

1 However this book does assume a basic knowledge of testing and assessment; readers who are new to the area are advised to read *Assessment: A Teacher's Guide to the Issues* (1993), by Gipps and Stobart first.
2 Formative assessment takes place during the course of teaching and is used essentially to feed back into the teaching/learning process. Summative assessment takes place at the end of a term or a course and is used to provide information about how much students have learned and how well a course has worked.

Chapter 2

Assessment and Learning

It is now widely accepted that testing has an effect on teaching, particularly in terms of curriculum coverage (see chapter 3). What is not so often acknowledged is that there is a relationship between assessment and the way in which subject matter is presented in teaching: this in turn affects — through the tasks in which pupils engage — what and how pupils learn.

In this chapter I want to explore some models of learning, both traditional and more recent, and what these imply for assessment.

Traditional Models of Learning

Critics of traditional testing, in particular standardized testing (for example, Resnick and Resnick, 1992), point out that psychometric testing is rooted in a 'traditional' educational model of teaching and testing routine basic skills; this is based on psychological theories of learning dating from the earlier part of this century. Two assumptions underlie this approach: decomposability and decontextualization.

'Traditional instructional theory assumes that knowledge and skill can be analyzed into component parts that function in the same way no matter where they are used' (Resnick, 1989, p. 3). Psychological theories of the 1920s assumed that learning of complex competencies could be broken down into discrete skills learnt separately, through developing individual stimulus-response bonds. This is called the 'building block' model of learning. The idea was that complex skills could be developed later, although the old theory did not make clear how. It supports a model of teaching and testing separate skills on the assumption that their composition into a complex performance can be reserved for some time later. But, assessing separate components will encourage the teaching and practice of isolated components, and this is not sufficient for learning problem solving or thinking skills. '. . . efforts to assess thinking and problem solving abilities by identifying separate components of those abilities and testing them independently will interfere with effectively teaching such abilities' (Resnick and Resnick, 1992, p. 43). Basic arithmetical computational skills can be treated in this way i.e. practising and testing isolated components, but for more complex thinking processes, for example solving an unstructured maths problem, testing isolated components will not work. Complex skills are not complex simply because of the number of components involved in them but because of the interactions among the components and the heuristics for calling upon them.

A basic tenet of the behaviourist school is that learning is seen as linear and sequential. Complex understandings occur only when elemental prerequisite learnings are mastered. Shepard (1991) notes that this building block model is the rationale for grade-retention (or *redoublement*): one cannot go on to higher levels until the prior level has been mastered and that repetition is the only way to remedy deficient skills acquisition. This notion is increasingly coming in to question as the importance of motivation and self-esteem to the learning process is recognized, as well as the view that practising higher order skills can help to develop or strengthen 'basic skills'. The more serious legacy of this model has been the delaying of teaching higher order skills until the prerequisite skills in the hierarchy have been mastered.

The second assumption of traditional instructional theory, that of decontextualization is linked to decomposability: '. . . . each component of a complex skill is fixed, and that it will take the same form no matter where it is used' (Resnick and Resnick, 1992, p. 43). In fact, what we understand now of cognitive processes indicates that there is an intimate connection between skills and the contexts in which they are used. 'Educationally this suggests that we cannot teach a skill component in one setting and expect it to be applied automatically in another. That means, in turn, that we cannot validly assess a competence in a context very different from the context in which it is practised or used' (*ibid*). Skills and knowledge are now understood to be dependent on the context in which they are learnt and practised; facts cannot be learned in isolation and then used in any context.

Research with young people in the Youth Training Scheme (Wolf *et al.*, 1990) on the transferability of complex problem-solving skills found that transferability was indeed limited. Trainees were given training on problem-solving tasks either within their own occupational group only or of deliberately very varied types; a control group was given no training at all. Results showed that both groups which received problem solving training improved their performance over the group which did not, and the group which had received training in a variety of contexts performed better on problem-solving tasks outside their occupational area than did the group with own-occupation training. The authors conclude that varied training encouraged generalized learning (i.e. that generalized skills do not develop from context-specific learning). Such doubts about transferability (and generalizability) of skills throw doubt on the move in the UK to assess common core or generic competencies independently of subject context (Atkins *et al.*, 1992).

The Resnicks' analysis of the content of standardized tests supports their claims — seemingly obvious once pointed out — about the low level nature of the tasks required, and emphasize that being able to recognize grammatical or correct alternatives in a test does not tell us whether the pupil is able to *produce* good prose or to communicate ideas clearly. The tests support the model of knowledge as collections of bits of information; they demand fast responses which militates against reflection; and the multiple-choice format indicates that the task is to find the correct answer (someone else's correct answer) rather than to engage in interpretation and thinking.

> Evidence is beginning to accumulate that traditional school-ing's focus on individual, isolated activity, on symbols cor-rectly manipulated but divorced from experience, and on de-contextualised skills may be partly responsible for our schools' difficulty in teaching processes of thinking and knowledge construction. (Resnick, 1989, p. 13)

Of course the Resnicks and Shepard are writing in the USA where standardized tests have a particularly powerful hold and their argu-ment is overstated for the UK. However, it is a powerful way of mak-ing us examine our taken-for-granted assumptions about the nature of knowledge, how testing can shape teaching and the way in which knowledge is presented.

The assumption made in the traditional, behaviourist testing/learning model is that one can specify and measure all important learning objectives, and furthermore that mastery on the test items implies mastery of the intended skills and concepts. Shepard's (1991) view is that these ideas took hold among the testing community because of the, then current, emphasis on content validity rather than construct validity (i.e. an examination of the test content directly rather than a study of correlation with external criteria) and because it matched with the evaluation models based on behaviourally specified objectives in use at the time.

Shepard (1991) examined the underlying beliefs about learning of a sample of district testing directors i.e. people in charge of testing programs within school districts (equivalent to LEAs). Her rationale for this was that it is important to understand the conceptions of teaching and learning these specialists call upon when they make decisions about testing practice, in other words to examine the implicit theories which guide their practice. What Shepard found was that approximately half her sample held beliefs about testing which imply acceptance of behaviourist learning theory i.e. which requires practice, repetition and testing of discrete basic skills prior to any teaching of higher-order thinking skills. This view of teaching/learning/testing has been passed on to teachers in the USA via testing programmes and has not been modified because of the time lag in getting new theories about learning into in-service and pre-service training.

The issue of the extent to which tests can reflect learning goals is central to this chapter. Can all required learning be specified through test content? In the USA this is exactly what has happened, with much of elementary education working on an objectives model linked to regular standardized testing. The dominance of this model is such that teachers have focused their instruction on these discrete skills and on the decontextualized test items, offering over-practice until mastery is achieved (or not in some cases).

Current learning theory, however, suggests that this approach is inappropriate. Isolated facts, if learnt, quickly disappear from the memory because they have no meaning and do not fit into the learner's conceptual map. Knowledge learnt in this way is of no use because it cannot be applied, generalized or retrieved. 'Meaning makes learning easier, because the learner knows where to put things in her mental framework, and meaning makes knowledge useful because likely purposes and applications are already part of the understanding' (Shepard, 1992a, p. 319).

Cognitive and Constructivist Models of Learning

An alternative to the linear hierarchy model of learning comes from recent work in cognitive and constructivist psychology; this shows learning in terms of networks with connections in many directions; not of an external map that is transposed directly into the student's head, but an organic process of reorganizing and restructuring as the student learns.

Cognitive theory suggests that learning is a process of knowledge construction; that learning is knowledge-dependent; and that learning is tuned to the situation in which it takes place. Learning occurs, not by recording information but by interpreting it so that instruction must be seen not as direct transfer of knowledge but as an intervention in an ongoing knowledge construction process (Resnick, 1989). Thus in constructivist learning theory students learn best by actively making sense of new knowledge — making meaning from it and mapping it in to their existing knowledge map/schema. (The social constructivist school sees this as happening within a shared social context.)

'Contemporary cognitive psychology has built on the very old idea that things are easier to learn if they make sense' (Shepard, 1991, p. 8). All learning requires us to make sense of what we are trying to learn and learning through the active construction of mental schemas applies even to young children's 'basic' learning.

Information-processing models of learning tend to have three elements, two of which overlap with constructivist models: a first stage in which through selective attention certain aspects of the environment are filtered for conscious processing; second, active mental engagement with the new input so as to make personal sense of it, using selectively recalled prior learning in the process; finally a structuring of the resultant learning in such a way that it can be stored usefully in the long-term memory (Atkins *et al.*, 1992). Thus knowledge is seen as something cohesive and holistic which provides a scaffolding for later learning.

This view of student learning built up during the 1970s and 1980s under the 'constructivist', label which sees students as active constructors of their own world view and which insists that to be useful new information must be linked to the knowledge structures, or schemata, already held in long-term memory, means that we can no longer use a model of assessment which atomizes knowledge. We need to assess level of understanding and complexity of understanding rather than recognition or recall of facts: 'The strength and frequency of calls for authenticity in assessment are evidence of the influence of such a view of student learning' (Wilson, 1992, p. 123).

The basis of most measurement theory underlying psychometrics is a view of the learner as a passive absorber of information and facts provided by the teacher. Standardized achievement tests test students' abilities to recall and apply facts learnt routinely; even items which are designed to assess higher level activities often require no more than the ability to recall the appropriate formula and to make substitutions to get the correct answer. But learners construct their own interpretations and relate this to their existing knowledge and understandings. Students who conceive of knowledge as collections of facts will use learning strategies that are aimed at successful memorization. This is influenced by their experience of 'schoolwork' as a required activity which is not directly related to knowledge and learning; their role in traditional schooling is to answer the teachers' questions. The result of this equation of learning with production of work is that learning becomes an incidental rather than an intentional process. Alternative forms of teaching in which students and teachers jointly engage in knowledge construction and in which teachers progressively turn over metacognitive functions to the students, so that students are taught how to learn, can result in learning being an intentional process. But first we need to change the way in which test developers, teachers and students view the learning of school knowledge.

These new conceptions of learning require a new assessment methodology with a focus on tests that show what the pupil knows and will facilitate good learning: 'Tests ought not to ask for demonstration of small, discrete skills practised in isolation. They should be more ambitious instruments aimed at detecting what mental representations students hold of important ideas and what facility students have in bringing these understandings to bear in solving their problems' (Shepard, 1991, p. 9).

Students can succeed on 'objective' tests without necessarily understanding the material they are learning. Recent research on learning and cognition, particularly in science, has shown a phenomenon called 'shallow learning' (White, 1992; Entwistle, 1992) with pupils showing widespread misconceptions and misunderstandings of both natural and scientific phenomena. Shallow learning has taken place when students are able to manipulate complex formulae and to work through involved exercises while not understanding fundamental principles. Constructivist models of learning are built on the precept that pupils have their own theories — of how things work, why the sun comes up every morning, interpretations of history etc — and that real learning involves becoming dissatisfied with this existing belief and finding the new concept intelligible and plausible. Shallow learning then is the acquisition of principles, from a teacher or other instructor, without commitment or deep consideration. The principles are often discarded as soon as the need for them has gone, for example, after a test or exam. The ability to hold conflicting views implies that the learner has not thought through what she/he is learning. Deep learning in 'good' learners, on the other hand involves thinking about the meaning of what is being learnt. This notion of purposeful or deep learning clearly has implications for curriculum and pedagogy and also for assessment.

Shallow learning clearly approximates to what Resnick, Shepard and other US commentators describe as being fostered in classroom approaches which are dominated by the demands of standardized, multiple-choice testing. Characteristics of deep learning, however:

> — an intention to understand material for oneself
> — interacting vigorously and critically with the content
> — relating ideas to previous knowledge and experience
> — using organizing principles to integrate ideas
> — relating evidence to conclusions
> and — examining the logic of the argument (Entwistle, 1992)

reflect cognitive and constructivist models of learning but demand a very different approach to teaching and assessment.

Programmes which have successfully taught higher order cognitive abilities or thinking skills have a number of common elements: they involve socially shared intellectual work, are organized around joint accomplishment of tasks so that elements of the skill take on meaning in the context of the whole; they use procedures (for example, modelling) that make hidden processes overt; they allow skills to build up bit by bit yet permit participation even for the relatively unskilled; they are organized around particular subject matter rather than general abilities (Resnick, 1989).

One of the concepts that has emerged from work in cognitive science is that of *metacognition*. Metacognition is a general term which refers to a second-order form of thinking: thinking about thinking. It includes a variety of self-awareness processes to help plan, monitor, orchestrate and control one's own learning. It is a process of being aware of and in control of one's own knowledge and thinking, and therefore learning (following Flavell's 1976 definition). Such learners control their learning using particular strategies which hinge on self-questioning in order to get the purpose of learning clear, searching for connections and conflicts with what is already known, creating images, and judging whether understanding of the material is sufficient for the task. An essential aspect of metacognition is that learners control their own learning and, in order to reflect on the meaning of what they are learning, pupils must feel commitment to it.

In the traditional model of teaching the curriculum is seen as a distinct body of information, specified in detail, that can be transmitted to the learner. Assessment here consists of checking whether the information has been received. These newer models of learning, which see learning as a process of personal knowledge construction and meaning making, describe a more complex and diverse process and therefore require assessment to be more diverse and to assess in more depth the structure and quality of students' learning and understanding. While, for example, standardized multiple choice or short answer type tests are efficient at sampling the acquisition of specific knowledge gained from teachers, more intense, even interactive assessment such as essays and performance assessments, small group tasks and projects, are needed to get at and encourage a deeper level of learning.

Work in cognitive science has also looked at learners in terms of novices and experts: they differ from each other not just in terms of quantity, that is the extent of their knowledge, but also in the types of models they have constructed for themselves, the types of conceptions and understandings they bring to a problem and the strategies and approaches they use (Glaser, 1990 op.cit.). Other research has pointed to the importance of learning which produces a qualitative change in the learner's conception of a phenomenon from a less sophisticated conception to a more expert understanding of that phenomenon.

All learning involves thinking and what we need is a curriculum and assessment model designed to produce 'intelligent novices', students who are able to learn in many domains: they may not have the background knowledge needed in a new field but they know how to go about gaining that knowledge (Brown *et al.*, 1993). As learning experts they will be better prepared to be inducted into the new field of study; given changing employment patterns and the explosion of knowledge content, what we need to do in school is to make children become intelligent novices in order to be flexible learners. Brown and colleagues see the school's role being to induct children as apprentice learners, learning how to think and reason in a variety of domains.

Assessment for Learning

The Thinking Curriculum is a term coined to denote a curriculum which focuses on the 'new basics' of thinking, reasoning and learning how to learn (Resnick and Resnick, 1992). These new basics have become important in the wake of global changes in technology and communication and the resulting impact on the global economy. In many industrialized countries the call is the same, for workers at all levels who can operate and *understand* technical systems, and be flexible, adaptive learners since we are educating a generation of pupils who, rather than have a trade or career for life as in our parents' and grandparents' day, are likely to have one or more changes of task *and* conditions of work during their working lives. The call is for schools to provide educational programmes that enable pupils to reason and think, not just to perform routine operations. This move, to require thinking and problem-solving programmes for *all* students rather than just for the elite or high achieving students, is new: the higher-order skills of interpreting unfamiliar texts, constructing convincing arguments, developing approaches to problems etc. have been, in the British and American systems, reserved for the elite.

Alongside these economic and cultural demands for a different curriculum, come the findings of research that thinking and reasoning do not have to wait until after the basic skills have been learned. Far from it, '. . . thinking and reasoning are intimately involved in successfully learning even elementary levels of reading, mathematics, and other school subjects' (*ibid*, p. 39). Even the simple learning of lists, or facts, requires the pupil to organize the knowledge if it is to be retained, since facts acquired without structure and rationale will quickly disappear as the critique of traditional learning theory made clear.

So we need to encourage deep learning, higher order thinking and self-monitoring, alongside the acquisition of knowledge, from the earliest stages of schooling.

As the New Zealand report *Assessment for Better Learning* (1989) has it assessment should be directed at higher order skills:

> such as understanding of principles, applying knowledge and skills to new tasks, and investigating, analysing, and discussing complex issues and problems

because

> such skills and understanding will generally prove of more enduring value and greater versatility and form the basis for further learning and appropriate interpretation of factual information. (p. 26)

Not only does higher order learning seem to be retained longer, but it is likely that it encourages the development of intrinsic motivation and positive attitudes to continued learning (Willis, 1992b).

Another key area is the pupil's role in assessment. If pupils are to become competent assessors of their own work, as developments in metacognition tell us they should, then they need sustained experience in ways of questioning and improving the quality of their work, and supported experience in assessing their work, in addition to understanding what counts as the standard expected and the criteria on which they will be assessed (Sadler, 1989).

There are two related but distinct issues at stake:

— what form of assessment do we need to properly reflect students' learning?
— what form of assessment should we use to ensure a beneficial impact on teaching and learning practice?

The work of Vygotsky is important in conceptualizing models of assessment which might both reflect and support learning.

Vygotsky pointed to the importance of tools and aids in human learning: the use of external supports is a key element in the development of mental functions. The increasing use of technological developments in both professional work and in school learning point to the significance of Vygotsky's ideas, developed as they were, before the technological revolution (Ivic, 1991). Assessment which, in the traditional examination and psychometric model, denies the pupil the use of external tools, reduces its usefulness/ecological validity: following Vygotsky's ideas we should develop assessment which allows the use of auxiliary tools in the process of assessment; this could reduce the emphasis on the ability to memorize and increase the emphasis on thinking and problem solving.

Vygotsky's most famous contribution to psychological theory, however, is the *zone of proximal development* (ZPD). This refers to the gap between the actual developmental level as shown by the child's unaided performance and her potential level as shown by her performance under adult guidance or in collaboration with more capable peers. The process of support and guidance offered by adults to help the child to perform at the higher level is known as scaffolding: the adult offers support which is gradually removed as the child becomes competent at that level.

Scaffolded assessment is a term which extends the scaffolding notion to assessment, to move beyond static assessment of what is known to be a more interactive model looking at learning potential (potential in Vygotskyian terms, rather than in terms of 'intelligence'). A good example of such an assessment would be the National Curriculum Assessment SATs for 7-year-olds in 1991/92. These active, performance-based tasks were individual or small group activities under the control of the teacher which could be used for diagnostic purposes. However, if teachers were to extend the questioning process and offer the child support to attempt the next level, then they would be able to see whether the child was at all close to a higher level of performance; this would be a scaffolded assessment and would provide more diagnostic information for the teacher.

A similar approach has been developed by Feuerstein with his Learning Potential Assessment Device (LPAD) used to assess potential in children who have been culturally and intellectually deprived. There is a range of assessment approaches called *dynamic assessments* (Brown *et al.*, 1992). Dynamic assessment based on Vygotskyian models of learning are used in a range of research settings (see Brown *et al.*, 1993). Building on the notion of the zone of proximal development, dynamic assessments present children with tasks one step beyond their competence. The assessor is also the teacher and helps the child to gain mastery. 'The degree of aid needed, both to learn new principles and to apply them, is carefully calibrated and measured. The required amount of aid provides a much better index of students' future learning trajectories in a domain than static pre-tests' (*ibid*, p. 28). As with scaffolded assessment, this form of assessment is somewhere between teaching and traditional examination in that the adult gives aid only as needed, allowing the child to show competence when s/he can.

Brown and colleagues offer an analysis of collaborative assessment environments and collaborative teaching environments within Vygotsky's ZPD conceptual framework (Brown *et al.*, 1992, p. 175), and show that there is in fact considerable overlap. Clearly one is for assessment and the other for learning but the only major difference is that, in assessment, aid is in the form of standardized hints while in the teaching paradigm aid is opportunistic.

Building on Vygotsky's definition of metacognition in relation to school learning viz: knowledge about one's own cognition in the process of systematic school learning which aids deliberate mastery, Ivic (1991) points out that in assessing school learning we focus on content knowledge and omit to assess metacognitive strategies. As Binet pointed out, it is not sufficient to have intelligence, but one must also use it intelligently. This suggests that one of the limitations of intelligence tests and (a cause of so called 'under'-' or 'over-achievement') is this lack of focus on metacognitive processes, for it is these which identify an efficient learner. Access to metacognitive processes for pupils can come from a process of guided or negotiated self-assessment, in which the pupil gains awareness of his/her own learning strategies and efficiency.

Ivic (*ibid*) also argues that, following Piagetian lines, tasks to assess children's thinking might include 'tasks of understanding, concept comparison, interconnection of knowledge, invention of new examples to illustrate acquired concepts, critical analysis of different statements and application of the same intellectual operations on different conceptual contents. In other words, the tasks for the testing of acquired knowledge would in themselves have to offer the student the opportunity to show himself as an active independent learner' (p. 20).

Scaffolded, dynamic and Piagetian-type assessments are widely used in research into the learning of subject matter and in research on learning. These are, however, clearly research tools and techniques for individual rather than classroom use; they are more than 'performance' assessments since they are essentially interactive and diagnostic. The question, as posed in the previous chapter, is whether this type of task and style of assessment can be incorporated into more standardized procedures, which can be given and marked by teachers?

Conclusions

The implication of work in cognitive science for the assessment of student learning (rather than performance) is that we need to focus on the models that students construct for themselves and their understandings. Wilson (1992) suggests that we may need to estimate students' understandings using a range of perspectives, for example, the student's, the teacher's and expert opinion, rather than measuring the number of facts and procedures students can reproduce.

> The challenge, then, is to find out enough about student understanding to design performances that will reflect these different understandings and then to design assessment techniques that can accurately reflect these different understandings. (*ibid*, p. 125).

In shifting to a new paradigm of assessment it seems that we have to take on some new principles. Instead of depriving the pupils of aids and equipment for intellectual work, the opposite could be done, this would allow assessment of problem solving, use of aids and the transfer and application of knowledge. But dynamic assessment, scaffolded assessment and other interactive approaches pose a considerable practical dilemma since they by their very nature imply individual administration by expert teachers. So, rather than try to develop tools such as these for classroom use (and certainly not for accountability purposes) a better approach would be to help teachers to be aware of 'new' notions about learning, particularly scaffolding and metacognition and to work on professional development programmes which develop teachers' skills in observation, questioning and interaction so that they can integrate this type of approach into their regular classroom teaching and assessment.

The psychometric model of assessment is a static one based on a normal distribution of achievement narrowly defined; this relates to its ideological underpinning of measuring existing individual or group differences in achievement with the overall aim of selection of students. An alternative model is a more dynamic one in which the student's learning *potential* is the focus, not potential in a 'static' sense in that the potential is determined, needs only to be measured accurately and cannot be changed, but potential which, in a dynamic and positive sense, is elastic and highly responsive to adult support and teaching. Current learning theory indicates that what we need in assessment is to be able to assess what the pupil already knows; her learning strategies; and her ability to be aware of and control her learning. In addition, interactive or scaffolded assessment will indicate not only what the pupil knows and can do but also what she nearly can do.

Finally, in order to encourage the teaching and development of higher order skills, thinking processes and problem solving we must use assessment which directly reflects these processes. New assessment models alone cannot bring about the changes in learning which have been described in this chapter, but sticking with traditional, narrow forms of testing will surely inhibit this process.

Chapter 3

Impact of Testing

Introduction

As early as 1984, Frederiksen published a paper called 'The real test bias', in which he suggested that because test information is important in attempting to hold schools accountable, the influence of tests on what is taught was potentially great. In 1987 Popham was advocating what he called 'measurement-driven instruction' (MDI) as the most cost-effective way of improving the quality of public education (Popham, 1987a). By 1988 there were several major reviews of the impact of testing on teaching and curriculum (Crooks, 1988; and Madaus, 1988); the information began to build that testing (as opposed to assessment) had significant effects not only on teaching, but also on the curriculum and student motivation. Now one of the universally accepted facts about testing, particularly high-stakes testing, is that it will indeed have powerful effects on the way that teachers construe the nature of their task.

Frederiksen's argument was that any test is likely to influence the behaviour of students and teachers, provided that they know about it in advance, because the students will want to do well and the teachers want their students to do well. So an increase tends to occur in the time and effort spent in learning and teaching what the tests measure, and, because the amount of time available is fixed, decreases efforts to learn and teach skills which are not measured by the tests. The result is that the abilities that are tested, because they can most easily and economically be tested, become the ones that are most taught. Frederiksen's concept of bias here relates to the impact of the test: introducing bias against teaching important skills which are not measured. As an example, Frederiksen gives the rapid increase in the use of standardized tests for accountability purposes after the 1981 Debra P case, in which the US Court of Appeal judged that Florida could not use a minimum competency test to satisfy a graduation requirement if there was insufficient evidence that the test measured what was actually taught in school. After this case, many schools and teachers attempted to make what they taught mesh fully with any accountability tests that were used. In the USA at the time this meant inevitably multiple choice standardized tests of the basic skills. Over the decade about which Frederiksen was writing the national surveys carried out by NAEP (the US National Assessment of Educational Progress) showed that items measuring basic skills did not show a decline in performance, but there had been a decline in performance on items reflecting more complex cognitive skills. Although there are many possible causes of the changes in performance shown by the NAEP tests, Frederiksen considered that the possibility must be entertained that the mandated use of minimum competency tests using multiple choice formats had discouraged the teaching of abilities that could not easily be measured in this way. This of course is the argument being repeated in this decade, particularly in the United States (see chapter 1).

> Efficient tests tend to drive out less efficient tests, leaving many important abilities untested — and untaught. An important task for educators and psychologists is to develop instruments to better reflect the whole domain of educational goals and find ways to use them in improving the educational process. (Frederiksen, 1984, p. 201)

Measurement-Driven Instruction

Measurement-driven instruction is defined as when a high-stakes test, because of the important contingencies associated with students' performance, influences the instructional programme that prepares students for the test (Popham, 1987a). Whether concerned about their own self-esteem, or their students' well-being and prospects, teachers clearly aim for their students to perform well on high-stakes tests. Stakes can be high, either for the students or for the teachers, and in some cases they are high for both. Teachers tend to spend a significant amount of their teaching time on the knowledge and skills assessed by such a test; a high-stakes test therefore serves as a powerful 'curricular magnet' (*ibid*, p. 680). Popham cites evidence to show that in a number of American states the introduction of MDI had led to significant improvement in basic skills amongst students. Furthermore, that this MDI was apparently reducing a performance gap between majority and minority students. Countering the criticism that these are only low-level skills, Popham points out that these are basic skills, required by all students, and in which many minority students had not previously been successful. 'Clearly effective assessment systems can go a long way toward reducing differences between majority and minority students in the mastery of skills' (*ibid*, p. 682). Popham's view was that, properly conceived, measurement-driven instruction can be a potent force for educational improvement. Clearly, care had to be taken to prevent the negative effects that are possible, including curricular distortion, but measurement-driven instruction he saw as having the potential for being a particularly cost-effective way of improving the quality of public education. Popham's conditions for MDI to be successful are:

— One: criterion-referenced tests must be used to clarify the skills and knowledge that will be measured, and to provide the instructional tasks for teachers.
— Two: non-trivial knowledge and skills must be measured.
— Three: a manageable number of skills or objectives must be measured, with the lower level ones subsumed by the higher level skills.
— Four: instructional clarity must come from the targets, so that teachers can use the targets or objectives for planning teaching.
— Five: instructional support, useful teaching materials, and suggestions for how skills can be taught must be part of the programme.

Airasian (1988a) takes the analysis of MDI further, and points out that the concept of high stakes is relative, not absolute, and therefore varies depending on the context in which testing takes place. He gives an example of a high school graduation test which firstly most pupils want to pass, as do their teachers but 'if the content examined on the test is fifth grade level, and if the standard for passing the test is very low, the impact of the test on instruction will not be great for most pupils' (*ibid*, p. 7). Airasian suggests that we look at both stakes and standards. Stakes and standards can each be high or low, and, Airasian suggests, the maximum instructional effect will occur when both the test standards and the stakes are high; that is, when the consequences associated with test performance are important and when the standard for passing is challenging yet attainable. By contrast, the least instructional effects will occur when the standards and the stakes are both low; ie when the test consequences are not particularly important and passing is not difficult. Although the greatest impact on teaching will occur when standards and stakes are both high, this is also the context in which the greatest number of test failures is likely to occur which exacerbates the stakes. Airasian cites as a classic example of high stakes, high standards testing programmes English public exams. He says '. . . it is well documented that such exams are very influential in driving the school curriculum' (*ibid*).

In an extended review of the influence of testing on the curriculum, Madaus (1988) gives the perceived benefits of MDI as these: if the skills are well chosen, and if the tests truly measure them, then the goals of instruction are explicit; teacher and student efforts are focused on well-defined targets; standards are clear and uniform; accountability at all levels is easier and more objective; and the public has concrete information on how well the schools are doing. Proponents of this form of testing, he points out, argue that the power of testing to influence what is taught, how it is taught, what is learned, and how it is learned, is a very beneficial attribute. Madaus also defines a high-stakes test as one whose results are seen, rightly or wrongly, by students, teachers, administrators, parents or the general public as being used to make important decisions. A low-stakes test, by contrast, is one that is perceived as not having important rewards, or sanctions tied directly to test performance. With this form of testing the results may still affect teachers' perceptions of students, and student placement decisions, but the important distinction is that teachers, students and parents do not perceive performance in these tests as being directly linked to reward.

The Impact of Testing on the Curriculum and Teaching

As a result of his survey of the impact of testing on the curriculum, Madaus posits a number of principles:

> *Principle 1*: 'The power of tests and exams to affect individuals, institutions, curriculum or instruction is a perceptual phenomenon. If students, teachers or administrators believe that the results of an examination are important, it matters very little whether this is really true or false. The effect is produced by what individuals perceive to be the case'. (*ibid*, p. 88)

So what matters is not whether a test is high stakes, but whether participants believe it to be high stakes. This explains the symbolic power of tests in the minds of policymakers and the public: policymakers realise the high symbolic value attached to testing; by requiring testing to take place, policymakers can be seen to be addressing critical reform issues. So a high-stakes testing programme is often a symbolic solution to a real educational problem. It offers the appearance of a solution, and indeed, as test scores rise over time, because of teaching to the test, policy makers can point to the wisdom of their action. However, the reality is that the testing programme may not be a cure for the educational problem.

Principle 2:   'The more any quantitative social indicator is used for social decision making, the more likely it will be to distort and corrupt the social processes it is intended to monitor'. (*ibid*, p. 89)

Madaus relates this to Heisenberg's 'uncertainty principle': one cannot measure things without affecting them. The point is that, while testing is seen historically as a relatively objective way of adjusting the system, the negative impact eventually outweighs any benefit, and when test results are used for important social decisions, the changes in the teaching system brought about by such a use can be both substantial and corrupting.

Principle 3:   'If important decisions are presumed to be related to test results, then teachers will teach to the test'. (*ibid*, p. 90)

High-stakes testing can indeed focus teaching on to that which is measured by the test. However, the evidence seems to make clear that it is the scores on the test which rise, and not necessarily the skill itself which improves, ie that the teaching is aimed at the test item, and the item format, rather than at the construct or the skill which it intends to measure. Madaus himself quotes examples of the effect of high-stakes testing on the curriculum in both the nineteenth and twentieth century in a range of countries, from India to Ireland, and from Japan to England. In the UK we have only to look to the example of the 11-plus test, and the profound effect that this had on the teaching of all primary school children (Gipps, 1990), and the effect of the old GCE 'O' level exam on the style and content of teaching in secondary schools (HMI, 1979). It is not that teachers want to narrow their teaching, nor to limit unduly students' educational experience, but if the test scores have significant effects on people's lives, then teachers see it as part of their professional duty to make sure that their pupils have the best possible chance they can to pass the test. We must remember, however, that this effect can also be used to bring in positive curricular change: a high-stakes test can bring in good curricular material. An example of this in England was the introduction of the GCSE exam at 16, which was designed specifically to counteract the damaging influence of the old 'O' level exam, and to bring in a wider range of student activity, moving away from a narrow, paper and pencil examination mode. Evidence from HMI indicates that this indeed is what happened, once teachers got used to the new system (HMI, 1988). The question remains whether even this kind of positive impact can also become corrupted after a number of years.

> *Principle 4*:   'In every setting where a high-stakes operates, a tradition of past exams develops, which eventually de facto defines the curriculum'. (*ibid*, p. 93)

Madaus argues that though this may not sound problematic, when in real life a teacher's professional worth is estimated in terms of exam results, they will corrupt the skills measured by reducing them to the level of strategies in which the pupil is drilled. The long-term effects of examination sanctions are profound in a high-stakes situation.

> *Principle 5*:   'Teachers pay particular attention to the form of the questions on a high-stakes test (for example, short answer essay, multiple choice) and adjust their instruction accordingly'. (*ibid*, p. 95)

The problem here, as I outline in chapters 1 and 2, is that the form of the test question can (of course it depends on the form of the question) narrow instruction and learning to the detriment of other skills.

> *Principle 6*:   'When test results are the sole, or even partial, arbiter of future educational or life choices, society tends to treat test results as the major goal of schooling, rather than as a useful but fallible indicator of achievement'. (*ibid*, p. 97)

Madaus considers that this may be the most damaging of all the effects attributed to tests. We need only look at the impact of Payment by Results in the nineteenth century, the powerful labelling effect of the

11+, the anxiety with which pupils wait for their public exam results, and now, the importance given by this government to league tables of schools' performance on National Curriculum assessment to find support for this principle.

> *Principle 7*:   'A high-stakes test transfers control over the curriculum to the agency which sets or controls the exam'. (*ibid*)

One can see that this is the case for the examination boards which run public exams in this country and in others — it is also the case where there is state control over a national testing programme. It is important to realize, Madaus says, that in the US, the state may be delegating this very real power over education to commercial companies (those who produce test material), whose interest is primarily financial and only secondarily educational.

Work done on standardized test use in America (Salmon Cox, 1981), in Ireland (Kellaghan, Madaus and Airasian, 1982), and in England (Gipps *et al.*, 1983) showed that teachers made little use of standardized test results when they were not high-stakes tests. The fact that this finding is common across different cultures and educational systems, I would suggest, supports the notion that where tests are not high stakes then their results may be ignored by teachers. Even more complex than that, what these studies seemed to show was that where teachers agreed with the outcomes of the tests, then they accepted them; if the results of the tests were unexpected, but in a positive direction, then they would also accept them. Where the results did not agree with teachers' assessments, however, and this resulted in a downgrading of student attainment, teachers would not accept the results; the negative discrepancy in standardized test results would be explained away by the teachers in terms of the student having a bad day, or the test not being a good one.

Madaus warns that the apparent improvement in performance resulting from the introduction of minimum competency tests, as a form of measurement-driven instruction, is that the gains may result from simply teaching to the test, as was the case in the Payment by Results situation. These improved test scores may not generalize to other measures of the same construct, and in fact the result may be to change the original construct which the test was designed to measure. Madaus' conclusion is that we need to lobby for a lowering of the stakes associated with test performance. We must instead persuade the general public and those in the education system that test information is only one piece of information, used alongside other indicators when decisions have to be made about pupils, teachers and school districts.

The second major review of the impact of assessment is by Crooks (1988), who focused on the effect of classroom evaluation practices on students. Crooks, in his review, does not focus solely on standardized testing; he makes the point that this has been widely researched and that, in any case, pupils spend a greater amount of time engaged in what he calls 'classroom evaluation activities' than in standardized testing. He includes in evaluation activities: formal teacher-made tests, curriculum-embedded tests, oral questions, and a wide variety of other performance activities, assessment of motivational and attitudinal variables and of learning skills. It is clearly a very wide-ranging review. Because of this, I will devote considerable space to the review, but the article itself repays reading.

It seems that teacher-made tests give greater emphasis to lower-level cognitive skills than teachers' intentions suggest; there is a case for reduced emphasis on testing recall and recognition of factual knowledge, since transfer is an important quality of learning, ie a crucial indicator of whether a pupil understands a concept or principle is whether he or she is able to apply it in different circumstances. Thus, if testing is to be for understanding, testing must take place in a range of circumstances and require students to use the factual knowledge, rather than just recall it. The review confirms the argument in chapter 2 of this book, that the style of assessment or evaluation will have an effect on the style of learning in which the students engage. Several studies show that students who use surface approaches to learning have difficulty adapting to evaluation that favours deep approaches; on the other hand, students who can successfully use deep approaches to learning can easily be persuaded to adopt surface approaches if the evaluation suggests that this will be successful. Crooks concludes that there is a strong case for encouraging the development of deep learning strategies from the early years of school; this would be facilitated by a greater emphasis on higher-level questioning in evaluation (*ibid*, p. 447).

In relation to frequency of testing, evidence suggests that moderate frequency is desirable for enhancing student performance. The use of cumulative tests, requiring repeated review of early material, is advantageous for performance in comprehensive end-of-course examinations. It seems that the benefit of regular testing is explained by three things: first, the testing makes the students attend to the content a second time, which is, in effect, another practice and this enhances retention; second, the testing encourages the student to actively process the content, and this is known to enhance learning and retention; third, the test directs attention to the topics and skills tested, which may focus the students' preparation for a subsequent test.

Crooks concludes that we need to place more emphasis on the role of assessment in helping students to learn, rather than simply grading them. Evaluation is integral to the teaching-learning process; he is particularly hard on the role of assessment for grading pupil achievement in a normative sense: the evidence which he reviews indicates clearly that normative grading, with the social comparison and competition between students which accompanies it, results in undesirable consequences for most students. His view is that it is hard to see any justification before the final year or so of high school for placing much emphasis on using classroom assessment for this normative purpose. The undesirable effects to which he refers include: lower levels of intrinsic motivation, increased anxiety, which hinders the learning process, attributions for ability that undermine pupil effort, lowered self efficacy for learning in poorer students, and poorer social relationships among pupils. Teachers' evaluation of pupils' work would more profitably be directed to giving useful feedback to students (as chapter 5 argues), and assessment for summative purposes should be not only less frequent, but also criterion referenced, to describe what students can and cannot do. 'The likely small reduction in reliability associated with counting fewer evaluations in the summative evaluation, would be a modest penalty to pay for the benefits described above, and the improved validity associated with greater emphasis on final competence, rather than on the mistakes made along the way' (*ibid*, p. 468).

The most effective forms of feedback are those which focus the pupils' attention on their progress in mastering the required task. This emphasis tends to enhance self-efficacy, encourages effort attribution, and reduces the focus on comparison with peers; it should take place while it is still relevant, ie soon after the task is completed; it should be specific and related to need, ie simple information about results should be provided consistently, with more detailed feedback only where this is necessary, to help the student work through misconceptions or other weaknesses in performance. Praise should be used sparingly, and should be task-specific. Above all, criticism is usually counter-productive.

Standards to be reached in assessment should be clearly specified to students, they should be high but attainable — and Crooks discusses the problems in making this true for all pupils in a mixed class; if all students are working on the same tasks, and trying to meet the same standards, some students will find the standards unattainable, while others will find them too easy. Several approaches are possible here: standards may be set for individual students, or flexibility provided through 'learning pathways' ie individualized teaching, or cooperative learning may be used in groups to reduce pressure on individuals and to compensate for strengths and weaknesses among the pupils. However learning is organized, the criteria and other requirements for good performance should be made very clear before an important task is attempted, to avoid misdirected effort and increased anxiety about the assessment (this echoes Sadler's arguments in relation to standards and formative assessment in chapter 7). Crooks concludes that

> the most vital of all the messages emerging from this review, is that, as educators, we must ensure that we give appropriate emphasis in our evaluations to the skills, knowledge and attitudes that we perceive to be the most important. Some of these important outcomes may be hard to evaluate, but it is important that we find ways to assess them. (p. 470) . . . classroom evaluation affects students in many different ways. For instance, it guides their judgment of what is important to learn, affects their motivation and self perceptions of competence, structures their approaches to and timing of personal study . . . consolidates learning, and affects the development of enduring learning strategies and skills. It appears to be one of the most potent forces influencing education (p. 467).

As well as the detailed information about the impact of assessment on learning, the important message from Crooks' review is that testing can have *positive* as well as negative effects; where we talk about the impact of assessment on the school system, teachers, and teaching we often do so in negative terms. It is important not only to remember that assessment can have good, positive impact, but that it is necessary to *plan* assessment in order that it does have this positive impact; that is the message of this book.

The Impact of Assessment on Motivation

A high level of motivation is not sufficient condition, but it is a necessary one for learning. Research has repeatedly shown (Crooks, 1988) that the responses of individual pupils to educational experiences and tasks are a complex function of their ability, personality, past educational experience, current attitude, self-perception and motivational state, together with the nature of the current task. Theories of achievement motivation (see chapter 5) put stress on the importance of students' self-perceptions in determining responses to educational and evaluative tasks. The attributions, or reasons, which students give for their success or failure, or their perceptions of their ability to perform well (self-efficacy) are highly important factors influencing their behaviour. Crooks' review of the impact of classroom evaluation on students deals in detail with motivation and classroom evaluation, but in essence the argument seems to be that students with high self-efficacy tend to make more use of deep learning strategies than other students; that they tend to persist in the face of failure or difficult tasks; and that self-efficacy is best enhanced if longer-term goals are supported by a carefully sequenced series of sub-goals with clear criteria that students find attainable. The important point here is that the goals must be attainable, and that in addition the standards must be clearly specified; both these factors have significant implications for teachers' strategies in relation to the level of work which is aimed at individual pupils, and the form of ongoing assessment which is carried out. Intrinsic motivation (that motivation which comes from within the self, rather than from external rewards) and self-regulated learning, are linked: self-regulated learning experiences tend to foster intrinsic motivation, intrinsic motivation in turn encourages students to be more independent as learners.

The effect of competition on motivation is also important. Competition is central to norm-referencing, which is a form of social comparison. This can lead to severe discouragement for students who have few academic successes in competition with their peers. It also discourages students from helping each other with their academic work, and encourages the covering up of misunderstandings. It threatens peer relationships, and tends to segregate groups into higher and lower achieving students. Neither does it encourage intrinsic motivation. It also tends to encourage students to attribute success and failure to ability, rather than to effort, which is especially harmful for low-achieving students. Crooks argues that we should reduce the amount of ability grouping and foster the use of cooperative learning approaches; the latter because one of the most potent forms of learning is receiving and giving elaborated explanations, and this tends to happen in cooperative learning settings, which also reduces the burden of failure on individual students. Performance feedback must also emphasize mastery and progress, rather than normative comparison. There should also be little emphasis on summative grading. Crooks concludes that '. . . if these conditions can be fostered, perceived ability stratification will be reduced, with consequent reductions in the serious differential changes of self-esteem that occur from about the age of 10' (*ibid*, p. 466).

Crooks emphasizes the significance of criterion-referenced evaluation (and by this he is referring not to strict criterion referencing, as we will discuss in chapter 6, but a form of standards or content referencing). In criterion-referenced evaluation, students are evaluated on the same tasks using the same standards; while this can become another type of competitive situation, there is at least some possibility of all students meeting specified passing standards. In addition the provision of repeated opportunities to meet these standards can be a factor in reducing the competitiveness of such assessment systems. But the best system of all, in relation to assessment and motivation is one in which the pupil's programme of work is individualized, and the emphasis in assessment is placed on each student's progress and learning (this is known as ipsative assessment); in such situations competitiveness is minimized, pupils are more inclined to help each other, and success and failure on a task are more likely to be attributed to effort rather than ability; this generates conditions that support intrinsic motivation.

Examinations at secondary level have traditionally been seen as having great motivating potential: they provide pupils with a powerful incentive to work, just at the age when they are becoming resistant to parental and teacher control, and more interested in the outside world (Gipps and Stobart, 1993). However, once youth unemployment began to appear on the scene in the UK, and there were few jobs available for school leavers, adolescents could see for themselves that a few qualifications could no longer guarantee employment, and the threat of exams was no longer sufficient to secure effort. Why should pupils continue to work at something in which they had little interest, when the reward was taken away? Here of course we are talking about extrinsic motivation, that is motivation external to the activity, doing something for a reward, rather than because of the enjoyment of, or interest in, the activity itself. Once it became obvious that teachers and parents could not use job success as a reason to work hard at school, other devices were sought. This happened with considerable speed, because of the political and public perception of the threat envisaged by the trends in youth unemployment and pupil behaviour (Hargreaves, 1988). For example, early records of achievement (RoA) schemes gave as one of their key strengths the development of motivation, particularly for the less able, which was the group most affected by the failure of the work-hard-to-get-some-exams-and-therefore-a-job argument.

The motivating properties of RoA are generally felt to include: recording experiences and achievements beyond the academic, thereby increasing the amount of success experienced by pupils, particularly the less academic; involving pupils in recording their own achievements, thus increasing their own independence and self-awareness; negotiating their assessments and future learning with teachers, thus encouraging them to feel that they have some control over their achievements and record; breaking up the curriculum into short units or modules, with assessment at the end of each one, because more immediate, achievable targets are more likely to retain enthusiasm than the long haul of public exams. Thus both extrinsic and intrinsic motivation are being addressed. There are, however, criticisms of using RoA to motivate pupils in this way. These relate to the role of education in shaping students' personal qualities to those required by employers, and the view that they are potentially a device for surveillance and control (Hargreaves, 1986).

Graded assessment too is felt to have motivating potential. First, the student has only to demonstrate what is required for a particular grade in order to achieve it, rather than their work being compared with the work of others. Second, shorter units of work with linked assessment are more motivating for many pupils than the two-year public exam syllabus. Third, taking the assessment only when ready to pass is clearly motivating in that the aim is to prevent failure; on the other hand, this presents severe organizational difficulties, particularly when teachers are used to teaching and assessing classes in lock step.

The GCSE also reflected a desire to improve motivation through its emphasis on positive achievement. Positive achievement sprang from the idea that the examination itself should allow all candidates to show what they *could* do, rather than to present many students with tasks which they were likely to fail (the 'examination as hurdle' model). Positive achievement was important in the early rhetoric about GCSEs; the aim was that all pupils would be able to show what they know, understand and can do, and that assessment should be a positive experience for all, rather than a dispiriting one for some. Therefore candidates should not be presented with tasks that were too difficult (SEC, 1985). If assessment was a positive experience, the argument went, motivation would be enhanced. However, since all candidates must be presented with tasks which they can do, the result is that differentiated papers are required in order to cope with the whole ability range. Owing to the need to allocate pupils to particular examination paths, and the consequent limit on grades which results, differentiation has in itself implications for motivation (for a discussion of differentiation in the GCSE see Gipps and Stobart, 1993, chapter 7). Another element of the GCSE which was designed to enhance motivation was the emphasis on coursework assessment. Research evidence indicates that for many pupils the coursework element has indeed enhanced their motivation and engagement in the work: the problem has often been one of pupils becoming over-involved in coursework assignments, to the detriment of routine classwork and homework (NEEDS project, 1990). The changes in content and teaching style accompanying GCSE have also affected intrinsic motivation (HMI, 1988), not least in modern languages, where the radical changes from 'O' level requirements have clearly encouraged many pupils. This is reflected in the dramatic increase in 'A' level entry from students who took GCSE.

It is important not to take too simplistic a view of assessment and motivation, since we must distinguish the form of assessment that we have in mind, and the type of motivation in which we are interested. Any form of assessment will have a motivating effect for those students who gain success, while for those who do not, traditional norm-referenced assessment is likely to result in further alienation from school learning. Self-assessment is believed to enhance motivation, however, the rationale for this is rarely explicitly stated, although as chapter 2 shows, self-assessment is linked with monitoring one's own learning, becoming an independent learner and as such is part of the metacognitive process in learning. However, unless student self-assessment is understood for how it can help motivation, and is handled well and in a positive, constructive way, rather than in a negative norm-referenced way, it will not greatly enhance motivation.

Kellaghan and Madaus (1993) suggest that policy-makers do not think clearly about the role of assessment in motivation, and offer the following as an example of naive thinking: 'A national examination and certification system will pressure schools to improve; entice students to put forth more effort; and, thereby, raise student achievement. These changes, in turn, will lead to a more skilled, productive and competitive workforce; and ultimately guarantee the quality of life for us and future generations' (Oakes, 1991, p. 17, quoted by Kellaghan and Madaus, 1993, p. 3).

Motivation is a complex concept, and was critiqued in much of the psychological literature in the fifties and sixties; it is only in more recent years that interest in it has re-emerged. However, problems remain in its definition, operationalization and measurement. Given the complexity of the concept of motivation, and its chequered role in the history of psychology it is extraordinary that such broad claims should be made for the effect of assessment in this area. However, as this chapter has shown, there can be little doubt, that if high stakes are attached to students' performance then at least some schools and some students will be motivated to work for the examinations. One way in which this may be achieved is that the examinations themselves make the goals of instruction explicit, so that students and teachers have well-defined targets to work towards. Examinations may provide standards of expected achievement (the explicit standards and goals in Sadler's version of formative assessment). For students who are not likely to do well on high stakes external tests, the possible negative effects are a serious concern. There is research evidence from a number of countries to show that where there are formal external assessments for graduation, or to stay in a year group, the assessment policy is implicated in increasing the drop out rate. Kellaghan and Madaus also make the point that many students in countries that have public exams are not motivated to do well in these for what they call sociocultural reasons, or on the basis of their estimate of present levels of achievement or ability. Thus they are likely to become alienated, not only from the exams but from the whole educational process. That around 10 per cent of students, mostly from disadvantaged backgrounds, avoid taking public exams before leaving school is regarded as a serious problem in several European countries. The group of pupils that is unlikely to pass high stakes tests, in their efforts to decrease personal anxiety and to protect their own self-esteem, will reduce their amount of effort and involvement in the examination in order to protect themselves, since they feel they are likely to fail.

The impact of high-stakes external tests on pupil motivation is complex and uncertain; what is clear is that it will not enhance motivation for all pupils. It is indeed much more likely to decrease motivation for that group of pupils who are at risk of scoring low. The setting of clear standards within a low-stakes assessment programme, including school-based assessment, together with positive, constructive feedback, and a focus on ipsative comparisons can however have positive effects on student motivation.

Teaching to the Test

Teaching to the test is an activity well-documented in the USA, but it is also a relatively well-understood activity in the UK, though here it might be called preparation for examinations. Practice on items similar to those which are going to be tested may in some circumstances be a useful form of instruction (Linn, 1981). But the important question is whether the skills thus taught and practised are transferable to other situations; we need evidence of the generalizability of the results. Learning the answer to a set of questions is not the same as coming to understand whatever the skill or concepts are that the questions represent; if there is too close a match between teaching material and the test itself we may not be able to gauge whether the important constructs and understanding are being assessed. Linn concludes that too close a match of teaching and testing, with an emphasis on practising the items that appear in the test, destroys the measurement value of the test, because we do not know whether attaining the items on the test means that the student actually understands and can apply the skills and concepts tested. To test whether a pupil can apply skills and knowledge, he/she must be given a new problem to solve, or must be asked about the concepts in a different context. What we need to know is that students have been taught, not the actual items in the test, but the skills and knowledge measured by the test, that is, that the students have been taught the construct, not just how to answer the items.

Test Score Pollution

The practice of teaching to the test, in order to raise test scores, is generally called in the US 'test score pollution'. Pollution here refers to an increase in the test score which is not connected to the construct being measured, that is it produces construct-irrelevant test score variance (see chapter 4). This is what Linn (1981) means by improving test scores without actually mastering the skills or constructs being assessed. Haladnya *et al.*, (1991) believe that test score pollution is pervasive in American education, and give three sources of test pollution:

(a) the way schools and personnel prepare students for tests;
(b) test administration activities or conditions;
(c) exogenous factors representing forces beyond the control of schools and teachers.

An example of exogenous factors is the reporting of test scores without acknowledging background factors, for example, family SES, student mother tongue, and other factors which can lead the general public and parents to draw invalid inferences from the test scores. The polluting practices include: teaching test taking skills, promoting pupil motivation for the test, developing a curriculum to match the test, preparing teaching objectives to match the test, preparing pupils on items similar to those in the test, using commercial materials specifically designed to test performance, and presenting before the test the actual items to be tested (p. 4). These are practices which, apart from the very last one, are well known in high performing schools in the UK. While the last example would be seen as cheating, the other activities would simply be seen as good examination preparation practice. According to Haladnya *et al.*, (1991), polluting practices also occur during the actual administration of the tests. These include doctoring the answer sheets by rubbing out wrong marks, allowing or encouraging low-achieving students to be absent on test days, and actual interference with responses by giving hints or answers. Haladnya *et al.*, (1991) go on to analyze these test polluting practices into ethical and unethical activities; I deal with these in detail in the chapter on ethics but include this information here to show how teaching to the test operates.

The 'Lake Wobegon' Effect

The *Lake Wobegon* story is about teaching to the test and test-score pollution. In 1987 an American physician, called John Cannell published a report stating that all fifty US states were reporting scores above the national average at all grades tested (Cannell, 1987). The impact of this in the US was profound. The official investigation concluded that, while there were a number of criticisms of the survey on which the report was based, they had to accept that the primary finding, that is that all fifty states were above average in the elementary grades, was correct (Phillips, 1990). John Cannell started his investigation because he discovered that West Virginia, which is the state with the highest percentage of adults without a college education, the second lowest per capita income, and the third lowest college entrance scores in the US, was actually producing results on a basic skills test which showed that in all fifty-five school districts students in the elementary grades were above the national average at all grades tested. Cannell wondered how West Virginia could do so well on a nationally normed test: if West Virginia was above the average, what state could be below the average? Cannell and the organization 'Friends for Education' then carried out their survey, and discovered that in all fifty states performance at the elementary levels was apparently above the average.

This was called the 'Lake Wobegon effect', in reference to Garrison Keillor's novel, *Lake Wobegon Days*, since in Lake Wobegon, (a mythical town in the US mid-west), all children are above average. But how could it be that all the states were able to produce these above average scores? Cannell suggested that it was a combination of inaccurate initial norms, and teaching to the test; the result he concluded was that no weight could be put on the high averages reported by every state. The evaluation of the Report for the US Department of Education (Phillips, 1990), suggested five reasons for these high scores:

1   The test users were choosing tests which best matched their local curriculum. This would give them an advantage over the students used in the 'norming' sample.
2   Test users may be more motivated to do well than students in the 'norming' sample, for whom the test did not matter.
3   Test familiarity: as the test is repeatedly used, schools become more and more familiar with the content and format. Again, this gives the user an advantage not shared by the norming sample.
4   The effect could be due to district response bias during the norming process. Since it is difficult to get school districts to co-operate in norming of tests, it may be that there was a particular overlap between the norming sample and the testing sample. If this is the case, then the performance of the testing sample would increase more over time, due to test familiarity.
5   The population of the school system tested and the norming sample may be different. The school system may exclude low-achieving students from the test, while these might be included in the norming sample.

Another reason put forward is the use of old, or outdated norms, since a number of factors could result in improvement on these old norms, including familiarity with the test in schools. Linn *et al.*, (1990) suggest that whenever results are reported, information should also be given about the date when the test was normed. Linn *et al.*, (1990) also point out that the gains on published tests are greater than the gains on the National Assessment of Educational Progress, which cannot be practised for. They thus suggest that although achievement scores may be rising, it is unlikely that true achievement is enhanced, ie that the test score gains are spurious or polluted. Whatever the reasons for the Lake Wobegon effect, the important outcome of this study and its critique was the focus on teaching to the test, and the effect that this had on what was taught, and how it was taught, ie the limiting effects of teaching to the test, rather than the misleading results.

Shepard (1990) concludes that forty out of the fifty states had high-stakes testing programmes, which placed pressure on head teachers to raise scores. Teaching to the test, she concludes exists in every state to some degree. It was the media, and the publications of results by the media, which was most likely to make teachers and head teachers anxious about performance. There is not only pressure to do well, but there is the opportunity to do well when the test is a familiar one, since in many states teachers give the same test in the classroom each year, and it is clear what this means in a high-stakes setting. Shepard concludes that, although test publishers might produce new tests more regularly, and thus update the norms, that this will not solve the basic problem of test-curriculum alignment, when less than perfect test objectives become the exclusive focus of instruction. Instead, she suggests, that since all tests are corruptible at high levels of pressure for accountability, the move should be towards tests which are not harmful to pedagogy and curriculum if teachers focus on teaching them. This is a call for the use of 'authentic' and performance-based assessments because teaching to these assessments is less damaging. 'In the context of high-stakes accountability, writing assessments, oral reading . . . interviews . . . student portfolios, and the like not only yield more trustworthy data on student performance, but pose less of a threat to the quality of instruction, if teachers use replicas as the templates for day-to-day instruction' (*ibid*, p. 21). Shepard's survey concluded that, without question, published norm-referenced tests are chosen so as to align as much as possible with the states' curriculum.

Koretz *et al.*, (1991) carried out a study in which they compared test results on a high-stakes test which had been used for several years in a large urban school district with those on a comparable test which had not been used in that district for several years. They found that high performance on the regularly-used test did not generalize to the other test for which students had not been specifically prepared, showing that the students had been prepared for the testing in a way which boosts scores rather than actual achievement in the domain that the tests are intended to measure. The conclusion is, from this and other studies, that teaching to a particular test invalidates the test results as indicators of more general learning. Using the same test year after year results in scores being raised without improving achievement on the broader domain. This threatens making valid inferences from the test score to the larger domain of achievement.

Why and How Teachers Teach to the Test

Smith (1991a) has carried out a detailed, qualitative study of the role of external testing in two elementary schools in the USA. Though the study is small, the data obtained are very detailed, and covered all aspects of school life over a period of fifteen months. Furthermore, much of what Smith concludes is in line with the findings of not only other research (although Smith's work extends beyond the findings of research into interpretation) and also with the findings of our evaluation of National Assessment in primary schools (NAPS)[1]. Smith's thesis is that teachers experience anxiety, shame, loss of esteem and alienation from the publication and use of test scores. These feelings are incorporated into the teachers' identities and subsequent definitions of teaching. Smith concludes that the effects of testing on teachers fall into a number of categories:

> 1 'The publication of test scores produces feelings of shame, embarrassment, guilt and anger in teachers, and the determination to do what is necessary to avoid such feelings in future'. (p. 9)

They react to these feelings by teaching to the test. However, there is a double-edged danger for teachers, in that too much teaching to the test can result in scores that are high enough to draw suspicions of cheating, and Smith cites the example of one such teacher, who gained very high test scores in a low SES district, and who was investigated, suspected of cheating.

> 2 'Beliefs about the invalidity of the test, and the necessity to raise scores, set up feelings of dissonance and alienation'. (*ibid*)

Because the tests do not match with teachers' beliefs about what is educationally valuable, they may end up feeling alienated 'why should we worry about the scores, when we know they are worthless?'

> 3 'Beliefs about the emotional impact of testing on young children generate feelings of anxiety and guilt among teachers'. (*ibid*)

Teachers feel anxious about the effect on younger children. They try a variety of techniques to ensure that the pupils do not feel over anxious. However, as Smith points out, not all teachers feel this way, and administrators tend to deny emotional effects on pupils, or blame pupils' emotional responses on the over-reaction of teachers. Still, this belief has salience for many teachers, and cannot be discounted.

> 4 'Testing programmes reduce the time available for instruction'. 'The focus on material that the test covers results in a narrowing of possible curriculum, and the reduction of teachers' ability to

adapt, create, or diverge. The received curriculum is increasingly viewed as not amenable to criticism or revision.' (p. 10)

The narrowing of curriculum and the neglect of untested subjects happened, as Smith put it, 'before our eyes' (*ibid*). However, teachers dealt with this tendency in two different ways. The first was accommodation 'faced with a packed curriculum', in other words, requirements which exceed the ability and time of any teacher to cover all competently. Some teachers did indeed align their teaching with the tested curriculum, discarding what was not going to be tested. The other stance was resistance. The teachers who resisted narrowing of the curriculum, who refused to give up doing for example, practical maths, or spending some time reading stories each day, were likely, in the setting which Smith describes, to pay a price for their resistance: in high stakes state testing programmes in the USA, such teachers are likely to be subject to frequent demands to defend their teaching programmes on other grounds, and suffer concern about sanctions in the case of low scores. A second form of resistance was that of political action; in the US, in the States studied by Smith, teachers were successful in encouraging legislation that did not require the testing of first grade pupils.

Smith's findings echo in a number of ways those of our research[1] in relation to teachers of 7-year-olds in the national assessment programme in England:

— the feelings of anger and guilt about the published results and the intention to avoid these in future;
— feelings of dissonance and alienation because of the perceived invalidity of the testing program;
— feelings of concern about the impact of testing on young children.

Eventually, their resistance, supported by colleagues teaching 14-year-olds, led to a withdrawal of the publication of school league tables at age 7.

Smith makes two final, and telling, points. First, the form of the test, whether norm-referenced or criterion-referenced, is not relevant to the impact which it has on teachers and teaching; it is the political and social uses made of the scores which determine its effect. Second, if teachers become too controlled, in terms of what they teach and how they teach it, by high stakes, narrow, tests, they will lose their capacity to teach other, untested topics, and other methods. 'A teacher who is able to teach only that which is determined from above, and can teach only by worksheets, is an unskilled worker. Far from the reflective practitioner, or the empowered teacher, those optimistic images of the 1980s, the image we project . . . is that of interchangeable technicians, receiving the standard curriculum from above, transmitting it as given . . .' (p. 11) The closeness of this observation to that made by Edmond Holmes in 1911 in his critique of the Payment by Results system in England is very marked:

> What the Department did to the teacher, it compelled him to do to the child. The teacher who is the slave of another's will cannot carry out his instructions except by making his pupils the slaves of his own will. The teacher who has been deprived by his superiors of freedom, initiative, and responsibility, cannot carry out his instructions except by depriving his pupils of the same vital qualities . . .

> . . . To be in bondage to a syllabus is a misfortune for a teacher, and a misfortune for the school that he teaches. To be in bondage to a syllabus which is binding on all schools alike, is a graver misfortune. To be in bondage to a bad syllabus which is binding on all schools alike, is of all misfortunes the gravest.

> Of the evils that are inherent in the examination system as such — of its tendency to arrest growth, to deaden life, to paralyse the higher faculties, to externalize what is inward, to materialize what is spiritual, to involve education in an atmosphere of unreality and self-deception — I have already spoken at some length. In the days of payment by results various circumstances conspired to raise those evil tendencies to the highest imaginable 'power'. When inspectors ceased to examine (in the stricter sense of the word) they realized what infinite mischief the yearly examination had done . . .

> . . . Not a thought was given, except in a small minority of the schools, to the real training of the child, to the fostering of his mental (and other) growth. To get him through the yearly examination by hook or by crook was the one concern of the teacher. As profound distrust of the teacher was the basis of the policy of the Department, so profound distrust of the child was the basis of the policy of the teacher. To leave the child to find out anything for himself, to work out anything for himself, would have been regarded as a proof of incapacity, not to say insanity, on the part of the teacher, and would have led to

results which, from the 'percentage' point of view, would probably have been disastrous. (Holmes, 1911, pp. 105–9)

Impact on the School System

Many educational innovations are adopted even though they have high levels of uncertainty; because of the nature of education the wisdom of adopting these innovations and the range of their effects are rarely known in advance (Airasian, 1988b). This is nowhere more so than in the imposition of testing programmes to raise standards (Gipps and Stobart, 1983). The fact is however, that despite this, there has been over the last fifteen years a rapid increase in the amount of high-stakes testing in order to raise standards and control curriculum. Airasian argues that the legitimacy of these assessment programme innovations derives, not from empirical evidence of their likely effectiveness, but from the perceptions which they evoke and the symbol which they offer of order and control, desired educational outcomes in traditional terms of certification and exam passes, and traditional moral values. Because of this symbolism, they strike a responsive chord with the public at large, and this helps to explain the widespread and speedy adoption of this form of innovation. The traditional values which the testing programmes endorse are the same as those endorsed by the existing culture, and this is the legitimization necessary to justify their widespread adoption. 'Given a different extant culture, state mandated, high-stakes testing programmes might have been considerably less warmly endorsed' (Airasian, 1988b, p. 311). Airasian's argument about the moral element of particular forms of testing programme is particularly interesting in relation to current developments in England, where a return to traditional teaching and traditional examination, is, in the view of the extreme right, linked with reasserting traditional moral values. Tests, Airasian concludes, are socially valid and respected symbols of a broad range of administrative, academic and moral virtues in society. With the added feature of central control together with sanctions for poor performance symbolic importance will be increased. The argument goes that, regardless of the actual impact that such high-stakes tests have on pupils, teachers or the curriculum, they are likely to have an important perceptual impact on the public at large. 'This perceptual impact underlies the social consensus, or social validation that provides the legitimisation of testing as a workable and desired reform strategy' (*ibid*, p. 312). Of course the public's view of the power of such tests to raise standards can be supported; in such a situation teachers will teach to the test and so student scores will rise. This is indeed what the British

government claimed in 1993 to be the case with regard to the introduction of National Curriculum and Assessment. Of course, as already
pointed out earlier in this chapter, what this rise might well be is
simply increased ability to perform the type of assessment task, rather
than enhanced performance in the construct or skills underlying those
tasks. This line of argument would, however, be unlikely to carry
much weight with those who demand mandated testing programmes.

Indeed there is evidence from close study of state-wide testing
programmes in the USA that the result of the imposition of such
testing programmes to reform schools in fact has rather the opposite
effect, as the focus of activity becomes not to reform schools but to
raise levels of performance on the test. Furthermore, the higher the
stakes involved, the more the response to the testing programme was
to raise scores rather than improve learning; the teachers tried to raise
test score levels to reduce the pressure on them. At the school district
level, the testing did not result in attempts to restructure or re-organize
the school, instead time, money and effort were redirected to some
parts of the system so that they could speedily increase their test scores,
while leaving the parts of the system which were producing good
scores well alone. It did not encourage the teachers to think about how
they should teach the subject matter, or administer the schools, they
simply addressed the parts of the system that felt the direct impact of
testing (Corbett and Wilson, 1990). In Corbett and Wilson's view, the
teachers are not at fault for teaching to the test, they are caught in a
double-bind, particularly since there are sanctions for poor performance.
Instead their view is that the policy-makers are using the wrong tool
to change schools and improve the system; if what is wanted is a
reexamination of schooling in terms of purpose, structure and process,
then testing programmes are the wrong vehicle for these reasons:

- Outcome measures stated in terms of student learning do not
  provide direction as to what school systems should do to produce different results.
- Testing programmes, both in terms of results and in the implications for action, ignore variations in district contexts that
  may affect the importance of the results, and the appropriateness of certain responses from community to community.
- State-wide testing policies tend to foster conditions anti-thetical
  to actual reform. (ibid, pp. 14–15)

Corbett and Wilson (1988) explain that a school district which is told
it is teaching reading poorly, on being told to raise scores, will tend to

teach reading poorly more intensively, without focusing on the more general question of how better to teach reading. If schools knew the right actions to take in order to enhance performance, they would take them anyway, in the absence of pressure. The testing programmes tend to identify individuals with weaknesses. This is not the same as diagnosing system weaknesses, and, Corbett and Wilson argue, without system diagnosis, little guidance is available as to what it is about existing purpose, structure and process that needs changing. Similarly, they point out that schools or districts with high test scores may not reflect good practice, but simply an advantaged pupil population, as the critics of the school league tables being published in the UK would argue. Corbett and Wilson found in their research that many teachers and heads themselves felt uncomfortable about their reaction to the high-stakes testing. What was happening, however, was that they felt pressure coming from the local community, often via the local newspaper; the knowledge of local performance on the test was the means of empowerment for various local constituencies. This links in with Smith's (1992) findings among elementary school teachers of anxiety about the publication of scores.

Although Corbett and Wilson, and Airasian were writing in relation to the introduction of minimum competency testing programmes to raise standards, the same argument is reverberating in the USA again in relation to using performance-based assessment in order to enhance the teach ing of higher order thinking and skills. As I made clear in chapter 1 simply instituting a particular form of assessment will in itself not change teachers' practice. For the introduction of perform-ance-based assessment to have any significant impact on teachers' teaching practice, it needs to be accompanied by an explanation of, and training in, the skills and processes which are felt to be lacking or being taught at a low level.

Shepard (1992b) refers to this as 'test-leveraged reform'. She con-cludes that, as a result of the introduction of high-stakes minimum competency testing, basic skills test scores have increased in the US at the expense of higher order thinking and problem-solving skills; hence the calls in the early 1990s for the introduction of authentic or per-formance-based assessment to ensure that student learning will be re-directed toward more challenging content. The tests will be expected to play the same role as before in bringing about reform, but, it is hypothesized that the effects will be different because of the different nature of the assessments. Shepherd's review of research leads to the following findings about the effects of high-stakes testing:

1   When test results are given high stakes by political pressure, and media attention, scores can become inflated, thus giving a false impression of student achievement.
2   High-stakes tests narrow the curriculum. Tested content is taught to the exclusion of non-tested content.
3   High-stakes testing misdirects instruction, even for the basic skills.
4   The kind of drill-and-practice instruction that tests reinforce is based on outmoded learning theory. Rather than improve learning, it actually denies students opportunities to develop thinking and problem-solving skills.
5   Because of the pressure on test scores, more hard-to-teach children are rejected by the system.
6   The dictates of externally mandated tests reduce both the professional knowledge and status of teachers.

Resnick and Resnick (1992) induce three principles as guidelines for accountability assessment and their impact:

(a)   you get what you assess;
(b)   you do not get what you do not assess;
(c)   build assessments toward which you want educators to teach.

Based on the lessons learned from previous accountability testing programmes, Shepard argues that the following factors need to be considered in any attempt to bring in performance-based assessment to change teaching. First, the performance tasks need to be incorruptible, since it is possible for teachers to teach to the tasks in performance-based assessment just as in multiple-choice tasks. What we want is to develop assessments which will encourage teachers to teach to the construct or broader domain, rather than the assessment task. To put it differently, practice on the task is in itself of no value, unless the performance will generalize to other, similar tasks. Second, an important element of enhancing teaching of higher-order thinking and skills is teacher training in curriculum and instruction; in other words the tests themselves cannot bring about the changes that we seek.

In the American situation where there is a lot of tracking, or streaming, and pupils may be held back to retake a year, Shepard argues that they need to look for high standards in the assessment in order to raise performance (rather than minimal competency tests, which have been demonstrated to keep averages low) whilst not making students who fail to meet the high standards be kept back. The evidence is that streaming, or tracking, and re-taking years, do not enhance the educational performance of the students thus categorized. Shepard points out that, in relation to equity, the question is not just whether the exams measure fairly, but what impact they have on educational opportunity, and this is a question of consequential validity. The greater the consequences of test use, the more important it is to be concerned about issues of validity and fairness in relation to test use.

Wiggins (1989b) offers an enthusiastic account of what teaching to authentic tests can do for teaching and learning:

> to talk with disdain of 'teaching to the test' is to misunderstand how we learn. The test is the point of leverage — for learning and for reform. The issue is the integrity of the test: the genuineness, effectiveness and aptness of the challenge . . . legitimate and effective assessment is as simple (!) as ensuring that tests, grades, diploma requirements and the structures and policies practise what we preach as essential. If we so honor our professed aims, the problems associated with standardized testing will take care of themselves. (p. 46)

In view of the discussions above about the power which published results have over teachers' practice, and teachers' inability to resist accountability pressures in many settings, (together with the lack of attention paid to developing teachers' practice through training) Wiggins' stance is probably overly naive and optimistic.

These detailed accounts of the impact of testing on curriculum, teaching, school systems, pupil motivation and teachers' practice should leave us in no doubt as to the power of testing, particularly high-stakes testing, to affect teaching and learning. How then can we harness this powerful tool so that assessment, in the broadest sense, can help to develop the kind of learning and the higher order skills and processes described in the previous chapter? A broader conceptualization of assessment within the educational assessment paradigm is certainly part of the way forward. By moving beyond narrowly defined standardized testing and examination we can allow such skills to be taught even within a system dominated by high stakes assessment. But before discussing types of assessment which are at the heart of educational assessment, we need first to address the technical issues of reliability and validity.

Note

1 *National Assessment in Primary Schools: An Evaluation*, ESRC project No R000232192

Chapter 4

Validity and Reliability

Validity

The traditional definition of validity is the extent to which a test measures what is was designed to measure. If it does not measure what it purports to measure, then its use is misleading.

Early writings about validity emphasized four *types* of validity: predictive validity, content validity, construct validity and concurrent validity. *Predictive* validity relates to whether the test predicts accurately or well some future performance for example, is 'A' level a good predictor of performance in higher education? One difficulty in calculating predictive validity that, in the case of this example, only those who pass the exam go on to university (generally speaking) and we do not know how well students who did not pass might have done (see Wood, 1991). Also, only a small proportion of the population takes 'A' level and the correlation between 'A' level grades and degree performance would be higher if the entire 18-year-old population were included in the 'A' level group.

Concurrent validity is concerned about whether the test correlates with, or gives substantially the same results as, another test of the same skill. Of course if the second test is not itself valid (in terms of content or construct) then we may have simply two tests which correlate with each other but are not valid for the purpose intended. An example here would be a reading test which correlated highly with the Schonell Graded Word Reading test which we now see as having very low construct validity.

Construct validity itself relates to whether the test is an adequate measure of the construct, that is the underlying (explanatory)skill being assessed. Important to the development of an assessment then is a clear and detailed definition of the construct; as explained in chapter 1 a full definition of reading as a construct would include not only reading aloud, but also reading comprehension, accuracy, and enjoyment of reading.

Content validity is more straightforward and likely to stem from construct validity; it concerns the coverage of appropriate and necessary content i.e. does the test cover the skills necessary for good performance, or all the aspects of the subject taught? Content validity tends to be based on professional judgments about the relevance of the test content to the content of a particular domain, for example measurement in mathematics, and the representativeness with which the content covers that domain.

Concurrent and predictive validity are often combined to give criterion validity because they both relate to predicting performance on some criterion either at the same time or in the future. There are other definitions of validity too (Wood, 1987; Wiliam, 1992) but those outlined above have been the main approaches.

Emphasis on these different types of validity has led to a situation in which, all too often, evidence is provided about only one or two of these types of validity in test development. More recently therefore the literature on validity has emphasized that validity is in fact a unitary concept with construct as the unifying theme (Messick, 1989a; Cronbach, 1988). The responsibility for valid test use is put on to the user not the test developer (assuming that there is evidence of construct validity). A third development is the emphasis, in developing performance assessment, on validity *rather* than technical reliability: the reverse of the situation with, for example, standardized tests.

Validity as a Unitary Concept

Messick (1989a) in his classic chapter on validity describes the testing profession's move toward recognizing

> 'validity as a unitary concept, in the sense that score meaning as embodied in construct validity underlies all score-based inferences. But for a fully unified view of validity, it must also be recognized that the appropriateness, meaningfulness and usefulness of score-based inferences depend as well on the social consequences of the testing. Therefore, social values cannot be ignored in considerations of validity'. (p. 19)

Messick therefore is operating with a notion of validity that relates to inferences drawn from test scores. 'Validity is an integrated evaluative judgment of the degree to which empirical evidence and theoretical rationales support the *adequacy* and *appropriateness* of *inferences* and *attitudes* based on test scores or other modes of assessment' (p. 13). Validity here, then, relates to the *evidence* available to support test inter-pretation and potential *consequences* of test use. This, clearly, is a different and more demanding conception of validity than 'the extent to which a test measures what it purports to measure', as Nuttall (1987) points out.

Messick (1989a) argues that 'Construct validity is based on any evidence that bears on the interpretation or meaning of the test scores' (p. 16), and gives a list of questions which he maintains must be addressed in the development of *any* assessment:

- Are we looking at the right things in the right balance?
- Has anything important been left out?
- Does our way of looking introduce sources of invalidity or irrelevant variance that bias the scores or judgments?
- Does our way of scoring reflect the manner in which domain processes combine to produce effects and is our score structure consistent with the structure of the domain about which inferences are to be drawn or predictions made?
- What evidence is there that our scores mean what we interpret them to mean, in particular, as reflections of knowledge and skill having plausible implications for educational action relative to personal or group standards?
- Are there plausible rival interpretations of score meaning or alternative implications for action, and, if so, by what evidence and arguments are they discounted?
- Are the judgments or scores reliable and are their properties and relationships generalizable across the contents and contexts of use as well as across pertinent population groups?
- Do the scores have utility for the proposed purposes in the applied settings?
- Are the scores applied fairly for these purposes?
- Are the short- and long-term consequences of score interpretation and use supportive of the general testing aims and are there any adverse side-effects? (Messick, 1992, p. 3)

The aim in asking these questions is to collect evidence and arguments to discount the two major threats to validity: construct underrepresentation and construct irrelevant variance.

An example of the latter is an emphasis on reading comprehension in a test of subject matter knowledge: the construct score will be, invalidly, low for poor readers because of the reading demands. Construct underrepresentation is just that and Messick advocates specifying the full breadth of the construct in the content specifications for a test; in the validation process we should use multiple measures and types of each construct under scrutiny.

'The essential purpose of construct validity is to justify a particular interpretation of a test score by explaining the behaviour that the test score summarises' (Moss, 1992, p. 233). Construct validation requires an explicit conceptual framework, hypotheses deduced from this which can be tested, and multiple lines of relevant evidence to do so. Searching for plausible rival hypotheses or alternative explanations of test scores is an important process after initially describing and specifying the construct. Evidence comes from patterns of relationships among items within a test, between test scores and other measures; studies of performance differences over time, across groups and settings, and in response to experimental treatments and manipulations; modelling of the processes underlying test responses; content relevance and representativeness; and criterion-relatedness. Thus, Messick concludes, almost all forms of validity evidence are subsumed under construct validity; the only missing evidence is appraisal of social consequences.

So, Messick (1989a and 1992) and Cronbach (1980 and 1988) have taken the discussion of validity beyond a conception based on the functional worth of the testing: construct validity is needed not only to support test interpretation, but also to justify test use. This is particularly pertinent to current test developments in the UK and USA, since programmes are being developed in order to have a major impact on curriculum and instruction.

Validity and the Consequences of Test Use

Consideration of the consequences of test use and interpretation — called consequential validity — is a relatively recent development but it is in tune with developments in the philosophy of science: science is no longer seen as a value-free activity, and Weber's ideal of a value-free social science is 'passé'. Messick quotes Kaplan (1964) 'all propositions . . . are judged on the basis of their implications and not just in terms of what they entail but also in terms of what they make more likely' (Messick, 1989a, p. 58). The same is true, according to Messick, in assessment: values, which we must explicitly address, have a role in determining or distorting the meaning of test score interpretations.

Messick was the first to suggest that two questions have to be asked: is the test any good as a measure of the characteristic we are supposed to assess and should the test be used for the proposed purpose? Thus what is being evaluated (as we pointed out above) is not just the test itself but the validity of each particular use of a test. A dramatic example used by Messick is should tests 'predictive of dire academic failure' be used to place children in special education programmes without explicitly addressing the intended and unintended consequences of such use?

The effects of test consequences include the systematic effects of recurrent or regular testing on schools and curriculum as described in the previous chapter. So we need to ask whether the potential or actual consequences of test interpretation and use are not only supportive of intended purposes but also consistent with other social values.

As an example of a social consequence of testing Messick cites females scoring low on a quantitative test; this is likely to have an adverse impact on the females and is due to *either* a source of test invalidity *or* reflects a valid aspect of the construct assessed — perhaps both. If it is the first, this affects the meaning of the test scores and if the second affects the meaning of the construct. Thus social consequences, construct validity and the meaning of test scores are interlinked.

Messick uses a two-by-two table to show the facets of the unitary concept of validity.

Table 4.1:   Facets of Validity

	Test Interpretation	Test Use
Evidential Basis	Construct Validity	Construct Validity + Relevance/utility
Consequential Basis	Value implications	Social consequences

(*ibid*, p. 20)

This table shows that the evidential basis of test interpretation is construct validity, as it is for use, although in the latter CV is combined with relevance (of the test to the specific purpose) and utility (of the test in the applied setting). The consequential basis of test interpretation is the appraisal of value implications of the construct, and of test use is the potential and actual social consequences of the testing together with construct validity, relevance/utility and value implications. It is construct validity, Messick claims, which binds the validity of test use to validity of test interpretation. For example, in the example given above if it is some aspect of the test that contributes to the gender differences adverse impact here is an issue of test invalidity. However, if these differences reflect valid properties of the construct tapped by the test they contribute to score meaning and are thus not a source of test invalidity. So, Messick concludes, if the sources of invalidity are not due to the test itself then the decision about whether to use the test, bearing in mind its adverse impact, is an issue of political or social policy. Evidence of construct validity and consequences must be weighed up in making such a decision.

Extending the social consequences argument Messick makes the point that judging whether a test does the job it is employed to do requires us to evaluate the intended or unintended social consequences of its use. 'It is not that the ends should not justify the means, for what else could possibly justify the means if not appraisal of the ends' (*ibid*, p. 85).

This approach begins to address issues of ethics in assessment which form the basis of a later chapter: what has come to be known as 'consequential validity' is a key issue in ethical considerations. One reason for this shift in emphasis within validity seems to be the role of legislation in testing in the USA: educational measurement experts have been called upon to defend the uses of tests in various circumstances and this has resulted in the move to widen the scope of validity studies.

With this expansion of the concept of validity to include consideration of social consequences the focus of validity evaluation becomes 'personal, institutional and societal goals', (Cronbach, 1980, p. 101). Messick and Cronbach, however, appear to hold different views about the relationship between consequences and test validity. Messick takes the view that adverse impact does not *itself* render the test invalid, if construct validity has been demonstrated, while Cronbach argues that adverse social consequences *of themselves* call the validity of a test use into question.

They also offer different advice about evaluating intended and unintended consequences. Messick suggests evaluating the proposed assessment against alternatives, for example, other forms of assessment or alternative means of serving the same purpose, including not assessing at all. Cronbach, on the other hand, suggests canvassing stakeholders and investigating how decisions which might be made would affect their interests, and being sensitive to these in the decision making process (Moss, 1992).

Although the importance of construct validity and the social consequences of test use has been a major theme over the last ten-fifteen years in the American academic literature, as Moss points out, most of the measurement textbooks as well as the most recent Standards for Educational and Psychological Testing (AERA, APA, NCME, 1985), continue to describe validity in terms of construct, criterion and content-related evidence and do not emphasize the importance of social consequences in consideration of validity. One suspects that this is so because the shift in the concepts has been so great that it will take some time for practitioners to take on the new frameworks.

Consequential validity relates more directly to use than to interpretation of scores. 'Washback' on teaching and the curriculum are long-established consequences of assessment, particularly high-stakes testing. These consequences may be sound educationally, such as encouraging the teaching of a broader range of skills, or negative as in a narrowing tendency to teach to the test. The current emphasis on performance-based assessment in the USA is driven by the desire to have a particular sort of consequence on teaching: encouraging the teaching of practical, problem-solving and higher order skills. However, 'if performance-based assessments are going to have a chance of realizing the potential that the major proponents in the movement hope for, it will be essential that the consequential basis of validity be given much greater prominence among the criteria that are used for forming assessments' (Linn *et al.*, 1991, p. 17). In other words in the development of performance assessment not only does evidence need to be collected about the intended and unintended effects on teaching and learning, but we need to be much more clear about what we wish the effects on teaching and learning to be.[1]

Systemic validity is a specific form of consequential validity (Frederiksen and Collins, 1989). 'A systemically valid test is one that induces in the education system curricular and instructional changes that foster the development of the cognitive skills that the test is designed to measure' (p. 27). As Frederiksen and Collins point out, since the education system tends to adapt itself to the characteristics of high stakes tests, introducing tests in to the system poses particular validity problems.

Linn (1989) points out that when individual pupils' results are aggregated up to give results at class, school and district level another validity question arises. We may conclude that interpretations and uses of test scores are fine for individual students but their validity may have to be reconsidered at the aggregated level. This is a highly significant issue, particularly in the UK in the context of national assessment. If a testing programme has, say, formative purposes at the pupil level, accountability purposes at the school and class level, and policy purposes at the district level this poses a hugely complex validation task. A test could be shown to have construct validity and positive impact at the pupil level but adverse impact at the school level if the results are to be used to put in league tables to encourage parents to choose high performing schools (which will penalize schools in poor areas with a disadvantaged intake). Since the uses are so clearly different at the different levels it seems highly unlikely that the same test can be considered equally valid at all levels, which is the same as saying that a test can not be valid for all purposes. Support for this comes from work on the UK national curriculum assessment program which shows that the same assessment cannot be used satisfactorily for a range of purposes (Harlen *et al.*, 1992; Gipps, 1992a).

The challenge to validity in such a situation is so great that it questions the conceptualization being put forward by Linn, Messick, etc. Control over use of results is neither possible nor practical; control over interpretation of results is even more difficult to specify. As Tittle (1989) points out, evidence describing teachers' interpretation and use of assessment has to be gathered as part of the validity enquiry process; we know, however, that such interpretations are hugely complex. The assessment result itself is only one piece of information which the teacher will use in making inferences and deciding on test use; the other pieces of information are the pupil's personal and learning history; the realities and constraints of the class or group setting; and the type of assessment information (whether it is detailed or a single figure, criterion-referenced or a standardized score etc). The teacher's interpretation of the test score is dependent upon other knowledge that she has, including how the pupil responded to the tasks that made up the assessment and how he/she will respond to the follow-up tasks and activities. Tittle's argument is that we need to extend validity enquiry to include the teacher's and student's perspective to add to the professional's perspective in the validation of what test scores mean and whether they are useful to teachers and learners. What adds to the complexity is that we cannot assume that the teacher shares the same frame of reference as the test developer, and furthermore that test use cannot be considered independently of local context (as Messick, 1989a and b, points out).

'Validity is thus a two pronged theory. On the one hand, it seeks to be based on generalisability. On the other hand, the test scores we hope to be valid cannot be generalizable' (Tittle, 1989, p. 8). The paradox is that the logico-scientific paradigm encourages generalizability and yet validity theory now suggests that inferences and uses can only be valid if interpreted in the local context. 'Valid inferences can only be constructed by the teacher, and valid use arises from the accuracy and appropriateness of the meaning teachers construct from test scores and the information system in which they are embedded' (*ibid*).

This line of argument takes Tittle to the (logical) conclusion that where test results are not used by teachers (of which there is plenty of evidence for example, Gipps *et al.*, 1989), then the test/testing system is invalid in that setting. Is the reason that the test results are not used because they do not fit the frame of reference of the teacher? Is the time frame wrong? Is there too much or too little information? Tittle argues that all these would be causes of test invalidity because they result in the results not being used (although Messick would not agree, if the test demonstrated construct validity).

To expand the scope of validity enquiry even further Tittle suggests that in the case of educational assessment for teaching and learning the model of the classroom and the educational goals of the teacher must be specified, as must the criteria for the selection of relevant constructs for assessment. The relationship between the model of the classroom, constructs and the assessment can be described as part of the validation process. Ideally, she maintains, validation studies would include case study examples of classroom uses of assessment; these can provide illustrative descriptions of school and classroom uses of assessment information by teachers (and pupils). Tittle describes a maths assessment programme in which she and her colleagues have developed assessment in conjunction with teachers based on the validity requirements explained above. In this way she has been able to develop assessment which can be built in to the planning-teaching-learning cycle. Of course, while such validation studies are possible, and would explicate the role of assessment in the teaching/learning process, this detailed evaluation will add considerably to test development costs. It is fairly unlikely that at a political and commercial level this is feasible for accountability assessment and could result in test developers only evaluating the technical aspects of validity while leaving the evaluation of interpretation, use and social consequences to others (as Shepard, 1993, has recently pointed out). This, of course, is the current situation which has led to concern and the reconceptualization of validity as a unitary concept.

To conclude, Messick is the key writer in relation to validity and in the USA he has certainly led the field in reconceptualizing validity theory. What is important in relation to our critique of psychometrics is that Messick has clearly moved away from claiming that what we need is ever more refined statistical analyses to solve problems which do not have a measurement base but a social base: Messick takes us firmly into a scenario in which educational, *and* social implications of assessment are addressed, and his work is to be welcomed for this. There is a danger, however, that the concept has become over-elaborated in relation to interpretation and use. If interpretation of assessment results is differently valid at different levels of the system and results can only be interpreted validly in the local context, as Linn and Tittle argue, then Messick's validation process is in danger of collapsing under its own weight. Messick in fact sets up this problem when he argues that construct validation is a never-ending process and proceeds to outline validation requirements of extensive proportion. We are then left with some serious questions:

- How much can we reasonably place at the door of validity studies?
- Is it naive to expect policy makers to act on social consequences if this would conflict with their policy requirements?
- How do we specify or control test use?

Reliability

School-based assessment such as coursework in the GCSE and Teacher Assessment in National Curriculum assessment have been introduced in order to enhance validity of the overall assessment. This is because the range of skills and type of task which can be assessed is thus expanded and construct validity is enhanced. Performance assessment and 'authentic' assessment are designed specifically to enhance construct validity and to have beneficial consequences on teaching and learning (see chapter 1). However they bring particular questions of reliability, the second main psychometric characteristic of assessment, which is often in tension with validity.

Reliability is concerned with the accuracy with which the test measures the skill or attainment it is designed to measure. The underlying reliability questions are: would an assessment produce the same or similar score on two occasions or if given by two assessors? Reliability therefore relates to consistency of pupil performance and consistency in assessing that performance: which we may term replicability and comparability.

The standard ways of assessing reliability of a test include — giving the same test a few days apart (*test-retest* procedure); using alternate forms of the 'same' test to compare performance of similar populations (*parallel* forms); if only one test is available or only one administration is possible then the test can be divided in half randomly and the comparability of performance on the two halves assessed (*split-half* procedure); an extension of this approach is a statistical analysis which averages all the possible correlations (ie across all possible divisions of the test), giving a coefficient of *internal consistency*. There is also consistency of marking to be considered: agreement between raters on the same assessment task is *inter-rater* reliability; agreement of the same rater's judgments on different occasions is *intra-rater* reliability.

Parallel forms of a test are not always easy to produce: how do we know for example that two tests of, for example, English comprehension are actually parallel (Wiliam, 1992)? It can also be difficult to persuade pupils to take two tests close together for test-retest studies, hence the development of the split-half and internal consistency approaches.

Of the four methods of calculating the reliability of the test, (as opposed to consistency of marking,) the latter two, both measures of internal consistency — are considered to be the least robust (Wood, 1991; AERA *et al.*, 1985) since they only identify consistent response behaviour: they say nothing about stability over time or across forms of a test. A test that was homogenous would almost certainly have a higher coefficient of internal consistency than a test that assessed many different abilities or attainments (ie was heterogeneous). The assumption of unidimensionality is, of course, a building block of psychometrics. There are four major sources of error in testing: variations arising within the measurement procedure; changes in the specific sample of tasks; changes in the individual from day to day; and changes in the individual's speed of work (most tests and examinations are timed). The parallel forms analysis, where the same individual takes a parallel form of the test a few days later, is the only one to take all the sources of variation into account. One problem with the logic of internal consistency measures is that if the assessment contains a mix of modes and contexts, so that all pupils have an optimum chance of doing well (see chapter 8), then expecting internal consistency is unjustified.

In a criterion-referenced system the concept of reliability as traditionally conceived is not appropriate: 'Traditional reliability measures, based on correlation techniques, are likely to be misleading, since they rest on the assumption of high levels of discrimination between pupils and wide variation in scoring' (Shorrocks *et al.*, 1992, p. 10). Since criterion-referenced assessments are not designed to emphasize differences among individuals the range of scores for any one group may be narrow — indeed all pupils could attain the criterion and scores will then be bunched. In addition, because there is usually no underlying mark scale, and because performance on individual aspects is aggregated using a range of combinations, alternative approaches need to be used to evaluate the consistency of measurement from one item to another or one occasion to another, and the stability of classification decisions. See chapter 5 for a detailed discussion of the technical issues in CRA.

In performance assessment we need to consider consistency of approach to the assessment task as well as consistency of standards in marking. Consistency of approach relates to the administration of the tasks; the way in which tasks are presented can affect children's performance quite markedly (James and Conner, 1993; Gipps, 1993a). Consistency of standards relates to ensuring that different markers interpret the assessment criteria in the same way; this is necessary whenever qualitative judgments have to be made, and in particular when assessment criteria are open to various interpretations.

Reliability in Marking

The standard ways of assessing reliability of marking are mark-remark procedures with different markers scoring the same piece of work (*inter-rater* reliability) or the same marker scoring the same pieces of work on different occasions (*intra-rater* reliability). If the marking is straightforward as in a multiple-choice, or other standardized tests with one word answers, then agreement across raters and within raters should be high. With essay answers and other performance-based assessment tasks there is more likely to be variance because of the complexity of the marking scheme and the subjectivity of the judgments made.

Research carried out on examinations has shown that essay-type questions are less reliably marked than structured, analytically marked questions (Murphy, 1982) and this would seem to be logical: the greater the amount of structure in the question and in the marking scheme the more likely it is that two people would agree on the result. This is in fact supported by research which shows that even for performance-based tasks when observers/raters are trained and scoring rubrics provided inter-rater reliability can be high (Brown, 1992; Shavelson *et al.*, 1992).

There is a considerable amount of evidence to show that markers are affected by the characteristics of the pupil and of the piece of work. Neatness of presentation and clear handwriting will affect marks in an upwards direction (Wood, 1991). Also gender — both of the pupil and of the marker — has a significant effect; the same piece of science writing received lower marks when assigned to girls than when assigned to boys (Goddard-Spear, 1983) by both male and female markers, an effect found also in academic writing: both male and female academics rated the same article more highly when it was attributed to John T McKay than to Joan T McKay (Paludi and Bower quoted by Linn, 1992, p. 28). While in design and technology surveys for the APU, there was some evidence that female markers marked girls' work higher than boys and male markers marked boys' work higher. The authors believed that in this case the curriculum background of the staff meant that they were more in tune with the work of pupils of the same gender: the female teachers were mostly home economics teachers by training and the male teachers CDT teachers (Gipps and Murphy, 1994).

Concerns over reliability between markers become concerns of bias whenever markers are influenced by group-related characteristics of an examinee that are irrelevant to the construct and purposes of the test. In some situations markers might either know an examinee personally or be able to infer group membership on the basis of the examinee's name, school designation or aspects of the response such as handwriting or characteristic surface errors. There the danger is that the assigned score may be influenced by the marker's conscious or unconscious expectations about an examinee based upon sex, ethnic origin, ability level, social class etc as with teacher expectation. Another way in which bias can arise is when responses valued by markers reflect skills, knowledge or values irrelevant to the construct of interest, for example content knowledge (when a test is intended to measure writing skill), writing skill or spelling (when a test is intended to measure content knowledge); these are potentially irrelevant influences on the scores. In these cases the groups of concern could be examinees with poor handwriting, inadequate knowledge of an arbitrary topic or limited facility with standard written English. Subjective judgments can be particularly difficult when the examinee and the markers do not share a common cultural heritage and hence common values about what constitutes competent performance. Although training and monitoring of markers can help to minimize threats of bias resulting from the influence of irrelevant factors, where cultural value differences between markers and examinees are present, it becomes especially important to guard against this and to specify the scoring criteria *in relation to the construct being assessed.* Although open-ended responses offer greater scope for biased marking and are thought to be least fair since markers are given more latitude, it must be remembered that a multiple-choice format, while offering no latitude to the marker, allows the assessor to become the marker and his/her biases are then built in to the alternatives offered.

To sum up, it seems that when markers can infer gender or ethnic group from the pupil's name, stereotypes come in to play, with curriculum area interacting. Even when names are not attached to scripts, surface effects such as neatness can affect marking. Ensuring reliability in marking/grading therefore needs to take these issues into account in order to reduce variability and to ensure fairness.

To conclude, we need to consider traditional reliability in relation to educational assessment. There are three major areas of critique. First, there is the assumption that it is possible to measure achievement 'accurately'; given everything that we know about the role of context and personal state in performance and how this interacts with assessment mode the suggestion that we can assess achievement, particularly of complex skills, 'accurately' is simply misleading.

Second, a condition which inheres in psychometric testing in order to ensure replicability is highly standardized administration of the test. Once we move beyond paper and pencil tests and examinations such standardization becomes difficult. Indeed in an educational assessment model where we wish to elicit best performance, such standardization is inappropriate.

Third, to achieve high measures of internal consistency, items in a test need to be homogenous and thus assess a unidimensional skill or attribute. Such unidimensionality is for many constructs artificial, and in any case, in order to offer all pupils a chance of doing well, assessments should contain a mix of modes and contexts; this is likely to reduce the internal consistency while enhancing fairness.

The reconceptualization of reliability will be addressed in the final chapter, but before leaving reliability we need to look at methods, other than psychometric ones, for enhancing consistency in assessment within the educational assessment paradigm. Educational assessment approaches can be used for monitoring and accountability procedures and in these, as well as classroom settings, we need to ensure consistency of approach and grading on the grounds of equity and fairness. Harlen and colleagues (Harlen, 1994) have conceptualized the issue as one of ensuring quality in assessment and categorized the approaches into those for quality assurance and quality control, which parallel the terms consistency of approach and consistency of standards.

Enhancing Consistency in Assessment

Quality assurance in assessment is an approach that aims for standardization or consistency of approach and thus it focuses on the process of assessment. Quality control on the other hand focuses on ensuring that the outcomes are judged in a comparable way. Generally these two processes, and others which support consistency in order to offer comparability, are termed, in the UK, moderation. Moderation is particularly important in any assessment programme which uses teachers' assessments of pupils' work.

The processes involved in moderation range from 'hard' statistical approaches which adjust score distributions (to ensure comparability of grading between schools, for example) — a quality control activity —

to 'soft' group discussion and judgmental review approaches called group moderation (DES, 1988) or social moderation (Linn, 1992) — a quality assurance approach. The latter looks at the products and how they are graded but may also involve discussion of the assessment process. Indeed logic would suggest that the process of moderation be better aimed at ensuring consistency has been achieved (quality assurance) rather than trying 'to impose it on an otherwise inconsistent assessment system' (NISEAC, 1991, para 10.1), which is what statistical moderation does.

Whatever approach is used, the aim of moderation is the same: to achieve consistency in assessment in order to enhance quality.

Methods of Moderation

A brief introduction to the methods of moderation is appropriate at this stage; this account draws heavily on Harlen (1994).

Statistical Moderation Through Use of Reference Tests or Scaling Techniques

This approach involves the use of statistical procedures to adjust students' marks on an assessment on the basis of their score on another assessment. This procedure does not require the involvement of the teacher. When a reference test is used then students' results on this common reference test may be used to moderate their teachers' assessments after the event. In this situation the rank order of the students assessed by one teacher, or school, stays the same but the scores of that group may be moved up or down, the point being to use the common, reference, scores to compensate for systematic variations in teachers' judgments. This approach is widely used in Australia. An example is the use of the Australian Scholastic Aptitude Test to moderate school-based assessment results, as used to be the practice in Queensland, for pupils who wished to go on to tertiary education.

Scaling is a statistical procedure carried out in order to examine comparability of standards across subjects. Some subjects, for example, maths and sciences, attract more able candidates and therefore it is harder to get a high grade on those subjects within a norm-referenced system. The process of scaling allows compensation for candidates who take the 'more difficult' subjects and for whom it is (in theory) more difficult to get a high grade.

The grade obtained by a particular candidate in a particular subject tells us little about the candidate's overall performance and nothing about the subject's severity. Given more grades for a candidate we begin to build up an overall picture of the capability of that candidate; given more candidates, with all their grades, a picture of the relative comparability of standards in the subject emerges. (Nuttall *et al.*, 1974, p. 32)

Essentially within a scaling system pupils are given a bonus for doing the 'hard' subjects, for example, chemistry and physics, and lose out by doing 'easier' subjects, for example, English. A commonly noted problem is that the rank order can change and boys are advantaged by this system because they tend more often to take the so-called difficult subjects.

There are two problems with statistical moderation:

1   the pattern of subject choice when compensated for during the scaling process favours boys, since boys are more likely to take the maths and science subjects. (Candidates aiming to go to university are playing the system in Australia by concentrating on maths and sciences courses regardless of their chosen subject at university level in order to score the highest possible ranking in the tertiary entrance score which is arrived at through a process of scaling.)

2   the reference test itself may be biased in favour of one group. If a reference test is biased or low in reliability the scaled scores will also be biased or low in reliability, and there has been considerable criticism of statistical scaling techniques in general in Australia. Work by Sadler (1992a) on actual test results in Queensland show that scaling errors may be serious for small group sizes and, even for groups of 100 or more students, substantial errors may be introduced into the adjusted scores of high ability candidates. 'Small differences in the adjusted scores or aggregates of such candidates should therefore be interpreted with caution' (*ibid*, p. 36).

To sum up, the aim of statistical moderation is to yield a score which is not influenced by factors such as subject selected (although note problem 1 above), teachers' inconsistencies in marking, the school attended and so on. This is therefore a 'strong' version of moderation.

Moderation by Inspection

In this procedure the body responsible for awarding grades/certificates inspects a sample of the examination papers or projects assessed in order to check that the tasks have been set as required and that they have been marked and graded according to instructions. This may be done by mail (for example, with GCSE coursework in England and Wales) in which case only written products can be inspected, or by visitation in which case a wider range of products can be moderated (and therefore assessed) and there is the possibility of dialogue between teacher and moderator about both the process and products of assessment (for example, the visiting moderation procedures of the Scottish Examination Board). Inspection through visitation is, of course, expensive and usually means that in the case of schools only a sample can be visited in any year. However, as with cross-school group moderation, where the visiting moderator observes and discusses with teachers the way in which assessment is carried out, then professional development of teachers is part of the benefit, alongside the enhancement of reliability. Examples of this procedure include visits of moderators to KS1 schools in the National Curriculum Assessments in 1991 and 1992 (James and Conner, 1993), and visits of verifiers to work places or colleges where NVQ assessments are being made. A particular version of moderation by visitation is external examining which is a widespread practice in higher education. In this case the institutions set and mark examinations and continuous assessment components internally, and grant their own degrees. There is thus considerable scope for variation in standards of awards across institutions. External examiners (from other institutions within the same system) comment on the standards of work attained and graded and may also comment on the process of assessment, ie the papers and the tasks set. Grades or marks would not be changed unless the entire set of papers for a particular course were inspected. The external examiner would, however, be asked to confirm failures and to adjudicate on borderline cases (at all levels).

Panel Review

Here a review is carried out focusing on the extent of agreement with the grade or rating scale point awarded to particular pieces of work. The purpose is solely to ensure that grades have been assigned as agreed rather than to affect the process of grading, as such it is a quality control rather than assurance procedure.

Consensus Moderation

This refers to the moderation of teachers' assessments by the common or consensus judgments of a group or panel of teachers and/or experts or moderators (SSABSA, 1988). This is called group moderation and may involve agreement panels.

Group Moderation

Here examples of work are discussed by groups of teachers or lecturers; the purpose is to arrive at shared understandings of the criteria in operation and thus both the processes and the products of assessment are considered. The groups may come from one school/institution or across a group of schools/institutions. Meetings across schools (as proposed for the English National Curriculum assessment programme in the TGAT Report, DES, 1988) serve to enhance the consistency of judgments at the system level. They are, of course, more costly than meetings within a school/institution, but need to be evaluated in terms of their potential for supporting professional development for teachers particularly in relation to the processes of assessment, what counts achievement and how it may be best produced (Gipps, 1993a). This process will be dealt with in detail in chapter 7 on teacher assessment.

Approval of Institutions

Another way of assuring quality in assessment is approval of institutions; the body which is responsible for particular awards approves an institution or centre as one which can provide the relevant course adequately and carry out the related assessment. The institution is visited, teaching and materials reviewed as is the assessment process. The aim is to cover many aspects of quality assurance and control, and responsibility for ensuring reliability of assessments may be devolved to the institution or centre.

Intrinsic Moderation

The Senior Secondary Assessment Board of South Australia (SSABSA) refers to intrinsic moderation in relation to externally set exams. In this context moderation occurs through experienced teachers as examiners using a common set of syllabus objectives to construct an examination and mark students' scripts using a team approach. Thus moderation involves the setting and marking of the exam and all students who take a course sit the same examination. 'Hence, the results of external examinations need no further subject moderation and should be held to be self-moderated' (SSABSA, 1988, p. 8). This notion of intrinsic moderation is essentially one of quality assurance and (rather arrogantly) denies the need for quality control.

Conclusions

Validity is traditionally considered to be more important than reliability: a highly reliable test is of little use if it is not valid, 'No body of reliability data, regardless of the elegance of the methods used to analyze it, is worth very much if the measure to which it applies is irrelevant or redundant' (Feldt and Brennan, 1989, quoted in Wood, 1991, p. 132); but a test cannot be valid — in classical test theory — if it does not have a basic level of reliability. However, although texts on educational measurement tend to maintain that validity is more important than reliability, in fact actual test development (in psychological and standardized testing) has tended to emphasize reliability. In the attempt to achieve highly accurate and replicable testing, the validity of the tests has often been neglected (see chapter 1). The move towards performance-based assessment and the development of school-based teacher assessment are part of an attempt to redress the balance between reliability and validity. What is needed, of course, is an appropriate balance between the two because they are in tension. Harlen (1994) suggests that we deal with this tension by considering the quality of a test which she defines as the maximum level of reliability appropriate for the test's purpose while maintaining high levels of (content and construct) validity.

Generalizability is the concept which links validity and reliability. Within traditional test theory assessment is based on a sample of behaviour and the intention is to generalize from the sample to the universe of that behaviour (Nuttall, 1987). Thus a score on a reading test is taken to be representative of reading ability beyond the items in the test more generally. Generalization is necessary because we cannot assess individuals on the whole domain, so we have to base the assessment on a sample of performance. In order to allow generalization with any confidence several conditions must be fulfilled: the universe of behaviour must be carefully defined (construct validity) and the assessment itself must be reliable: if the assessment is unreliable then generalizing across raters and across tasks is unsafe.

> Different aspects of generalisability are sometimes in tension, since the pressure for standardisation and uniformity arising from the need for generalizing across assessors and occasions can conflict with establishing conditions that will allow a faithful sampling of the behaviour of interest. (*ibid*, p. 110)

As the foregoing discussion on validity made clear, it is not so much the test score itself that matters but the inference that is made from it, and we therefore need to be certain that it is reasonable to make inferences from scores. One of the major challenges to generalizability is context: we need to ask whether the score is context-specific or whether it generalizes across contexts. The more practical or performance-based the assessment is the less we seem justified in generalizing from the assessment context to other contexts. As Moss (1992) points out the more recent advice of authors such as Anastasi, Cronbach and Messick is that a cautious approach should be taken to the issue of context; the range of context to which a test applies should be specified and the use of the test and interpretation of scores should be kept within those contextual boundaries.

Linn (1993a) concludes that in performance assessment increasing the number of tasks assessed is the most effective way of enhancing generalizability '. . . low levels of generalizability across tasks limit the validity of inferences about performance for a domain and pose serious problems regarding comparability and fairness to individuals who are judged against performance standards based on a small number . . . of tasks' (pp. 12 and 13). An alternative view point for some forms of assessment is to abandon notions of sampling and generalizability and look instead at eliciting best performance within a meaningful and well explained context. A fuller discussion of this issue will be found in chapter 6.

Linn *et al.*, (1991) argue that the concept of reliability also needs to be expanded; focusing on internal consistency or reliability in parallel forms is not sufficient: we need also to enquire whether we can generalize from the specific assessment task to the broader domain of achievement. They make the point that although standardized multiple choice tests are more reliable than performance-based tasks there are nevertheless serious questions over generalizability to tasks beyond those in the test: we need to ask whether skills and knowledge which lead to success on multiple-choice tasks transfer to other tasks, a question which has not traditionally been asked.

In this chapter I have set the scene in relation to validity, reliability and methods of enhancing reliability; in future chapters I shall deal with these aspects in relation to various forms of assessment. Ensuring comparability is a particular issue for teacher/school-based assessment and for performance assessment, since these procedures are the least standardized. Given the importance of these approaches within educational assessment, and the need to enhance public confidence in them, I shall devote a whole section to the process of ensuring quality and comparability through moderation in teacher assessment and to reliability and validity in performance assessment.

Note

1 Moss (1992) gives a detailed analysis of the components of validity inquiry including the sources of evidence used, aspects of inquiry, and criteria for conclusions put forward by Messick and Cronbach, together with those discussed in relation to performance assessment by Frederiksen and Collins (1989), Haertel (1991) and Linn, Baker and Dunbar (1991). I shall not repeat the analysis here, but refer the interested reader to Moss instead.

Chapter 5

Criterion-Referenced Assessment

In 1963 Glaser published his seminal paper on criterion-referenced testing (Glaser, 1963) which signalled the emergence of educational assessment as a separate enterprise from psychometrics and psychological measurement. Indeed, Glaser specifically defined criterion referenced testing in terms of its difference from norm-referenced testing.

> What I shall call criterion-referenced measures depend upon an absolute standard of quality, while what I term norm-referenced measures depend upon a relative standard. (*ibid*, p. 519)

and

> Measures which assess student achievement in terms of a criterion standard thus provide information as to the degree of competence attained by a particular student which is independent of reference to the performance of others. (*ibid*, p. 520)

Glaser's thesis was that classical test theory was built on the particular requirements of aptitude measurement with high levels of prediction and correlation; measurement of *achievement* on the other hand requires different underlying principles — concern is with current levels of performance not prediction, and there is a concept of a continuum of knowledge acquisition ranging from no proficiency at all to perfect performance: a student's achievement on the test indicates his/her performance in relation to the criteria which articulate the continuum.

As chapter 1 explains the key feature which distinguishes educational from psychological measurement is that it is concerned with an individual's growth (rather than variation between individuals) and testing is linked to content matter taught. The question to be answered by criterion referenced testing is therefore 'Can X and Y do Z?' rather than 'Did X score higher than Y on Z?'

There is, however, an argument that norm-referenced assessment and criterion-referenced assessment are closely linked and that norms may be used to set criteria, for example 'better than an absolute beginner' (Skehan, 1984, quoted in Wood, 1991), and that a norm-referenced interpretation can be put on a criterion-referenced measure, for example, most children of 7 will be at Level Two.

Making comparisons is part of human mental activity and some assessment specialists believe that criterion-referenced assessment will inevitably be used for normative purposes. Madaus (1992a) gives an example from the US of how, unwittingly, the rhetoric of criterion-referenced assessment is used in a norm-referenced situation:

> . . . in my state of Massachusetts, the democratic leadership, enthralled by the powerful reform rhetoric, proposed in their Educational Excellence and Accountability Act, adopting 'new, performance-based learning assessments that are benchmarked to the skills and knowledge of students in the most educationally advanced regions of America, Europe and Asia'; major assessment tests given at three grade levels will be used 'to compare our students' progress . . . with our most advanced economic competitors throughout the world' (Commonwealth of Massachusetts Joint Committee on Education, 1992). What could be more normative? (p. 5)

A clear example of norm-referenced/criterion-referenced interaction is the German grading system the *Notenskala*. The grading framework is criterion-referenced, for example, 1 = very good, well above the required standard, 2 = good, fully meets the required standard etc. The knowledge and skills which should be mastered and taught at each stage are published by the states; the standards are pre-determined and therefore can be described as criterion-referenced. But, what constitutes 'good performance' in a particular class is only assessed through a norm-referenced process (Phillips, 1991): teachers are encouraged to take into account the type of secondary school (whether for example vocational or highly academic) so that there are different evaluations of 'good' depending on the type of school attended. This means that there is variation from one school type to another and that consistency from one state to another is likely to be even less robust, an issue which does not concern the German system unduly (DES, 1986) until the school leaving exam. Perhaps this is not only because the *Notenskala* has been in operation for some considerable time and everyone understands it, but also because it has a criterion-referenced element however loosely interpreted. The British concern with external examination in order to offer high levels of consistency across schools and local education authorities may be in part due to the absence of criterion-referencing in what is a highly norm-referenced system.

One of the boosts to the development of criterion-referenced testing in the 1970s was that norm-referenced tests when used to evaluate educational innovations and programmes regularly showed 'no significant differences' (Popham, 1987b); this was due in part to the way in which the tests are developed: items on which most students perform well are dropped because they do not contribute to the test's discrimination value (see chapter 1). However, these items may well be the very ones which are important to teachers and students may do well on them because of the programme they have been involved in. The very generalized descriptions of what those tests measure also make it difficult to articulate what the programme's effects actually were:

> The chief dividend of a well-constructed criterion-referenced test, at least from the perspective of educational evaluators, is that it yields an explicit description of what is being measured. This, in time, permits more accurate inferences to be made regarding the meaning of test scores. And, finally, because of such heightened clarity, educational evaluators can provide decision-makers with more meaningfully interpretable data. (*ibid*, p. 37)

In addition Popham claims that the clarity of description in a well constructed criterion-referenced testing allows teachers to direct their teaching to the areas on which a pupil does not perform well whereas on a norm-referenced test the teacher would have to look at performance item-by-item in order to know where to aim teaching. As a consequence of the interest in criterion-referenced testing publishers in the USA added criterion-referenced interpretations to many norm-referenced tests (Popham, 1992) .

Criterion-referenced testing was adopted widely in the USA, mostly in the guise of minimum competency tests and mastery learning programmes. A modified version was taken up in the UK with graded assessment; and then in the mid-1980s it was decided that both GCSE and National Curriculum assessment were to be criterion-referenced.

The distinguishing characteristic of criterion-referenced testing is now taken to be the detailed specification of the content or domain to be assessed, rather than the referencing of scores to criterion performance as in Glaser's original paper (Shepard, 1991). (Domain here refers to an area of subject knowledge, for example, measurement within mathematics.) Domain-referenced testing is a version of criterion-referenced testing: in this model the domain is clearly defined and all the possible content of this domain (called the universe of content) described. Items for a test are selected from this universe according to a formal sampling rule. The candidate's performance on the test then gives an indication of the proportion of the domain s/he has mastered.

Domain-referenced testing is different from criterion-referenced testing in a number of ways; this distinction may seem esoteric but it is important to understand the difference since in equating the two models some of the criticisms of domain-referenced testing are in danger of being applied to criterion-referenced testing (Linn, 1993b). Both forms of assessment share a focus on *content*, but domain-referenced testing, in its pure form, requires the 'specification of rules that determine membership in the domain and a procedure for sampling individual elements so that inferences can be made from the sample to the domain' (*ibid*, p. 5). Such detailed specification (or 'pseudo precision' as Linn calls it) is possible only for very narrow domains. The example commonly given is that of adding 100 possible pairs of single digit numbers: the percentage that the pupil gets correct indicates the proportion of the domain that the pupil has mastered. This highly specific approach leads inevitably to reductionism, where the content is specified more and more minutely and attention is diverted away from broader achievements. This is one of the criticisms of criterion-referenced testing but, as Linn points out, it is not a requirement of criterion-referenced testing to focus on detailed, specified tasks; Linn argues that because it is not possible to specify all the elements in most domains in criterion-referenced testing attention can be focused on broader descriptions.

Indeed the grade-related criteria which were developed for GCSE were an attempt to map the domain and to specify predetermined standards of performance which examiners were to apply in their grading (although this was not domain-referenced testing since there were no formal sampling rules) the overall description was to tell the user of the grade what was and was not mastered. In fact grade-related criteria were extremely difficult to produce and the 'grade-descriptions' are simpler, more generalized statements about the skills and knowledge mastered by the majority of candidates who have obtained a certain grade (Orr and Nuttall, 1983).

Technical Issues

The differing concepts underlying norm-referenced testing and criterion-referenced testing have implications for test design. Items for norm-referenced testing must discriminate among those tested in order to spread scores along the normal distribution. Thus, as already mentioned, items which do not have a high discrimination index are dropped. Criterion-referenced tests are not built to discriminate in the same way; what matters is to identify the tasks which pupils can and cannot perform. Thus items which do not discriminate between candidates because they are particularly easy or difficult would be included if they are important elements of the area of study; the important factor in criterion-referenced tests is not high discrimination, but to represent a continuum of relevant tasks.

Reliability in Criterion-Referenced Assessment

Classical test theory methods for estimating reliability are not suitable for criterion-referenced assessment because they assume an underlying score scale (for example, 1–100) and on the basis of this employ correlation techniques. In some instances criterion-referenced assessment developers either use psychometric techniques to estimate reliability or ignore reliability issues altogether. Further complications are added by the fact that aggregation (of performance on sub-tests, or elements of an assessment) may be based on logical combinations rather than an arithmetic method, for example, calculating a mean.

Criterion-referenced assessment is generally scored on a mastery classification basis; it is less precise than domain-referenced assessment scoring (but then criterion-referenced assessment is a less precise form of domain-referenced assessment). The score on a domain-referenced assessment is the proportion of items sampled from the domain which the pupil gets correct and this is extrapolated to the full domain, giving an estimated score. In criterion-referenced assessment a pupil who achieves more than the specified proportion of the assessment tasks, or achieves the criterion performance, is classified as a master, and a pupil who achieves less is classified as a non-master.

In this circumstance, reliability can be considered in relation to the correctness of classification (Wiliam, 1992). One can have four situations:

- a **true master** where a candidate is **correctly classified as a master**;
- a **false master** where a candidate is **incorrectly classified as a master**;

> **a true non-master** where a candidate is **correctly classified as a non-master;**
> **a false non-master** where a candidate is **incorrectly classified as a non-master.**

In this situation the reliability coefficient is an index of decision consistency, and the process attempts to estimate the cost associated with incorrect decisions.

The American Psychological Association's Standards for Testing recommend, with reference to 'pass-fail' decisions, that the percentage of candidates consistently classified be reported (APA, 1985, Standard 2,12). Schagen and Hutchison (1991) give a detailed account of measures of reliability used when developing criterion-referenced assessment in relation to National Curriculum assessment. In trialling reliability procedures for use specifically with National Curriculum assessment these authors concluded that a useful statistic is the percent of the 'population classified correctly, for example the probability of correct classification at Level 2' (*ibid*, p. 136). Even better, however, they report would be to display the proportions classified into each level of attainment in a stratum diagram.

Since traditional reliability measures, based on correlation techniques, are inappropriate for criterion-referenced assessment with mastery/non-mastery classification, the research team evaluating National Curriculum assessment at Key Stage 1 in 1991 used instead the term *dependability* and their focus, too, was whether classification decisions were relatively stable, since the purpose of the assessment is to classify pupils as masters or non-masters of the levels in the ATs. The team addressed this by comparing the classification of pupils by three separate assessment approaches: the teacher assessments, the SATs, and the specially developed ENCA assessment. The authors admit that this is a less than satisfactory approach (Shorrocks *et al.*, 1992, p. 235) given the different assessment approaches and contexts involved.

What this brief discussion indicates, I hope, is the lack of consensus about a range of adequate approaches to evaluating reliability in criterion-referenced assessment. We can also see that in National Curriculum assessment measures of reliability will be rather crude, particularly since the two types of misclassification are treated equally (whereas it maybe more significant to have false positives, or masters, than false negatives) but the difference between the levels is so large (an average of two years' progress) that the assessment does not, in theory, need to be particularly 'accurate' to have a low misclassification rate.

In criterion-referenced assessment such as GCSE where there is no concept of a pass/fail score and the exams produce marks (which discriminate among students and which are then used to allocate grades) the traditional reliability measures are more appropriate and Wood (1991) suggests that improved reliability may ensue from tightening up the specifications and targeting marking in relation to grade descriptions.

Generalizability is another area of difference between norm-referenced testing and criterion-referenced testing; in norm-referenced testing performance is generalized, not to the body of content, but in relation to the 'norm' group.

> It is of limited value, and rarely appropriate, to generalize student performance to a body of content because of the way in which test items are selected for inclusion in a norm-referenced test. (Hambleton and Rogers, 1991, p. 9).

By contrast proponents of criterion-referenced testing argue that because test items in a well-designed criterion-referenced test can be matched to domains of content, generalization can be made from the items on a test to the larger content domain. Thus, a crucial factor in determining the quality of a criterion-referenced test seems to be a full description of the content area, and the items included in the test must be adequate exemplars of the tasks identified in the analysis of the content area (Pilliner, 1979). Then generalization is possible from the performance on the tasks to the content area (but see comments on context below).

Aggregation

A major problem for criterion-referenced assessment is aggregation, i.e. the 'collapsing' of the detailed performance profile for each individual into a single reporting figure, or grade. Aggregating detailed assessment information into a crude single grade compromises the information offered by the assessment. A final summative aggregated grade does not help the pupil or employer: it obscures more than it clarifies. If an exam assesses five domains, elements or components, candidates with a high overall grade may have done well on (any) three or four and poorly on the other(s). The high grade, therefore, tells us little about what the pupil is capable of doing (Gipps and Stobart, 1993).

Of course there would be no need to aggregate to a single level or grade were it not for the requirement to report in a simple quantifiable form. It is much more in keeping with the educational assessment function of criterion-referenced assessment that attainment be reported in terms of a descriptive profile, as a list of tasks completed, or a series of stages reached:

> The ultimate aim would be to provide individualised descriptions of what pupils have learned, in simple prose, . . . (Drever, 1988, p. 103)

Not only should this be so in order not to label children simplistically

> There should be, after all, . . . no such thing as a 'Level 2' child. (Shorrocks *et al.*, 1992, p. 94)

but also because with complex systems of weighting and aggregating final scores can be distorted and mastery states camouflaged. For example if pupils can be evaluated as being at Level 3 in maths without having attained every assessment criteria in the different aspects of the specified maths curriculum (the ATs) we do not know whether they failed to master any elements and if so, which.

An example of complex aggregation rules which lead to difficulty in getting meaning from the final grade or level (see Brown, 1991 and 1992) can be found in the National Curriculum assessment system where the number of assessment criteria at any level varies. Where the aggregation mastery rule is n-1 (all tasks except one must be achieved in order to attain that level) then attaining that level becomes increasingly more demanding as the number of assessment criteria increase. This is because the content domain increases and with it the number of items a pupil has to be able to achieve. Thus, where the number of assessment criteria is variable, it will be more difficult to show mastery of some aspects of the curriculum. Furthermore, the aggregation process does not allow for differing levels of difficulty of assessment criteria or the tasks used to assess them — it assumes equal difficulty by ignoring it.

Aggregation is part of the process of assigning a grade or level and is thus part of the process of mastery classification. The setting of cut-off scores (i.e. to determine at what level of performance mastery is assumed) is a judgmental matter according to Hambleton and Rogers (1991) best done by individuals who are familiar with the test content, understand the standard setting process, have access to performance data and understand the social and political context in which the tests are being used. One cannot help feeling that this approach has much to recommend it, having observed the use of 'random' aggregation procedures in National Curriculum assessment.

Validity

Validity in criterion-referenced assessment has generally been taken to relate mainly to content validity (Linn, 1980) and in relation to criterion-referenced assessment it has three elements: is the domain adequately defined; does the content (the items as sampled) adequately represent the domain or construct of interest; and do the assessment items adequately reflect the construct, (that is, do the items assess what we think we are assessing eg. the ability to measure in centimetres?). Where the assessment criteria are imprecise then validity is threatened.

Criterion-referenced assessment is supposed, as Wood (1991) points out, to be a low-inference procedure, because of the careful specification of the domain or construct and thorough sampling from it. In order to keep inference low we have to specify the skills and objectives very tightly and this is the Catch 22 situation for criterion-referenced assessment — too narrowly and tightly defined assessment criteria lead to fragmentation and an overburdening of discrete assessment tasks — while too generally and loosely defined criteria limit the validity and dependability of the assessment. Having promoted criterion-referenced assessment for its content validity in the early 1980s, developers sometimes did not adequately define the domain or articulate the construct, for example what we mean by basic literacy? (Messick, 1981). Is a basic skill one that facilitates later learning in the same area, or does it enable performance at a basic level in a wide variety of situations?

Linn (1980) points out in criterion-referenced assessment as much as in other forms of assessment:

> Compartmentalization of thinking about validity into the traditional types of validity tends to perpetuate the notion that there are alternative approaches or 'roads to psychometric salvation' (Guion, 1980, p. 4) and that one must merely pick one of them. (as quoted by Linn, 1980, p. 552)

In the new conceptualization of validity the uses and interpretations of criterion-referenced assessment scores must also be considered. According to Hambleton and Rogers (1991) expert judgment is the main mode of investigating a criterion-referenced test's content validity, and they regard content validity as important whatever the test use. For a detailed account of methods of assessing validity in criterion-referenced assessment see Hambleton and Rogers, who review current advances in methodology in relation to criterion-referenced assessment; they take the view that during the 1980s validity questions in relation to criterion-referenced assessment began to be properly framed and good validity studies reported. In their review Hambleton and Rogers outline a range of approaches and techniques suitable for use with criterion-referenced assessment but caution that:

> Accumulating validation evidence can be a never-ending process. The amount of time and energy that should be expended on the validation of test scores and mastery classifications should be directly related to the importance of the test use. (*ibid*, p. 27)

Another major technical problem for criterion-referenced assessment is the crucial importance of context in performance: once the domain is specified and items sampled from it, if both are done rigorously and in sufficient detail then the notion was that the test items generated should be 'functionally homogeneous, that is, essentially interchangeable' (Popham, 1984, p. 39). In fact research shows that context factors will critically affect pupil performance, and that even in such a simple test task such as 'adds two digit figures' the task is more difficult if presented horizontally than vertically; and that 11 + 11 is easier than 99 + 99.

It is not possible therefore to decontextualize test items, nor to produce specifications so precise that it is possible to produce 'identical' test items. An alternative approach is to aim assessment specifications at particular groups and to base assessments on high levels of shared meaning. 'Specifications which seem unclear to the general reader may nonetheless, among experts, generate equivalent assessments and, consequently, clear substantive statements about candidates' performances' (Wolf, 1993, p. 13).

In the case of NVQ qualifications in the UK where assessment decisions are mastery-based candidates are credited with an element, a unit or an award (see Johnson and Blinkhorn (1992) who offer a comprehensive review of this field). Range statements serve to indicate the range of applications to which an assessed element applies. The list of range of applications is used both for teaching and assessment purposes, to ensure that a skill has been learnt and can be demonstrated in a range of contexts. Range statements can therefore act either to broaden or to limit the range of contexts in which mastery can be assumed (Jessup, 1991).

As an example of the problems in developing criterion-assessment the development of the GCSE examination will be described in some detail.

GCSE[1]

One of the reasons for the interest of the DES and Secondary Examinations Council (SEC) in the development of criterion-referencing within GCSE was concern over comparability, or rather the lack of it, in GCSE grades from different examination boards. With a single, consistent, system of clearly-defined grades, the idea was that all the boards would apply the same standards in awarding grades (Orr and Nuttall, 1983).

Another reason for the introduction of GCSE was an attempt to boost standards: Sir Keith Joseph's aim was to get 80–90 per cent of 16-year-olds up to the level previously deemed to be average. On norm-referenced tests there is no point in trying to get every pupil to achieve an average or above-average score since, by definition, these tests are designed to have half the population scoring above and half below the mean. With criterion-referenced assessment in theory everyone can achieve the top grade.

However, it is important not to understate the difficulties in designing criterion-referenced assessment, particularly in relation to advanced levels of assessment in complex subject areas. The main problem is that, as the requirements become more abstract and demanding, so the task of defining the performance clearly becomes more complex and unreliable. Thus while criterion-referencing may be ideal for simply defined competencies ('can swim fifty metres'), it is less so as the task becomes more complex: either the assessment must become more complex (for example, the driving test requires intensive one-to-one assessment) or the criteria must become more general. If the criteria are more general they are less reliable, since differences in interpretation are bound to occur. An example of this comes from the statements of attainment in National Curriculum English; the first SoA in level 9 Speaking and Listening (En1) reads:

> . . . give a presentation expressing a personal point of view on a complex subject persuasively, cogently and clearly, integrating talk with writing and other media where appropriate, and respond to the presentations of others.

This SoA clearly requires a great deal of exemplification before any two teachers are likely to interpret it in the same way.

Specifying the criteria has proved to be a particular problem in GCSE. Sir Keith Joseph's announcement of the new GCSE in 1984 included a reference to grade-related criteria — the criteria which students would have to meet in order to gain a particular grade:

> examination grades should have a clearer meaning and pupils and teachers need clearer goals. We accordingly need grade-related criteria which will specify the knowledge, understanding and skills expected for the award of particular grades. (DES, 1987b)

There were already grade descriptions in the GCSE subject criteria which gave a broad idea of the performance likely to have been shown by a candidate awarded a particular grade, but what was wanted were more specific descriptions of performance. Working parties were set up in each of the main subjects to develop grade criteria. These working parties first identified 'domains': coherent and defined areas of knowledge, understanding and skills within each subject. The groups then broke the domains down into abilities and produced definitions of performance, or criteria, required for achievement at different levels. These draft grade criteria were then put out for consultation, in 1985. Two key issues emerged from this.

First, the complexity of the draft grade criteria militated against their usefulness, 'particularly to employers' (*ibid*). What had happened was that the working parties had produced numerous and often complex criteria which made their assessment unmanageable. In history, for example, there were ten sub-elements across three domains and criteria were given for four levels of performance within each sub-element, adding up to forty statements of performance to be used not only by those doing the assessment but also by those interpreting candidates' performance. In English the problem lay in the rather broad criteria formulated, which made reliable differentiation between performance at different grades very difficult. An example taken from the domain of writing will make this clear: to get a grade A/B a candidate should 'Give a coherent and perceptive account of both actual and imagined experience', while to get a grade F/G he/she should 'Give a coherent account of personal experience'. At the other extreme, the maths group produced eighty detailed criteria for one domain at a single grade level (Brown, 1988).

Second, care was needed to make sure that teaching and assessment strategies based on the draft grade criteria would not lead to the breaking down of subjects into isolated tasks. This, of course, is bound to be a danger where there is a highly specified curriculum and/or assessment. The SEC had been aware of this problem for some time

(Murphy, 1986) and in the briefing paper to the draft grade criteria subject working parties said that:

> The rigorous specification of full criterion-referencing for assessment in the GCSE would result in very tightly defined syllabuses and patterns of assessment which would not allow the flexibility of approach that characterises education in this country. (SEC, 1984, p. 2)

In order to refine and develop the draft grade criteria the SEC funded a remarking exercise. This involved the remarking of the 1986 joint 'O'-level/CSE exam scripts according to the draft criteria. This exercise threw up a host of problems. First, there was a poor match between the domains and levels produced by the working parties and the content of the exam papers studied; this was not particularly surprising since these exam papers had not been designed to cover the domains and levels. More importantly, however there were ambiguities in the criteria: the hierarchies of performance given by the draft grade criteria bore little relationship to the actual responses of candidates to specific questions; and there was a lack of equivalence between the same levels of performance on different questions and across different domains. It was concluded that the draft grade criteria were largely unworkable (Kingdon and Stobart, 1987).

At this point, the draft grade criteria were dropped. As the DES paper put it:

> In the light of this outcome from the remarking exercise, the SEC decided to approach from a different angle the task of making GCSE grades more objective. (DES, 1987b, para 13.)

This new angle involved the development of performance matrices, which meant starting the other way round. The starting point was some of the existing approved GCSE syllabuses and the task was to develop, for these particular syllabuses specific descriptions of performance, 'attributes', at different levels. These attributes defined as 'a quality developed in students who follow a particular course' were described at different levels of performance (for example, grades A, C and F) and combined into domains. (Quite how the introduction of the concept of attributes was to help in an already hugely complicated area is not at all clear!) The point about performance matrices is that they relate to individual syllabuses rather than the whole subject, and they are based on examiners' articulation of their implicit judgments in awarding grades.

The final reports of the working parties were produced in mid-1988 with varied reactions to the viability of performance matrices. But when the SEC was superseded by the School Examinations and Assessment Council (SEAC) at the end of 1988, one of the first things it did was to freeze work on performance matrices (SEAC, 1989).

In the summer of 1988, the first GCSE papers were graded on the basis of the original (loose) grade descriptions. This approach continued throughout the first five years of GCSE awarding and looks likely to continue until the national curriculum replaces the GCSE criteria.

With the advent of a 'criterion-referenced' national assessment system there seemed little point in continuing the search for performance matrices or grade-related criteria. The GCSE will have to follow the attainment targets for Key Stage 4, and these will form the basis for criterion-referencing. However, as we have intimated already, the imprecision of the ATs and SoAs and the problems of aggregation are likely, at best, to produce only a loosely criterion-referenced system.

Syllabuses will be based on the National Curriculum programmes of study and assessment was to be reported on the ten-level scale. The model proposed by SEAC for the 1994 Key Stage 4 awards was mark-based (SEAC, 1992). Pupils were to receive their subject level on their combined marks from each AT, not from aggregating and averaging the AT levels as at Key Stage 3. Similarly, within an AT the level was to be determined by the total marks across all the levels. For example, if the level 8 boundary is set at 70 per cent, pupils may achieve it by gaining high marks on the lower level questions and fewer marks on questions targeted at levels 9 and 10. The objection to this approach is that this degree of compensation weakens the criterion-referenced basis of the assessment. A pupil might even gain a level 8 simply by being highly consistent at lower levels and gaining hardly any marks at level 8. The argument for this approach is a technical one because a mark-based approach allows calculation of reliability using traditional statistical approaches.

Another example of the difficulty in aggregating complex data is the process of 'compensation' in which a poor performance in one part can be offset by a good performance elsewhere, a process which is traditionally offered in examination marking. In a marked-based approach, it simply means that low and high marks are combined to produce a 'middling' overall mark. Strict criterion-referencing does not work like this — pilots, for example, are expected to master every aspect of flying, and failure on one part leads to overall failure. It would be of little comfort to know that a pilot is extremely good at taking off and that this compensates for poor landing skills. If strict criterion-referencing were translated into exam performance, however it would mean that the final subject level would be determined by the *worst* skill areas. For example, if algebra was only grade F, then the subject grade would have to be F; to give an overall grade C because geometry was grade A would be misleading, as grade C level competence has not been shown in all areas of the subject.

In 1993 the whole process of shifting to reporting GCSE in terms of National Curriculum levels was halted, awaiting the outcome of a review of the National Curriculum and its assessment. The decision made was that GCSE would not be reported on the ten level scale, but continue to be graded as before.

Conclusion

In order to meet the requirements for strict criterion-referenced assessment, criteria need to be specified in fine detail; however, this leads to over-specification and a focus on narrow, tightly defined objectives. Popham, one of the strongest supporters of criterion-referenced assessment in the USA, has retracted his former enthusiasm for detailed objectives, and now argues in favour of stating only a few broad objectives (Popham, 1987b and 1993a). It seems that all attempts to develop criterion-referenced assessment have met the same problem.

> A careful path needs to be found between the extremes of vague and nebulous criteria on the one hand, and a proliferation of detailed and trivial objectives on the other. The essence seems to lie in formulating measurable criteria which have educational aims and specifications. (Shorrocks *et al.*, 1992, p. 109)

This move away from over-specification towards an anti-analytic, more holistic approach is in line with the general shift in educational assessment towards designing assessments to reflect the actual tasks and skills which we want pupils to learn. However, the broader nature of such objectives causes problems in assessing them dependably. Examples of work reaching particular standards or exemplifying certain criteria will help to enhance comparability as will training of teachers and group moderation approaches.

An example of an approach which aims to move away from norm-referenced assessment without going as far as full criterion-referenced assessment is standards-referenced assessment.

Standards-referenced assessment has been conceptualized in the main by Sadler (1987 and 1992b) in Australia. His critique of criterion-referenced assessment (1987) is that first it relies on relatively sophisticated statistical and technological approaches. Because of this complexity much of the responsibility for grading and assessment is taken away from the teacher (and as a consequence the student). This he feels is inappropriate given the increased emphasis being given in educational assessment to assessment approaches involving the student. Second, criterion-referenced assessment with 'objective testing' and tight specification of domains is inappropriate for many subjects, in particular where the quality of student work can be best assessed only by direct qualitative human judgment.

Standards-referenced assessment draws upon the professional ability of competent teachers to make qualitative judgments which they do in everyday teaching. Another characteristic of standards-referenced assessment is that instead of using a total score for arriving at a final grade or level, 'it is the *configuration* or pattern of performance, over a series of testing episodes and assessment tasks, which takes precedence' (Sandler, 1987, p. 193).

Sadler argues that standards-referenced assessment is a feasible and credible form of assessment because teachers' qualitative judgments can be made dependable, provided that standards are developed and promulgated in appropriate forms and that teachers are given the relevant conceptual tools and practical training. The way to specify standards he argues is through a combination of verbal description and exemplars. Exemplars, which are chosen to be typical of designated levels of performance, are not the standards themselves but specify the standards. Verbal descriptions of standards set out the properties that characterize the designated level of quality. This combination of verbal description and concrete exemplar offers an efficient way of specifying standards, and if not kept centralized and secretive can help pupils to become self-monitoring learners (see chapters 2 and 7).

> The use of natural-language descriptions together with exemplars is unlikely to provide a complete substitute for, or render superfluous, the tacit knowledge of human appraisers, simply because external formulations cannot be exhaustive and cover every conceivable case. But by providing a definite framework within which educational assessments can be made, the dual approach has the potential not only for achieving comparability among schools, but also for helping students to acquire evaluative expertise themselves. (p. 207, 1987)

In Tasmania the model adopted has the following features:

— assessment is on a four-point rating scale against assessment criteria which are stated in each syllabus;
— standards for determining the appropriate rating are developed by a process of moderation involving meetings of teachers from all schools where the syllabus is taught;
— examples of work at the standard of each rating are made available to support this process;
— the ratings are aggregated to produce subject awards which are on a three-point scale:
   SA-Satisfactory Achievement of the objectives of the course;
   HA-High Achievement of the objectives of the course;
   OA-Outstanding Achievement of the objectives of the course. (Grosvenor, 1993)

Another, similar, example is the development of Target-Related Assessment in Hong Kong (Clark, 1993) which takes a criterion-referenced stance but with holistic goals or targets. There is an emphasis on:

— production and performance in assessment tasks;
— complex assessment tasks with a range of response modes;
— tasks which model good instruction.

and, as with standards-referenced approaches in Australia, the targets are described in the syllabus; teachers are given explicit criteria for judging student performance; and there are descriptions of what students typically do at any particular stage (i.e. exemplars).

Taken together the learning targets, the explicit criteria for judging learner performance and the descriptions in the bands of performance provide a powerful means for achieving a common understanding among teachers and learners of what represents progress, and a powerful way of achieving reliability in the monitoring of it across schools. (*ibid*, p. 10)

This system was in development in 1993, and not yet proven, but it offers a pattern for an assessment model which is neither norm-referenced nor criterion-referenced.

We need to stop thinking of weak versions of criterion-referenced assessment for example, grade-related criteria in the Scottish and English examination systems, as a step down or back from criterion-referencing, and to see them in a more positive light. Strict criterion-referenced assessment is clearly unmanageable and undesirable, particularly in an educational assessment framework. Developments such as standards-referenced assessment are strong models in their own right and offer, not a compromise on criterion-referenced assessment, but a development from it, criterion-referenced assessment having proved to be educationally and technically an unsound model.

Another route is to think in terms of criterion-referenced or standards-referenced *reporting* as opposed to criterion-referenced *assessment* — in other words to specify performance standards and to allow schools (or school districts) to assess students' performance in any way they wish with the proviso being that performance is reported in relation to the standards. This is an approach currently being pursued in the USA and in Australia, but of course it has huge problems in terms of comparability across assessments. Given the relevance of context to performance and the contextualization of complex skills it is important to have a notion of the context in which the pupil is able to perform the task, and this suggests much fuller reporting procedures, as in NVQ.

Interestingly Linn (1993b) has recently argued that criterion-referenced assessment provides a conceptual framework for thinking about performance-based and authentic assessments. Linn returned to Glaser's original conception and identified four 'interpretations' of criterion-referenced assessment that go beyond the essential core:

- the view that norm-referenced and criterion-referenced interpretations cannot co-exist for a single measure;
- the interpretation that there must be a cut-off score to determine mastery;
- the equating of criterion-referenced assessment and domain-referenced assessment;
- limitation of criterion-referenced assessment to a narrow behaviourist conception of discrete, and typically hierarchical, skills and behaviours.

Linn's argument is that the value of criterion-referenced assessment is that it focuses attention on performance resulting from instruction. Because it is not possible to define all the elements of the domain in complex tasks, such as the one suggested by Glaser in his 1963 paper — the preparation of an experimental report or dissertation — attention is forced towards the valued outcomes of instruction; this focus is consistent with the authentic assessment movement. The aim of both approaches, Linn claims, is to close the gap between the test and the aims of instruction. Although this may sound very far from the usual understanding of criterion-referenced assessment with its basis in the learning theory of behaviourism (Shepard, 1991) Linn's view is that criterion-referenced assessment's development has been corrupted and that this path was not essential to the original conception of criterion-referenced assessment. The concept of criterion-referenced assessment, Linn argues, is much richer than that commonly viewed for it and matches Lindquist's (1951) notion of the primary goal in constructing an achievement test: that the test question should require the examinee to do the *same* things however complex that are required in the criterion situation (Lindquist, 1951, quoted by Linn, 1993b). This is the philosophy underpinning current moves in developing various forms of educational assessment: it seems that the rationale for what makes a good assessment has come full-circle, having been down some very mechanistic side-tracks.

Note

1   This section draws on Gipps and Stobart, 1993.

Chapter 6

Performance Assessment

Introduction

Performance assessment, as already explained in earlier chapters, is a term currently in wide use by those who wish to move away from traditional standardized multiple-choice testing. The term is, however, very loosely used. In the USA for example it is commonly taken to mean any form of assessment other than multiple choice. The first task of this chapter then will be to make clear the sense in which the term is used in this book.

Performance assessments aim to model the *real* learning activities that we wish students to engage with, oral and written communication skills, problem solving activities etc, rather than to fragment them, as do multiple-choice tests; the aim is that the assessments do not distort teaching. In the USA performance assessment may include portfolio assessment and what we in the UK call teacher assessment, that is school based teacher-made assessment of pupils' performance. In this book however I shall deal with the latter under teacher assessment while for performance assessment I will deal exclusively with assessment carried out using tasks which are performance-based. In the UK this definition therefore includes Standard Assessment Tasks and the GCSE examination.

It is also important to distinguish performance assessment from what is called authentic assessment in the USA: authentic assessment is performance assessment carried out in an authentic context, i.e., it is produced in the classroom as part of normal work rather than as a specific task for assessment. While not all performance assessments are authentic, it is difficult to imagine an authentic assessment that would not also be a performance assessment, that is authentic assessment is a special case of performance assessment. An example of an authentic assessment would be a portfolio — the portfolio contains examples of *actual* student performance: 'best' performance elicited under normal classroom conditions in the classroom context. Meyer (1992) suggests that in using the term 'authentic assessment' assessors should specify in which respects the assessment is authentic: the stimulus; task complexity; locus of control; motivation; spontaneity; resources; conditions; criteria; standards; and consequences. The list is daunting but the point is to be rigorous in our definition and address the question 'authentic to what?' Authentic has become a buzz word in assessment parlance in the USA and clarity and precision need to be injected into the debate.

Despite the fact that most of the experience with performance assessment lies on the English side of the Atlantic, particularly coming out of the work of the Assessment of Performance Unit (Gipps and Goldstein, 1983) much of the *writing* on performance assessment as a distinct mode of assessment, and much of the recent research on technical issues, stems from the American side of the Atlantic. Notwithstanding current interest in performance assessment in the USA it is clear that educational measurement specialists were writing about it as early as the 1950s (Stiggins and Bridgeford, 1982) and an integration of these early definitions created a working definition for Stiggins — one of the strongest proponents of classroom-based assessment in more recent times:

> Performance assessment is defined as a systematic attempt to measure a learner's ability to use previously acquired knowledge in solving novel problems or completing specific tasks. In performance assessment, real life or simulated assessment exercises are used to elicit original responses which are directly observed and rated by a qualified judge. (*ibid*, p. 1)

Ten years on there is agreement in the educational assessment profession that: 'Performance measurement calls for examinees to demonstrate their capabilities directly, by creating some product or engaging in some activity'. (Haertel, 1992) and that there is heavy reliance on observation and/or professional judgment in the evaluation of the response (Mehrens, 1992) including teacher-examiners grading coursework and marking essay scripts.

Testing for accountability purposes is essentially large-scale testing and for this reason it commonly relies on tests that are relatively cheap, brief, offer broad but shallow coverage, are easy to score and reliable. Performance assessment by contrast is: time-consuming, tends to provide detailed multi-dimensional information about a particular skill or area, (and, because of the time factor, depth may be exchanged for breadth); scoring is generally complex and usually involves the classroom teacher; standardization of the performance is not possible and therefore reliability in the traditional sense is not high. All these features, which render performance assessment valuable for assessment to support learning, become problematic when performance assessment is to be used for accountability purposes (Frechtling, 1991). As pointed out in chapter 1, the more interactive types of performance assessment emerged from research in subject matter learning, rather than as a result of psychometric test development. Given the impact of the style of test on teaching and learning practice, it is important to see in what circumstances performance assessment *can* be used for large-scale testing. The technical aspects of performance assessment are interesting in themselves given the relatively new nature of this mode of assessment; but they are brought into sharp focus by any attempt to use performance assessment for high stakes purposes.

Validity in Performance Assessment

Performance assessment is important in educational assessment terms for what it offers by way of enhanced validity and the opportunity to assess higher order skills; the idea is that both construct and consequential aspects of validity are high.

Performance assessment does tend to have good 'face validity' ie the assessments appear to be assessing the sort of tasks that we know as practical maths, investigational science etc and face validity is in itself important, particularly for public acceptability (Mehrens, 1992). However, there is some criticism about inadequate attention to construct validity and inadequate definition of the domain.

> In studying the validity of performance assessments, one should think carefully about whether the right domains are being assessed, whether they are well defined, whether they are well sampled, whether — even if well-sampled — one can infer to the domain . . . (*ibid*, p. 7)

Messick (1992) refers to this issue as task-driven rather than construct-driven performance assessment. He criticizes some measurement practitioners for focusing on particular products or performances while using 'construct language' to infer score meaning, ignoring issues of domain coverage and generalizability.

It would probably be helpful here to recap on some terms: mathematics is a *domain*; in the domain of mathematics a sub-domain or *category* would be measurement (though confusingly the sub-domain or category is often referred to as a domain); a *sub-category* would be units; an assessment item on centimetres could be measuring the *construct* 'knowledge of understanding about centimetres'. Construct validity is threatened if the test does not sample some parts of the performance domain it is supposed to represent; this is referred to as *construct underrepresentation*. Construct validity is also threatened if performance depends on knowledge or skills from outside that domain, this is *construct-irrelevant variance*. Examples of performance assessment which have been developed following rigorous specification of domain and consideration of the construct being assessed can be found in Baker (1992) and Shavelson *et al.*, (1992).

An approach which Haertel advocates for studying the construct validity of performance assessment (Haertel, 1992) involves investigating the processes used by students in carrying out the tasks, for example getting the student to talk through the task during the assessment activity, or using a post-task interview to probe the skills on which the task draws.

Consequential validity is an important issue for performance assessment given the 'promises' being made by its advocates: that such tasks can be a faithful reflection of intended and important learning outcomes, and can encourage a tendency to direct teaching towards higher order skills and processes. Dunbar, Koretz and Hoover (1991) argue that ensuring quality control of performance assessment focusing on both evidential and consequential bases of validity (see Messick's table in chapter 4) is particularly important for performance assessment given its popularity and the promises being made for it. 'Just because a task is authentic doesn't mean it's valid for inferring mastery of a complex capacity' (Wiggins, 1992, p. 36). Baker, O'Neil and Linn (1991) (writing about performance assessment and authentic assessment without distinction), point out that although proponents of performance assessment intend the student to bring higher order thinking skills to bear in the assessment they have been remiss in giving clear-cut conceptual frameworks of the student learning they wish to assess and enhance. Thus the underlying cognitive requirements of assessment tasks must be clearly stated. In any case, intentions to measure higher order thinking can be subverted by practice on the task and intended higher order tasks can be transformed into rote tasks: it is possible to teach to the performance assessment task and thus subvert it. Shepard (1992b), among others, warns that any high-stakes test is corruptible and that teachers will teach to performance *tasks* in such a setting. If we wish performance assessment to impact on teaching in a beneficial way then we need to encourage teachers to teach to the domain or sub-domain rather than to the task.

Given the promises made for performance assessment, Frederiksen and Collins' (1989) concept of systemic validity is relevant: a test is systemically valid to the extent that it induces in the education system curriculum change and teaching approaches which foster the development of the cognitive skills the test is designed to measure. The main characteristics which Fredericksen and Collins identify as contributing to systemic validity are the directness of the cognitive assessment and the degree of judgment required in assigning a score. Direct tests involve evaluating the cognitive skill of interest *directly* rather than indirectly, for example, through a more or less abstract task. Frederiksen and Collins argue that the advantage of such direct tests is that instruction which improves the test score will also result in improved performance on the extended task and on the expression of the cognitive skill within the context of the task (ie, teaching to the task will be teaching to the domain). If the assessment involves judgment, reflection and analysis on the part of the scorer, then the scorer must understand the scoring categories and be taught how to use them. Training is expensive *but* may be seen as an aspect of professional development. In this model the assessment system provides a basis for developing metacognitive awareness of what are important characteristics of good problem solving, good historical analysis etc.

The directness and instructional value of the task, together with the subjective element of scoring, are key features of performance assessment which appear in all the literature dealing with conceptual and technical issues in performance assessment and therefore must be part of any definition of performance assessment.

Linn, Baker and Dunbar (1991) identify criteria for evaluating the validity of performance assessments, pointing out that face validity is not sufficient, and following Messick, that validity has been viewed too narrowly. They stress the need for greater consideration of consequences: evidence about the intended and unintended effects on teaching must be collected routinely in the validation of performance assessment. They also point up the need to consider afresh the equity issues in performance assessment: we cannot assume that because we are shifting to a more professionally acceptable form of assessment for educational purposes that these assessments will necessarily be more fair to minority groups. 'Gaps in performance among groups exist because of differences in familiarity, exposure, and motivation on the tasks of interest' (*ibid*, p. 18); shifting to a different model of assessment will not necessarily in itself reduce the gaps. Furthermore, the smaller number of tasks used in performance assessment means that it will be more difficult to achieve a balance of content, context and response mode which we know is crucial in minimizing the effect of group differences in prior knowledge (see also Gipps and Murphy, 1994).

The judgmental nature of the scoring is a particularly vulnerable aspect of performance assessment in relation to fairness: the perceptions and biases of the rater must not be reflected in the student's score. The training of raters and moderation of results are clearly important here as explained in chapter 4.

Linn *et al.*, (1991) also include various criteria for validity evaluation which come under the overall heading of construct validity mentioned above; these are cognitive complexity of the task, analysis of which goes beyond 'face validity'; content quality: the tasks in themselves must be worth students' time and effort, this is particularly so because of the small number of tasks used for any one domain; the involvement of subject experts in test design is important because of the 'promise' that performance assessment will impact on teaching — if there are gaps in content coverage for assessment there will be gaps in teaching. This latter is an area in which performance assessment is undoubtedly vulnerable. Performance assessment is able to sample a domain in depth, but because of the time taken to do the tasks breadth of coverage is often sacrificed to depth; breadth of coverage is important in that it relates to our ability to generalize from the assessment to the broader domain.

Reliability in Performance Assessment

As chapter 4 makes clear the technical term reliability refers to the accuracy with which the test measures the skill or attainment it is designed to measure. Reliability can be broken down into consistency of pupil performance (replicability), and consistency in assessing that performance (comparability).

If traditional test development has over-emphasized reliability at the expense of validity, performance assessment has in the same way over-emphasized validity at the expense of reliability. This is because the use of performance assessment is part of a move away from highly standardized procedures. However, if performance assessment is to be used beyond the classroom setting for accountability or certification purposes then we must address questions of reliability. Again fitness for purpose is the guiding concept: each assessment must have acceptable levels of reliability and validity for its particular purpose.

Where reliability is examined in the development of performance assessment attention tends to focus on the agreement of different raters, ie comparability of rating across judges considering a single task administered on a single occasion. This, of course, is because of the performance assessment criterion of high subjectivity in the marking process which relies heavily on professional judgment, thus a focus for evaluation has been inter-judge consistency. A detailed account of the evidence on inter-rater reliability can be found in Dunbar, Koretz and Hoover (1991) and in Linn (1993a). These studies indicate that inter-judge agreement can be high on performance assessment tasks but that this has to be achieved through careful training of raters and the provision of scoring rubrics.

The Pittsburgh portfolio program used only external assessors who went through a rigorous training and there was a regular checking procedure which led to re-training if acceptable judgements fell below a certain level. Inter-judge reliabilities here were at a consistently high level of 0.90 (Le Mahieu, 1993). The Vermont portfolio program by contrast used teachers in the schools to carry out the rating with less rigorous training and no checking procedure and attained IRR levels of between 0.34 to 0.43 for the unstandardized writing assignments but 0.67 to 0.75 for standardized performance assessment in writing. (Koretz *et al.*, 1993). Koretz and colleagues considered that these figures limited the use to which the Vermont portfolio assessment could be put.

What emerges clearly from these two developments is that with standardized performance assessment, clear rubrics and training for markers, and exemplars of performance at each point or grade, levels of IRR can be high. However, portfolio assessment is often adopted for professional development purposes as much as for assessment purposes; training therefore tends to be spread thinly across a broad population of teachers rather than involving in-depth work with a small cadre of markers; in this situation IRR is more likely to be low than high.

Linn (1993a) concludes that:

> . . . with careful design of scoring rubrics and training of raters, the magnitude of the variance components due to raters or interactions of raters with examinees can be kept at levels substantially smaller than other sources of error variance . . . (p. 10).

Rather less attention has been paid to consistency of performance across tasks and over repeated occasions. 'As with objective tests, length . . . in terms of . . . additional samples of behaviour, is critical to the reduction of chance errors in performance assessments' (Dunbar *et al.*, 1991, p. 291).

The weight of evidence reviewed by Linn and Dunbar *et al.*, indicates that score reliability is generally low, lower than rater reliability and more resistant to being raised than is IRR through training etc. The evidence is that performance on performance assessment tasks is highly task-specific; that is performance on different tasks from the same domain, or on tasks that appear to be similar, will only be moderately related. The actual task set leads to variability in performance; the method of assessment (observation, notebook, computer simulation) also affects measured performance, since each method provides different insights into what students know and can do (Shavelson *et al.*, 1992). Increasing the number of tasks in an assessment tends to increase the score reliability more than does increasing the number of raters, and Linn (1993a) advocates increasing the number of tasks to enhance generalizability.

Generalizability

Generalizability is a particular problem for performance assessment: since direct assessments of complex performance do not generalize well from one task to another (because performance is heavily task dependent) we cannot take performance on one task to imply that the student could do other tasks in the domain. This is in any event a problem for performance assessment but is more serious if the performance assessment is to be used for anything other than formative, classroom-based purposes. This task specificity is compounded by limited sampling from a domain and the difficulty then of generalizing from the performance to the whole domain. Mehrens (1992) separates out the limited sampling from any domain which limits generalizability, from the lack of internal consistency which itself influences generalizability. In the learning of some skills for example, a second language (Swain, 1990) variation in performance may be part of the learning process, in which case high internal consistency is not an appropriate criterion to use in seeking a valid assessment.

Linn (1993a) argues that to overcome these problems we should increase the number of tasks and ensure comprehensive coverage of the domain in order to improve generalizability. Shavelson *et al.*, (1992) suggest the use of a range of tasks and types of assessment activity together with a reemphasis on assessment for professional purposes rather than for accountability or school reform. Swain (1990) argues that, in relation to second language measures, we need to rethink the whole concept of accuracy and consistency: 'Perhaps we may have to begin a search for 'meaningful quality criteria' for the inclusion of test items rather than rely on a measure of internal consistency' (p. 411). Moss (1992) too calls for the development of alternative models for warranting validity conclusions. Increasing the number of tasks to aid generalizability will of course increase the, already considerable, amount of time taken to carry out the assessments. Linn argues that this can be justified on the grounds that the assessment task itself is a useful part of instruction. But increasing the assessment load, without carrying the politicians' or the public's understanding of what these assessments are for, or are trying to do, will cause problems with public acceptability (Mehrens, 1992) as the UK story clearly shows.

Messick (1992) advises that because of the trade-off in performance assessment between domain coverage and generalizability on the one hand, and the time-intensive in-depth examination on the other, assessment batteries should use a mix of structured exercises and less structured open-ended tasks.

Linn, Baker and Dunbar (1991) point out that in order to evaluate the generalizability of assessments we need evidence on task reliability *and* rater reliability, ie the magnitude of variability due to raters and due to the sampling of tasks. The limited generalizability generally found in performance assessment from task to task is consistent, they point out, with what research in cognition and learning tells us about the context-specific nature of thinking and learning. They take the view that reliability in terms of internal consistency is not a sufficient indicator of generalizability: generalization from the specific assessment tasks to the broader domain of achievement needs to be justified, but this is the case for all forms of assessment.

One way of dealing with coverage is to use a grid design approach: the range of the domain is specified in advance and assessment tasks created to represent systematically critical dimensions. In this way, tasks should sample all specified aspects of the domain and overall, then, the performance on the domain. This is useful if time is not an issue at the pupil level and each pupil can take each task, or if matrix sampling is used and pupils take only some of the tasks, giving performance data for the cohort or the school etc. This latter approach is, however, not suitable where individual data is needed for certification or reporting purposes.

Baker *et al.*, (1991) simply accept that the high degree of task specificity in performance assessment suggests that substantial amounts of time will be needed for assessment when generalizability across tasks is required. The degree of generalizability possible appears to be influenced by two aspects:

— the extent to which tasks share comparable features; and
— the type of instruction received by students.

Haertel (1993) clarifies the issues by pointing out that generalizability in relation to performance assessment can be viewed in terms of four levels:

- first, replicable scoring of a single performance
  (can we score a single instance of a task in a consistent way?)
- second, replicability of a specific task
  (does the same performance task have a constant meaning across times and places?)
- third, generalizability across tasks which are presumed to be assessing the same construct
  (can we generalize across parallel tasks?)
- fourth, generalizability across heterogeneous task domains
  (can we generalize across tasks that are not parallel?)

In fact the levels are nested, so that each successive level incorporates all of the problems at the preceding levels.

As we have already seen, the first level (IRR) is not problematic, provided that there are clear scoring rubrics and raters are given training. The second level, replicability of a specific task, however depends, according to Haertel, on three factors: task administration, this involves whether specifications are made about the amount of time allowed, what the teacher is allowed to say, rules about collaboration among pupils, about what constitutes coaching and so on (see the later section on the 7-year-old assessment in England as an example of performance assessment programme where lack of such specification led to very low levels of replicability across tasks). The second factor is the role of ancillary abilities in successful performance on the task, for example, reading ability or listening comprehension: if this is a part of the requirement for being able to complete the assessment tasks then competence in these ancillary abilities will affect individuals' performance on the task differentially, i.e. it is a source of construct-irrelevant variance. An assessment can only have the same meaning across different administrations if the pupils who are taking it all have common access to the ancillary skills or abilities. The third factor is antecedent instruction. This is always crucial to performance, but Haertel argues is particularly so in the assessment of higher-order skills/activities, since this always requires the transfer or application of something familiar or learnt into something new, so the same task will have different meanings if it is given in different times or places following different relevant instruction.

Generalization across parallel tasks is also heavily dependent on the involvement of ancillary abilities — whether they differ from one task to another — and on antecedent instruction. Haertel concludes (as do Shavelson, Linn and Dunbar) that, even in a tightly constrained situation in which parallel tasks are kept similar, it is difficult to make two tasks function the same way. Furthermore, if pupils are given a task for which they have been prepared then we cannot say that this performance will generalize to other tasks in the domain.

As for the final level — generalization across heterogeneous domains — all the evidence suggests that this is fairly unlikely: from research in cognitive psychology and cross-cultural studies comes an understanding that much expertise is domain-specific and that variations in context greatly influence performance. We are left with a serious question of coverage if we wish to generalize across domains.

Baker *et al.*, also make the point, however, that new types of assessment are built on a model which is *not* that of psychometrics. The aim is not to estimate and predict future performance on a construct such as mathematics understanding, but in some cases is simply to credit a specific complex accomplishment in and of itself without the assumption of generalizability or prediction, as with a thesis or dissertation. Moss (1992) extends this line of argument: in evaluating performance assessment we should change our epistemological approach and follow the interpretative research tradition rather than the psychometric tradition. The interpretative approach focuses on participants' own perspectives in conceptualizing and reconstructing their experiences and world view. Such a paradigm would place subjects' and users' interpretations of generalizability at the forefront in any evaluation of a test's validity.

The point is not to standardize performance assessment to such an extent to achieve reliability that validity and attention to higher order skills are compromised. Careful specification of the domain with mapping of performance assessment tasks on to it, so that it is clear what the tasks are assessing is, however, important.

Issues in the Use of Performance Assessment

Much of the performance assessment in the USA has been developed for classroom based assessment for diagnostic and teaching purposes (Mehrens, 1992). There is, however, a considerable amount of large-scale performance assessment currently in the USA: since the middle

1980s, more than forty states have adopted writing samples instead of multiple choice to assess their children's writing abilities (Mitchell and Kane, 1992). In the late 80s at least nine states had adopted state policies of changing from standardized to performance assessment, mostly with the explicit intention of influencing instruction in the direction of conceptual, holistic teaching and learning. (Only two of the states, Vermont and Maryland, had, however, reached the stage of large-scale implementation by mid-1992.) Other states may have performance assessment just for the youngest children (Georgia, for example, has out-lawed the use of machine-scorable tests for young children) or pre-graduation (Michigan has an 'employability portfolio' for grades 9–12 emphasizing workforce readiness). At a national level performance assessments are being trialled in the New Standards Project and are suggested for the national examination system proposed by the National Education Goals Panel. The use of performance assessment for accountability purposes, however, immediately makes them high-stakes and the technical demands on them change dramatically; for this purpose they need to be: administratively feasible, professionally credible, publicly acceptable, legally defensible and economically affordable (Baratz-Snowden quoted by Mehrens, 1992).

According to Baker, O'Neil and Linn (1991) the following needs to be done in order to assure the comparability which is required for high stakes purposes:

- specification: of cognitive demands, scoring criteria, performance standards and context quality to assure quality of assessment development;
- calibration: to monitor and adjust scores of different raters to make them comparable;
- moderation: to allow raters to acquire shared understandings of performance standards;
- training: of raters to rate performance to agreed-upon standards;
- verification and audit: to double check scoring and assessment content to ensure that appropriate assessment standards are met. (p. 18)

This comprehensive list of requirements indicates how much needs to be done to make performance assessment comparable across pupils and raters.

However, the extra work and cost involved in using humans rather than machines to score the tasks should be welcomed because, not only does it yield more valid data, but also because involving the teacher can become a professional development exercise (and, assessing the right kind of tasks can encourage a different form of teaching). Shepard argues that the time and expense involved can be dealt with if policy makers were willing to test either fewer students (ie using light sampling procedures) at fewer ages or in fewer subject areas. 'The idea that accountability testing requires every pupil in every grade in every subject has to be given up to make it feasible to institute performance assessments' (Shepard, 1992a, p. 326). What we need then to emphasize to policy makers is the collateral benefit to teachers' professional development.

What is rarely brought up in this debate is that in England, Wales and Northern Ireland, a performance assessment is used at 16+ for school leaving certification *and* accountability purposes on a national scale. Every subject assessed in the General Certificate of Secondary Education (GCSE) which is taken by around 80 per cent of the age cohort, contains some element of performance assessment (Nuttall, 1992). These include investigational work in maths and science, oral assessment in English and modern languages, portfolios of work in English, and project investigations (written up at some length) in history, geography, economics/business studies etc. Examinations at this level have always had an oral 'examination' for modern languages, though not for English language, but the extent of this assessment is now greater in GCSE. Portfolios and investigational work are referred to as coursework, or more properly the coursework-assessed element, and they make up anything from 20 to 100 per cent of the final grade. The activities are laid down by the examination boards which organize the examinations, with some element of student choice or control possible. Marking is done by the students' own teachers within detailed guidelines laid down by the exam boards. This is monitored by two methods of moderation: either a sample, the details of which are carefully specified, is sent by the school to the exam board for checking or a moderator will visit the school to inspect assessed work. Moderators (who are generally experienced teachers) will themselves be supervised by a Chief Moderator who is responsible for training the moderators.

The written examination element employs virtually no multiple choice assessment, responses are almost exclusively essays or short answers; the written exam is therefore a performance assessment itself in North American terms though it is similar to most European examinations.

The point that needs to be made, however, is that very considerable amounts of pupil, teacher and examiner time is necessary to ensure coverage of the domains, and consistency of assessment and scoring.

This is feasible within the UK because it only takes place at one age (the introduction of similarly performance-based National Curriculum assessment at three other ages in addition to GCSE has proved to be insupportable) and examination at this stage of schooling has traditionally been a highly significant and time consuming activity. Thus, following the requirements identified by Baratz-Snowden they are administratively feasible and economically affordable. They are professionally credible because of the high status of the examination boards and the procedures for moderation and marking (although there is only limited information available about the reliability etc of public exams in general, see Satterly in Harlen ed. (1994).) Coursework has generally been a very popular activity with teachers and schools and has had a beneficial effect on teaching, bringing investigative, practical and oral work to the fore and engaging the pupils more deeply with the subject matter (see Gipps and Stobart, 1993). GCSE has, however, suffered from mixed levels of public acceptability: in England assessment for accountability and certification purposes is traditionally set and marked outside the school, since teacher involvement is deemed to be inappropriate for this assessment purpose. The teachers' role in coursework has therefore been viewed with some suspicion (mostly by those to whom the new examination was seen as something of a left wing educationalists' ploy to lower standards). Parents of many 16-year-olds have, come to see that coursework is in fact more demanding over the whole year, than is the classic four week 'cram' for a series of two hour examinations. Parents have, however, raised another problem in that pupils could, and in many cases did, get help with the coursework at home. A major cause of concern in relation to equity was that children from middle class homes were advantaged through having desk space, and word processors, access to books and a quiet room in which to work more freely available than children from less advantaged homes. To counter this genuine concern much of coursework is now done at school in rather more controlled conditions and for some boards the teacher must certify that the final piece of work is in fact the candidate's own.

So the GCSE, is a complex, true performance-based assessment which is used for high-stakes certification and accountability purposes. It had the desired impact on teaching and on student learning (although evidence on the latter is circumstantial rather than solid), and once the new system had bedded down it was manageable and valued by the majority of teachers and HMI. It has, however, fallen foul of the political body which cannot be persuaded that these moves towards enhancing the educational aspects of assessment are appropriate; as a result the amount of coursework is being decreased. As Professor Paul Black, the author of the ill-fated TGAT Report put it, the Right believes that the only examinations worth taking are ones which most people fail! (Black, 1993a).

National Curriculum Assessment at Age 7

Another example, which illustrates the pitfalls of *introducing* performance assessment on a wide scale, is the National Curriculum assessment programme for 7-year-olds, at the end of the first Key Stage of schooling in England and Wales. The requirements are that during the spring and early summer term of the year in which pupils reach the age of 7 (year 2) teachers make an assessment of each pupil's level of attainment on levels 1–4 of the National Curriculum scale in relation to the attainment targets of the core National Curriculum subjects. Teachers may make these assessments in any way they wish, but observation, regular informal assessment and keeping examples of work, are all encouraged. In the first half of the summer term and the second half of the spring term the pupils are given, by their teacher, a series of standard assessment tasks (SATs)[1] covering a sample of the core attainment targets.

Although *performance assessment* is not a term used widely in the UK, the SATs as originally proposed were clearly performance assessments, using the criteria of authenticity, directness, cognitive complexity (Moss, 1992) and 'subjective' scoring. The blueprint TGAT report (DES, 1988) suggested that a mixture of instruments including tests, practical tasks and observations be used in order to minimize curriculum distortion and that a broad range of assessment instruments sampling a broad range of attainment targets would discourage the narrowing tendency to teach to the test.

In the event, the SATs used for the first time with 7-year-olds in 1991 were a watered down version of the original proposals. The style of assessment was however active and similar to good infant school practice: for example, the reading task at Level 2 involved reading aloud a short passage from a children's book chosen from a list of popular titles, using dice to play maths 'games', using objects to sort etc. Despite the reduction in the scope of the curriculum assessed the Key Stage 1 SAT administration in 1991 took a minimum of forty hours for a class of twenty-five to thirty pupils and was rarely managed without support for the class teacher, since most of the SATs were done with groups of four pupils.

For example, multiplication, subtraction and addition were assessed through children throwing dice as in a game and having to add or multiply the numbers thrown on the dice; floating and sinking in science was assessed through a practical task in which the children were provided with a range of objects and a large tank of water. The children had to predict which objects would float or sink and try and develop a hypothesis (since it could take a week or more to assess a whole class of children on this particular task at one point in the summer term every infant school classroom could be seen to be full of water, waterlogged objects and rotting pieces of fruit: all the children were reported to have enjoyed it!); at level two reading was assessed by children reading aloud from a book chosen from a range of good children's story books (the list of twenty story books to be used at this level was published first in a national newspaper, within a week the books were out of stock from book shops); they were assessed by their teachers for fluency as they read and then asked questions when they had finished reading in order to test their comprehension. In addition there were some paper and pencil tasks to be done in maths on an illustrated work sheet and a story to be written in order to assess writing. In the majority of tasks, however, the children did not have to write their answers. Teachers were allowed to help the children produce the written answer in science, and were allowed to make their own judgments about whether the child understood or was able to do the task in hand. Bilingual children were allowed to have an interpreter for the maths and the science tasks. Listening and speaking was not assessed by a SAT: early on in the development process it was decided that this was better assessed by teachers' own judgment.

However, the program hit a number of problems. In response to the widespread publicity about the amount of time the 7-year-old SATs were taking, the Prime Minister announced in the summer of 1991 that for 1992 there would be shorter standardized paper and pencil tests. (This announcement was made *before* formal evaluations of the programme was available.) Thus the 1992 SATs contained a reduced number of active tasks, and offered, for a number of SATs, the option of a 'whole-class' administrative procedure, which in fact few teachers used. The reading SAT stayed as a reading aloud task with the teachers making a running record and in addition an accuracy score. There were also two extra tests: a traditional group reading comprehension test with written response, and a group spelling test. The reading test was optional at Level 2 and above and the spelling test was compulsory for Level 3 and above. These two scores had to be reported separately alongside the maths 'number' score, as well as the overall levels for

English, maths and science. For 1993 there were further changes with spelling and reading comprehension tests compulsory for all except level one as well as the reading and writing SATs. Different parts of the curriculum in maths and science are covered each year so that in 1993 7-year-olds were to be assessed on algebra and physics. The testing package took around thirty hours of classroom time in 1992. However, by 1993 teacher unrest was such that all national assessment was boycotted.

The issue at stake in the KS1 performance assessment was not so much political as physical: the assessment load of the SATs was high in itself but combined with the requirement for teacher assessment meant that the assessment program was unmanageable, particularly in the first year. Due to the style of assessment, with children having to be assessed individually or in small groups, considerable changes were required to school organization in order to support the class teachers and to cater for the children who were not being assessed (Gipps *et al.*, 1992). Considerable changes were made in some schools to support the administration of the testing. This often had a knock on effect on other staff and where disruption was widespread, for example, removal of all in-class support from other classes to the year 2 class, removal of year 2 teachers from all playground and other duties, it contributed to stress within the school as a whole. However, collegial support for year 2 teachers was the rule rather than the exception: colleagues offered high levels of support in order to protect the year 2 teachers from what was seen as an appallingly difficult, stressful and time-consuming activity rather than to perform the assessments particularly well or quickly.

Stress was due not just to the added pressure of having to do the assessment but also to the enormously high level of publicity that the assessments received, hitherto unheard of at primary level, and to many teachers' anxiety about formally assessing children as young as this with assessments which they felt could be used for labelling children. The culture of British primary teachers maintains that assessment of young children should be only for diagnostic purposes, that labelling, and indeed sorting children according to ability, is improper particularly at an age as young as 7 where many children will only have had five full terms of schooling. Teachers are all too well aware of the effect of different lengths of time in school due to birth date, different types of pre-school provision, different family and social backgrounds (especially for ethnic minority children from non-English speaking homes) on children's performance. Thus stress was due to a range of factors related to: a major innovation, the fact of assessment, and the high profile of the activity.

The 1992 exercise was managed with less stress, partly because it was the second time around and schools knew what to expect, partly because two long practical tasks were dropped. However, the testing still took a considerable amount of time and the administration was by no means standardized so that reliability and manageability were still major issues. Assessing a class of twenty-five to thirty children took forty to forty-five hours of direct teacher time in 1991, twenty-four hours plus the time for the reading assessments in 1992 (NFER/BGC, 1992) and arrangements had to be made for other children while individuals or small groups were being tested by the teacher. So, manageability was still a public and professional issue.

Lessons Learned About Reliability and Validity from this Assessment Programme

The administration of SATs is quite different from that of standardized tests: in the SATs the most important consideration was that pupils should understand what was expected of them. Thus there was no restriction on what was said, or on the use of the skills of another adult who was normally present in the classroom. There was no restriction on non-linguistic methods of presentation, there was no limit on pupils working in whatever language or combination of languages they normally used in mathematics or science. However, pupils were not allowed to explain tasks to each other nor could children whose mother tongue is not English have the English tasks explained to them in their mother tongue. Whilst the emphasis on understanding the task is of course entirely appropriate for assessing very young children, the lack of standardized introduction for the assessment tasks meant that, as we observed, there was great variation in administration, not only across teachers but also between administrations by the same teacher (see also James and Conner, 1993; and Broadfoot, 1993).

Other aspects which contributed to variability were: the choice of group for small group testing; choice of objects, for example, for the sorting or floating tasks; and in 1992 choice of work sheet or practical task. The make-up of a small group for an assessment task can have an effect on the performance of individuals within it, and teachers sometimes consciously chose to put shy children into groups which they felt would allow them to perform at their best. In fact we know rather little about the dynamics of small group assessment but they clearly can affect performance. In addition, teachers were allowed to choose the sets of objects for the sorting task, for example, and children in some classrooms sorted sets which appeared to be much easier to classify and sort than in other classrooms, with obvious effects on comparability of performance. Allowing teachers to choose the objects was no doubt meant to reduce the test development load and to provide objects with which the children were familiar, but detailed guidelines and/or lists of objects to be used would have helped to reduce the variability.

Performance assessments cannot be done in large groups with very young children; in order to deal with the manageability issue the assessments for 1992 were less time consuming and less performance-based so that they could be given to whole classes of children or small groups (in fact, most teachers chose *not* to use the whole class format). But offering the assessment as a whole class or a small group activity in itself is likely to alter the difficulty of the task.

Furthermore, sometimes the task could be offered as a practical task *or* done using a work sheet; this, of course, changes the nature of the task and is an unnecessary additional cause of variability. Studies by Shavelson *et al.*, (1992) and Koretz *et al.*, (1991) suggest that testing similar content in different assessment modes is unlikely to produce similar results; standardized (multiple-choice) tests are probably assessing different aspects of the domain than are the performance-based assessments.

Finally, the assessment criteria, the statements of attainment, were not always sufficiently clear to allow teachers to make unambiguous judgments about performance; the criteria in this criterion-referenced assessment system were not specific enough for assessment purposes. In some schools, teachers discussed criteria and standards of performance among themselves and in these schools it is likely that assessments were more standardized and more comparable across classes than in other schools (Gipps, 1992a), a finding supported by the official evaluation in 1992 (NFER/BGC, 1992). In the schools where discussion did take place it was partly because of the woolliness of the assessment criteria that these discussions were started.

Owing to the problems with the statements of attainment there was some concern over inter-rater (or judge) reliability. The technical evaluations carried out in 1991 indicate that SoAs were indeed interpreted differently by different teachers (NFER/BGC, 1991) and that assessments made of the same attainment target by teacher assessment, SAT and an alternative test had unacceptable levels of variation (Shorrocks *et al.*, 1992). The 1992 evaluation (NFER/BGC, 1992) found that the match between TA levels and SAT levels was significantly greater in the second year of the assessment. A range of factors could be causing this, one at least being an artefact of the system rather than necessarily being due to teachers' changing assessment skills. In 1992 teachers did *not* have to commit themselves to their TA levels until *after* the SATs were done; it is possible then that the teachers' own assessments were affected by the SAT results; it is also possible that some teachers did not make a separate TA but simply used the SAT result where an attainment target was assessed by both.

The evidence on inter-rater reliability is limited in the UK other than the comparison of teachers' own assessment and the performance assessment (SAT) score. However, the supervising body the Schools Examination and Assessment Council (SEAC), has admitted that there were good reasons for TA and SAT results *not* to align. TA, although less standardized, covers a wider range of attainments over a longer period of time. It may be less reliable than SAT assessment but is more thorough and offers a better description of overall attainment. 'The two forms of assessment should not therefore be regarded as identical' (SEAC, 1991, p. 34). The determination of mastery was also an issue in 1991 and 1992: for the SATs all but one SoA had to be achieved to gain a particular level while in TA there was no such rule, and we do not know how teachers made their mastery decisions, again suggesting variation between teachers' assessments and the performance assessment score.

There is some evidence (James and Conner, 1993; NFER/BGC, 1992) which our case studies would support that teachers in schools who made the opportunity to discuss standards of performance, that is engaged in group moderation, are developing common standards for assessment. Furthermore, the process of moderation had forced teachers to interact, negotiate meaning for SoAs, standardize judgments about individual children and discuss 'levelness' (McCallum *et al.*, 1993). However, concern about wider, national, levels of consistency remain. The process of group moderation (called social moderation by Linn 1992), in which groups of teachers with or without a 'moderator', or external expert, come together and discuss pieces of work or what counts as performance, greatly aids comparability. In some schools this process was going on but it needs to be supported and routinized if it is to have any serious impact on variability.

There is also evidence from the development of performance based maths tasks for national assessment at age 14 that inter-rater reliability was higher on these than on the written tests (Brown, 1992). This rather tentative finding is supported by the work of Shavelson *et al.*, (1992) that when observers are trained and scoring rubrics provided inter-rater reliability for performance-based tasks is high. By contrast, the standardized paper and pencil tests of reading comprehension and spelling that were introduced into the 1992 KSI national assessment in order to enhance 'objectivity' were not scored particularly reliably. When booklets were remarked in the reading test the original mark and the remark corresponded exactly in only 55 per cent of cases and 72 per cent of cases for the spelling test (NFER/BGC, 1992).

The style of the SAT was premised on an attempt to enhance the content and construct validity of the task and with the espoused intention of preventing negative consequences on teaching. This was welcomed since in the UK the consequential aspect of validity has received relatively little attention which is unfortunate, given the accountability uses to which the results are put at the school and district level, and the likely uses (selection, grouping) at the individual level.

Descriptions already given of the SATs indicate their likely content and construct validity. The case study work of James and Conner (1993) carried out in four districts suggests, however, that according to teachers a number of the assessments did not validly represent either the content or the construct being assessed, for example in relation to the writing task where use of full stops and capital letters was important but no judgment was required of the quality of ideas expressed in the writing. This is an issue for the test developers as the 1992 evaluation recognized (NFER/BGC, 1992). This reports some criticism of the quality of the pupil materials and notes that in moving away from practical tasks to paper and pencil tasks they need to take 'even greater care in ensuring that pupil materials are of high quality' (p. 158). The authors also report that many teachers who did not use these materials but stayed with a practical approach did so because they were concerned about the validity of the tasks. This in itself suggests an enormous increase in teachers' understanding of assessment issues (in contrast with Gipps *et al.*, 1983).

In attempting to enhance validity through the use of performance-based SATs reliability was often compromised. The reading assessment offers a good example of the tension between reliability and validity which ensued. The reading assessment for Level 2 (the expected level of performance for most 7-year-olds) involved children reading aloud from real books and then being asked questions about the content and future events. It was high on content, even construct, validity in that it matches what we think of as real reading for average 7-year-olds. However, part of the attempt to enhance validity was a very cause of the unreliability: there was a choice allowed from a range of twenty books and it was not uncommon for children to be reading from a book which they, it turned out, knew well. Thus obviously for some children the task was much easier since they already knew the story and had practised the reading.

Another aspect which enhances validity is that the teacher makes informal observational assessments of the child's fluency and other skills which relate to the statements of attainment for reading. However, these factors limit the reliability of the assessment because given the choice of texts we cannot assume that the task is comparable, or of comparable difficulty, for all the children, and given the reliance on judgmental factors in the assessment we cannot be sure that all teachers are assessing children at the same level in the same way. These factors tend to limit the comparability of the assessment. Thus we have an assessment that is more valid and less reliable while a standardized reading test would be more reliable and less valid. The problem lies in getting the most appropriate balance between these two requirements. This tension between reliability and validity is well understood within the literature (see Dunbar *et al.*, 1991).

In discussing consequential validity the use of National Curriculum assessment results has to be considered at a number of levels. At the level of the individual child we know that the close observation of children's performance on a range of tasks in English, maths and science against a set of (not always clear) criteria has been an illuminating, if exhausting, activity for many teachers. Despite early claims (Gipps *et al.*, 1992a) that the assessments told them nothing new, we have evidence that by late 1992 over half our sample of headteachers believed they could see the beneficial effects of this close observation and detailed assessment on teachers' practice. They felt that testing alone had not been of particular value but the close observation of children against the detailed curriculum statements had focused teachers' attention on the curriculum, improved their understandings of what children could do and raised expectations. We were also able to document some changes in teaching practice (*ibid*) which resulted both in an emphasis on the basics of spelling, punctuation and mental arithmetic (and the results for 1992 indicate that this had an effect on scores the following year — NFER/BGC, 1992), and a broadening of teaching to include more practical maths and science work. For some teachers, too, it brought the introduction of group and independent work (Gipps, 1992a). (It should be said, however, that the majority of infant school teachers already use group and independent work.) Thus, at this level we can see some positive consequences of the assessment.

The original intention was that school level results would be used to put schools into rank-ordered league tables; as a result of the 1993 teacher boycott the Government has retreated from league-tables at age 7 and 14. At both a moral and technical level one can critique this approach: encouraging schools to be compared on the basis of academic performance alone downgrades the other important tasks which schools, particularly primary schools, are trying to do and inevitably advantages schools with privileged intakes. At a technical level it should be clear from what has been said about reliability that given the undependable nature of results the data is simply not robust enough to be used for this purpose.

The same has to be said about local education authority or school district league tables: despite evidence that the 1991 national assessment results for Key Stage 1 were undependable, the publication of the league table went ahead. The school district at the bottom was pilloried in the popular press (*TES*, 28 February 1993, p. 8 'Dunce city leads league table battle') although two reasons are apparent for its low performance: large numbers of disadvantaged families and children whose first language is not English, and guidance that was given to local teachers to be conservative in their assessments (at the time it was believed that the 1991 results would not be reported — the school district's advice might have been different had they known they would be published, particularly in this form).

As a postscript, at the national level the Government has been able to claim that standards have risen from 1991 to 1992 since the percentage of the 7-year-old population reaching higher levels has risen in reading, spelling *and* maths (DFE, 21 December 1992, 'Seven year olds results show improving standards'). Of course one is left wondering what such a 'rise in standards' means or is worth. Given the changes in assessment from 1991 to 1992 and the undependability of results we would be inclined to say that such changes in patterns of performance should be treated with extreme caution.

Conclusion

As a number of writers have observed (for example, Mehrens, 1992; Linn, 1993a) there are problems with using performance assessments for accountability purposes. These problems hinge essentially around issues of manageability, reliability and validity. It is, however, possible to resolve these issues, as the GCSE shows.

But as Linn *et al.*, (1991) have it '. . . if great weight is attached to the traditional criteria of efficiency, reliability and comparability of assessments from year to year, the more complex and time-consuming performance-based measures will compare unfavourably with traditional standardised tests'. Since no one has yet suggested an alternative means of warranting assessment-based conclusions '. . . standardized assessment continues to be privileged by commonly accepted validity criteria' (Moss, 1992, p. 251).

Moderation is a key element in performance assessment, not only in terms of improving inter-rater reliability, but to moderate the *process* of assessment too. If we wish to be able to 'warrant assessment-based conclusions' without resorting to highly standardized procedures with all that this implies for poor validity then we must ensure that teachers have common understandings of the criterion performance and the circumstances and contexts which elicit best performance. This suggests that for some purposes we should move towards a performance model (see Frederiksen and Collins, 1989) rather than a sampling model i.e. concern is with the quality of the performance and fairness in scoring rather than with replicability and generalization.

The disadvantage of group moderation is that it is time consuming and this may then be seen to add to any unmanageability. Its great advantage on the other hand lies in its effect on teachers' practice. In the UK (and to a certain extent in the Vermont study, Koretz *et al.*, 1992) it has been found that where teachers come together to discuss performance standards or criteria it becomes a process of teacher development with wash-back on teaching. It seems that coming together to discuss performance or scoring is less personally and professionally threatening than discussing, for example, pedagogy. But discussion of assessment does not end there: issues of production of work follow on and this broadens the scope of discussion and impacts on teaching.

There are some very specific issues related to the age of the children being assessed which indicate that very young children require a different format for an assessment programme. For example, our teachers commonly tried to get the best performance out of the children: by reassuring them, helping them, offering preparation and emotional support and sometimes even a second chance. This is one of the criteria for educational assessment (see chapter 1) and definitely runs counter to the notion of assessment as examination or hurdle. This we felt was not due to teachers' particular models of assessment but rather to their view of what is appropriate for children of this age. Teachers were concerned about 'failure' and 'labelling' for such young children and there was some tension between offering children the chance to try the next advanced level in the assessment programme or indeed to keep plugging away at a particular assessment task, and the need to prevent the children experiencing failure. Our teachers also went to enormous lengths to hide the fact that this was testing; despite the stress and anxiety reported by teachers there was very little of this observed when the children were being assessed. The children were generally unaware of the purpose and importance of the tasks that they were engaged in.

It also seems to be the case that when teachers of young children assess those children, either individually or in small groups, it is almost inevitable that they will vary the way in which they introduce the task, whether they are given highly specific instructions or not; this is because what the teacher sees is not a testing situation but individual children whom she/he knows well and who need to have things explained to them in different ways, or presented in different ways, because of the children's own backgrounds, abilities and immediate past history. If this is the case then it will not be possible (and one might say not desirable) to have standardized performance assessments with young children.

Large scale performance assessment of every pupil *can* only cover a limited range of activities, because the tasks are time-consuming; this has problems for generalizability. We can either propose light sampling of pupils, or if we have to asses every pupil, we can design a high-quality assessment programme which combines high quality, time consuming performance assessment which covers a changing, smaller number of skills, complemented by more standardized procedures and teacher assessment of a much wider range of skills. Such a combination of assessment can better cover the full range of the curriculum giving due weight to processes and higher order skills and thus support teaching. We need also to remember the strengths of performance assessment: it is a powerful tool for assessing a broad range of skills in various modes; where necessary we can ensure comparability and consistency by assuring that the stimulus content is presented in the same way, and response content evaluated according to the same rules, by all assessors.

Notes

1   From 1993 SATs were called Standard Tasks at age 7, and Standard Tests at 11 and 14.

Chapter 7

Teacher Assessment and Formative Assessment

Introduction

Assessment made by teachers of pupils' attainment, knowledge and understanding is called variously teacher assessment (although in the USA this refers to assessment of teachers), school-based assessment and formative assessment. The last of these terms is not always appropriate since 'formative' refers to a function rather than the person who makes the assessment: formative assessment *can* be based on external tests or pupils' own self-assessment while teacher assessment can be summative rather than formative. There is also in England and Wales the teacher-assessed element of National Curriculum assessment called Teacher Assessment (TA).

In this chapter I shall deal first with teacher assessment, that is assessment made by teachers (of which National Curriculum assessment TA is a particular version) and then with formative assessment, that is assessment (made by any means or individual) that is used to feedback into the teaching/learning process.

Teacher Assessment

Teacher assessment is essentially an informal activity: the teacher may pose questions, observe activities, evaluate pupils' work in a planned and systematic or ad hoc way (see McCallum *et al.*, 1993). The information which the teacher thus obtains may be partial or fragmentary; it will not at the time allow the teacher to make a firm evaluation of the pupils' competence in reading, for example, or understanding of a mathematical process. But repeated assessment of this sort, over a period of time, and in a range of contexts *will* allow the teacher to build up a solid and broadly-based understanding of the pupil's attainment. Because of these characteristics teacher assessment may be seen as having a high validity in relation to content and construct (see chapter 4). If the teacher assessment is used for formative purposes which then results in improved learning then the assessment can be said to have consequential validity, to the extent that it has the consequences expected/required of it. If the assessment has sampled broadly across the domain *and* in depth within it then the assessment is likely to be generalizable (within that domain), since the teacher's evaluation of for example the pupil's ability to read at a certain level or to be able to manipulate single digits, will be based on a broad sample of tasks and assessments. An external test, on the other hand, will provide more limited information based as it is on a one-off occasion covering a limited sample of tasks.

The rationale of teacher assessment is linked with the constructivist model of learning. In this model it is important to understand what the child knows and how she articulates it in order to develop her knowledge and understanding. We need to take a child's initial ideas seriously so as to ensure that any change or development of these ideas and the supporting evidence for them makes sense and, in this way, become "owned" by the child. In this model it is learning with understanding which counts and to this end information about existing ideas and skills is essential. Work in psychology and learning tells us similarly that for effective learning the task must be matched to the child's current level of understanding (Gipps, 1992b) and either pitched at that level to provide practice or slightly higher in order to extend and develop the child's skills. If the new task is much too easy the child can become bored, if much too difficult the child can become demotivated. Assessment to find out what and how children know is thus part of good teaching practice and in helping the teacher to decide what and how to teach next is formative assessment. However, if it is to be really fruitful it seems that the pupil must also be involved, since teachers need to explain to pupils what they need to do to improve their work or the next steps in the learning process.

Formative Assessment

Formative assessment involves using assessment information to feed back into the teaching/learning process; some believe that assessment is only truly formative if it involves the pupil, others that it can be a process which involves only the teacher who feeds back into curriculum planning.

Sadler (1989) conceptualizes formative assessment as being concerned with how judgments about the quality of students' responses can be used to shape and improve their competence by short-circuiting the randomness and inefficiency of trial-and-error learning. The key difference between formative assessment and summative assessment is not timing, but purpose and effect: assessments made *during* the course of a unit or session may be used for summative or grading purposes rather than for truly formative purposes.

In Sadler's classic paper (*ibid.*) formative assessment is initially connected with feedback and for him feedback to teacher and pupil are separated:

> Teachers use feedback to make programmatic decisions with respect to readiness, diagnosis and remediation. Students use it to monitor the strengths and weaknesses of their performances, so that aspects associated with success or high quality can be recognized and reinforced, and unsatisfactory aspects modified or improved. (p. 120)

Sadler's work in theorizing formative assessment stems from the 'common but puzzling' observation that even when teachers give students valid and reliable judgments about their work improvement does not necessarily follow. In order for the student to improve she must have: a notion of the desired standard or goal, be able to compare the actual performance with the desired performance and to engage in appropriate action to close the gap between the two. Feedback from the teacher, which helps the student with the second of these stages, needs to be of the kind and detail which tells the student what to do to improve; the use of grades or 'good, 7/10' marking cannot do this. Grades may in fact shift attention away from the criteria and be counter-productive for formative purposes. In Sadler's model, grades do not count as feedback: information fed back to the student is only feedback when it can be used to close the gap.

Diagnostic assessment is another term used within this framework for assessment. It refers to assessment which identifies particular problems which individual pupils may have in learning particular subject matter or skills. Diagnostic assessment tends to be seen as a specialist activity: more the role of the psychologist or specialist support teacher than the classroom teacher. However, this is not necessarily the case: when teachers have a good understanding of the details of the subject and skills which the children are to learn and when they have training in observation and questioning (which we may call diagnostic questioning) then they can carry out diagnostic assessment. Indeed teachers, as a profession, should be trained to be able to carry out diagnostic assessment, since it is essentially a sub-set of formative assessment which itself is a crucial part of the skill of teaching.

A key development in the formative assessment process, and an indispensable condition for improvement, is that the student comes to hold a notion of the standard or desired quality similar to that of the teacher, is able to monitor the quality of what is being produced at the time of production, and is able to regulate their work appropriately. When the student reaches this stage the process is referred to as self-monitoring (rather than feedback from the teacher). Competent learners are those who self-monitor their work, although this does not mean that the need for feedback from the teacher decreases: such feedback will continue to be necessary whenever a new subject, standard or criterion is introduced. Sadler's conceptualization of formative assessment can be seen to be in line with theories of metacognition as outlined in chapter 2; which lends it strength since models of assessment need to be based on theories of learning.

The optimum size of gap between the student's current ability and the goal for which s/he aiming will vary from student to student. The teacher can set the goal with the student but ultimately in the self-monitoring model, the aim is for the student to set the goal for him or herself. Indeed an essential element of the learning process is improving one's criteria: 'without the reflection and deliberation that come with the critical revision of the means by which one judges quality of performance, one cannot make use of one's learning' (Blanchard, personal communication). A range of research supports the setting of standards for students to work towards in terms of goals. Goals which are specific and clear, challenging (but not out of the student's reach) have the most effect on performance (Sadler, 1989). 'By contrast, do-one's-best goals often turn out to be not much more effective than no goals at all' (p. 129).

Torrance (1993a) is concerned with the claims made for formative assessment and our relatively poor conceptualization of how it might fit into the teaching-learning cycle, given what we know about the complexities and nuances in teacher-pupil interaction. Sweeping generalizations such as this: 'Teachers should . . . create . . . the time and opportunity for assessment and diagnosis to take place, using both observation and interaction . . . (and) combine assessment of work completed with assessment of work in progress so as to understand the pupil's thinking as it happens . . .' (Alexander, Rose and Woodhead, 1992, p. 39) in policy documents suggest that the process is unproblematic and well understood. Torrance sees formative assessment fitting into constructivist approaches to learning with the teacher-child interaction supporting the child in moving the child through the ZPD, while pointing out that we have little evidence about how assessment fits into this framework (see also chapter 2).

Issues in Teacher Assessment

Where school-based teacher assessment is to be used for summative purposes then the relationship between teacher and pupil can become strained: the teacher may be seen as judge rather than facilitator. This uneasy dual role for the teacher which ensues is a result of the formative/summative tension. If the teacher assessment were not to be used for summative purposes then the relationship could stay in the supportive mode.

The formative/summative tension is well-captured by Sadler (1989):

> Continuous assessment cannot, however, function formatively when it is *cumulative*, that is, when each attempt or piece of work submitted is scored and the scores are added together at the end of the course. This practice tends to produce in students the mindset that if a piece of work does not contribute towards the total, it is not worth doing. (p. 141)

Harlen however, makes a distinction between 'summing-up' and 'checking-up' in assessment (Harlen *et al.*, 1992). In the former, information collected over a period of time is simply 'summed' every so often to see how students are getting on. This collection of pieces of formative assessment can be put together in an RoA since, in order to preserve the richness of the data, it is best kept in a detailed profile rather than aggregated. The summing-up provides a picture of current achievements derived from information gathered over a period of time and used in that time for formative purposes. Checking-up, however, is when summative assessment is done through the use of tests or tasks specifically devised for the purpose of recording performance at a particular time. End of year exams and end of unit tests are examples of this type of summative assessment. Harlen maintains that assessment for summative purposes should be separated into 'checking-up' and 'summing-up' types and that formative assessment can be used for summing up purposes without impairing its feedback role.

Questioning is a key device for understanding a child's interpretation and conceptualization of an issue and also taking that conceptualization or questioning further. But a number of research studies have shown that teacher questioning has a particular role in the classroom, being used to establish the teacher's control of the classroom and to sequence the lesson. Thus questioning can be seen to have a social function as much as (or more than) an intellectual function. Furthermore, much teacher questioning is 'closed' and children develop strategies to discover the answer the teacher wants before actually committing themselves to it (Edwards and Mercer, 1989; Pollard, 1985). In such a climate for questioning, attempts by the teacher to engage in detailed diagnostic questioning may be misinterpreted; as Edwards and Mercer (1989) point out: 'Repeated questions imply wrong answers' (p. 45) and the pupil may change tack in order to give the 'correct' answer and stop the questioning process rather than become engaged in an interactive process with the teacher. This is not to suggest that questioning is problematic in the classroom, but that teachers need to understand the role of different types of questioning and to be sensitive to the pupils' construction of the classroom context.

Sadler's conceptualization of formative assessment is based on the assessment of complex learning areas when qualitative judgments are involved in appraising performance and the outcomes cannot be characterized as correct/incorrect. However, I would argue that what Sadler is describing is relevant to most subjects and situations in which teachers engage in feedback for formative assessment. Even in the case of mathematics, when answers can be correct/incorrect some of the same processes apply: the teacher's standards must be available to the student and feedback from the teacher must allow the student to reach this standard. A real problem in this process is that of making teachers' criteria or standards explicit to students: these are often implicit, in the heads of teachers, and judgments are often made on the basis of ranking students' work rather than evaluating it against criteria. Where teachers are not given criteria or find it hard to develop them, then the use of descriptive statements and exemplars is a useful way to set about providing guidance for students. Sadler also points out that some teachers may give partial credit for a task well done or well-put together but off-target. This, in the long run is, counterproductive since the student is being deflected from the criteria or standards.

The age at which students can take on these evaluative and self-monitoring strategies is open to debate. Many teachers feel that this is an activity for older pupils, others that even young children can and should be engaged in such activity. Records of Achievement which have been taken on at primary as well as at secondary level essentially involve this process. The PRAISE team, in their evaluation of Records of Achievement (Broadfoot *et al.*, 1988), found that secondary pupils found self-assessment difficult partly because they were unused to it and partly because the assessment criteria caused problems. Often clear assessment criteria were not available and even when they were, students tended to make norm-referenced judgments of their achievement i.e. in relation to their perception of the range of achievement in their teaching groups rather than directly in relation to the categories. It also appears that pupils' perceptions of teacher expectations, their views on what is socially acceptable and their anxiety not to lose face affect their self evaluation. Furthermore, there appear to be differences in relation to gender and ethnic group in approach to the process of self-assessment and 'negotiation' with teachers. Boys tend to be more likely to challenge a teacher's assessment and have a keen sense of the audience for the final record, while girls tend to enter into a discussion and to negotiate more fully. Where pupils and teachers do not share a common cultural group, pupils may be disadvantaged by teachers not recognizing fully their achievements.

It is clear that if pupil self-assessment and teacher assessment of their work is to be empowering to pupils then considerable development will be required of teachers and preparation of pupils. In the process of developing formative assessment teachers may encourage pupils' understanding of marking criteria and encourage pupils to reflect on their strengths and weaknesses. As Torrance (1991) puts it:

> In some respects these two approaches reflect a basic tension that seems to inhabit much discussion of profiling — on the one hand making curriculum objectives and assessment criteria much more manifest in the belief that clarity of intention will aid learning, on the other, encouraging self-reflection and more idiographic approaches to curriculum and assessment in the belief that self-knowledge and intrinsic interest are the keys to learning. In either case, however, it is still, at least in the first instance, the teacher who sets the agenda for discussion, and often it is an agenda that pupils struggle to make sense of. (p. 234)

Feedback in Assessment

Feedback, in the process of teaching, is considered to be important for two reasons: it contributes directly to progress in learning through the process of formative assessment, and indirectly through its effect on pupils' academic self-esteem. Feedback has long been recognized as a crucial feature of the teaching-learning process. The model by Bloom (1976), for example, includes feedback, correctives and reinforcements (such as praise, blame, encouragement and other rewards and punishments that are used to sustain learning) as important elements of the instructional process. A later model by Bennett (1982) also includes teacher feedback which is regarded as crucial for both pupil involvement and comprehension and hence achievement. Bennett considers feedback to be one of the structuring conditions for learning and it is included alongside such variables as task presentation, sequencing, level and pacing of content and teacher expectations.

In teaching terms this means teachers using their judgments of children's knowledge or understanding of skills, concepts or facts to feed back into the teaching process and to determine for individual children whether to reexplain the task, to give further practice on it, or move onto the next stage. (Gipps, 1990). Such evaluations by teachers are also seen as crucial in the process of setting tasks which are appropriate or matched to the learner (Bennett and Desforges, 1985).

Such judgments by teachers during the teaching process may be incomplete, fuzzy, qualitative and based on a limited range of potential criteria. Describing and analyzing teachers' informal formative assessment is therefore a complex, and little attempted task. However, what we do know is that feedback defined in terms of how successfully something is being, or has been, done is a key feature in formative assessment. The importance of this 'correction' function of feedback is attested to in the research literature:

> (Feedback) confirms correct responses, telling the students how well the content is being understood, and it identifies and corrects errors — or allows the learner to correct them. This correction function is probably the most important aspect of feedback . . . (Kulhavy, 1977, p. 229)

In his review of research on the impact of classroom evaluation on students, Crooks (1988) concludes that feedback assists learning unless the material is too difficult for the students, in which case feedback appears to become demoralizing. Feedback of the global grades or simply confirming correct answers has little effect on subsequent performance, while detailed factual feedback, conceptual help or feedback on strategies used are more effective. A meta analysis by Kulik, Kulik and Bangert-Drowns (1990) showed the crucial role of feedback and remediation in improving learning at all levels of schooling; while the studies they reviewed showed that this was true at all levels of attainment, in general the gain was greater for lower attainers than for high attainers. Crooks concludes that teachers need to make more use of learning-related feedback to students and less use of feedback for evaluative or grading purposes. As already pointed out, Sadler argues that clear performance criteria are necessary so that the student knows explicitly and reliably what s/he is expected to do. (Sadler, 1989).

Feedback is also incorporated into recent models of primary teaching. In an extensive study into the quality of pupil learning experiences, Bennett *et al.*, (1984) utilized a model of task processes which incorporates teacher feedback as an important element in the process of ascribing tasks in classrooms. A simplified version of this model is presented in Bennett and Kell (1989). According to Bennett and Kell, teacher assessment 'concerns the judgments of right and wrong that teachers tend to make, including ticking and crossing, written comments, and the like' (p. 29). Teachers are adept at this, argues Bennett, but are less good at diagnosis, i.e. the ascertaining of misunderstandings and misconceptions through careful questioning.

In Pollard's (1990) social-constructivist model of the teaching/learning process, he stresses the importance of the teacher as a 'reflective agent'. In this role, the teacher provides 'meaningful and appropriate guidance and extension to the cognitive structuring and skill development arising from the child's initial experiences. This supports the child's attempts to 'make sense' and enables them to cross the zone of proximal development (z.p.d.). Their thinking is thus restructured in the course of further experiences' (p. 18). He argues that this role is dependent on the sensitive and accurate assessment of a child's needs and places a premium on formative teacher assessment.

Pollard does not comment on the nature and type of feedback required, while Bennett (1982) highlights the importance of diagnostic information in relation to praise. In order to have pay-off, praise needs to relate to the topic under consideration and be genuine and credible. Bennett concludes that a gap exists in our understanding of the quality of the information fed back: 'An informal assessment of the types of marking in exercise books or work books would indicate that the 'tick, good' or 'four out of ten' is still endemic, a practice which is less than useful in feedback terms' (*ibid*). The mere provision of feedback is insufficient for optimal learning; it must also indicate what the pupil can do to improve performance. Dweck and colleagues (1978) argue that in the classroom frequent use of evaluative feedback for non-intellectual behaviour (for example, conduct and neatness of work) increases the ambiguity of that feedback and impairs its meaning as an evaluation of the intellectual quality of the child's work.

Feedback has an impact on not only the teaching-learning process, but also sends messages to children about their effectiveness and worth.

Coopersmith(1967) defined self-esteem as:

> the evaluation which the individual makes and customarily maintains with regard to himself — it expresses an attitude of approval or disapproval and indicates the extent to which an individual believes himself to be capable, significant, successful and worthy. (pp. 4–5)

In a review of research on self-esteem enhancement in children Gurney (1987) points out that in the context of school: self-esteem is found to be positively associated with school achievement; that self-esteem is learned; that the causal relationship with academic achievement is not clear although there seems to be some evidence that academic improvement precedes self-esteem enhancement, while a minimum level of self-esteem is necessary for learning to take place.

A major determinant of self-esteem is feedback from significant others, thus childrens' self-evaluations are to a large extent a reflection of significant others' evaluations, i.e. parents, teachers and peers. As far as academic self-esteem is concerned, teachers' evaluations are most crucial, particularly in the early years of schooling. Children develop their 'self-image' in school through observing and feeling not only how the teacher interacts with them but also how the teacher interacts with the rest of the class (Crocker and Cheeseman, 1988a and 1988b): the development of a favourable self-concept in children is dependent upon perceiving themselves as successful, this in turn will depend on the way the child interprets the teachers' reaction to his/her performances.

Equally, children's images of themselves can greatly affect the benefit they receive from learning opportunities. Jensen (1985) points out that enhancing self-concept has been a major goal of federally funded early education programmes in the USA, such as Head Start, as a fundamental attitude for school success. Since children cannot escape school, failure in school easily generalizes to global self-esteem (Lawrence, 1987); while adults can enhance their self-esteem in a number of ways outside the work setting, for young children this is much more difficult.

According to Jensen's review, self-concept as it develops during the pre-school years is a global entity; as children mature, however, they make more discrete or differentiated self-evaluative judgments which appear around the age of 8. In Russia the age of 6 to 7, is considered to be a period of great 'perestroika' for the child in terms of self-concept and esteem, hence the delay of formal schooling until 7+ (which the rigour and formality of Russian schooling would in any case suggest). This tumultuous time is not an appropriate one for the pressures and anxieties of the first year in school (Gipps, 1991). Chapman (1988) reports that perceptions of ability decline for most children around the age of 7 or 8 but this is more marked for children experiencing frequent academic failure; for low achievers self-esteem declines over time as failures accumulate.

Teachers are constantly acting as feedback agents in terms of performance comments. Since these comments are evaluative and fairly frequent, particularly to some children, they will be crucial in confirming (or otherwise) self-concept and self-esteem levels (Gurney, 1988). Because society and schools put a high value on academic success, it becomes increasingly the yardstick by which children judge themselves as they move through primary and on to secondary school.

The classic study of feedback to young children and its effect was carried out by Dweck and colleagues (1978) and they hypothesized the concept of 'learned helplessness'. They found that girls attributed failure to lack of ability rather than motivation; this was because teachers' feedback to boys and girls was such that it would lead to girls feeling less able, while allowing boys to explain their failure through lack of effort or poor behaviour. This reaction to feedback was only so for teacher feedback; peer feedback did not have this stereotypical effect. Dweck and colleagues worked with fourth and fifth grade children in the USA, first carrying out an observational study of evaluative feedback from teachers, and then a small experimental study with feedback from tasks and a question about cause of failure. In essence, the learned helplessness model implies that some students may 'give up trying' because they do not see themselves as capable of success. Whether or not effort is applied, the outcome will be the same: failure. Logically, there is little to be gained by trying, and nothing to be lost by not trying (Craske, 1988).

People who hold positive self-perceptions usually try harder and persist longer when faced with difficult or challenging tasks. On the other hand students who feel relatively worthless and ineffectual tend to reduce their effort or give up altogether when work is difficult, what Dweck calls 'learned helplessness' (Dweck, 1986). Children with poor academic self-concept appear to be particularly susceptible to learned helplessness (Butkowsky and Willows, 1980). Females are more likely than males to exhibit learned helplessness (for example,

Dweck and Gilliard, 1975; Le Unes *et al.*, 1980). It is possible that a self-reinforcing cycle exists with a low self-concept predisposing attributions to lack of ability which then mediate reduced persistence and attainment levels. These in turn serve to maintain the self-concept at a low level.

Motivation is, of course, one of the links between self-concept/ self-esteem and learning behaviour, and achievement motivation is the theory most commonly used to explain the effect of teacher feedback on children's performance.

Motivational patterns generally may be either adaptive or maladaptive.

> Adaptive motivational patterns are those that promote the establishment, maintenance, and attainment of personally challenging and personally valued achievement goals. Maladaptive patterns, then, are associated with a failure to establish reasonable, valued goals, to maintain effective striving toward those goals, or, ultimately, to attain valued goals that are potentially within one's reach. (Dweck, 1986, p. 1040)

The adaptive pattern may be characterized as mastery-oriented; the maladaptive pattern as learned helplessness. In this model the role of the teacher in setting tasks and in providing feedback is crucial and has an important influence on the fostering of motivational patterns.

Pintrich and Blumenfeld (1985) studied second and sixth graders' classroom experience in relation to their self-perceptions of ability, effort and conduct. They report that younger children conflate the concepts of ability and effort and perceive their ability, effort and conduct more positively than older children. Children who were praised more for their work thought they were 'smarter' and worked harder than those children who had lower levels of work praise; they feel that this points to the importance of assigning tasks matched to students' skill levels and providing frequent opportunities for feedback. Criticism of performance did not have a negative effect on students' perceptions, possibly because it signified low effort rather than low ability.

Van Oudenhoven and Siero (1985) looked at teachers' evaluative feedback to children as a possible determinant of the teacher expectancy effect, since other research had shown that teachers give different evaluative feedback to students for whom they hold high and low expectations. Working with second graders in Holland, they observed children whom teachers classified as likely to bloom or not to bloom. The latter group were given more negative *non-verbal* evaluative feedback but also more positive, encouraging remarks. They concluded that if teachers hold low expectations they show this non-verbally for it is more difficult to control non-verbal behaviour. On the other hand teachers gave more personal negative feedback to those they considered under-achievers, for example, 'you could do much better' which possibly serves to strengthen the children's feelings of competence. Both these studies show that what is important is the *meaning* which teacher evaluative feedback has for the child, rather than the actual content.

Crocker and Cheeseman (1988a) found that with 5, 6 and 7-year-old children (in three schools in the Midlands) there was a high degree of correlation among the children's self-estimate of rank position 'at school work', their peer estimate and the teachers' estimate. They conclude that the children could rank themselves and each other with a high degree of agreement and that by the age of 6 the criteria used were predominantly academic.

Tizard and colleagues (1988), in their study of children in London infant schools, found, contrary to Crocker and Cheeseman, that 7-year-olds were not particularly accurate at estimating their academic achievement and feel that this is similar to others' findings that up to the age of 8 children tend to overrate their ability and performance. The Tizard study used different methods to the Crocker and Cheeseman one and is probably more robust. Children compared themselves with their classmates in maths, reading and writing ability (as good as, better, worse than) and these were compared with standardized assessments made by the researchers. Their findings show that the children, especially the boys, tended to over estimate their achievements at age 7; bad behaviour was seen by teachers as interfering with learning; the teacher's praise and especially her blame made important contributions to the children's happiness and enjoyment of a subject.

Tizard's research also found different types of feedback to children according to gender and ethnic group. White girls received the least criticism and disapproval from their teachers; however they also received less praise. Tizard suggests that these girls were 'invisible'. Black boys on the other hand received the most disapproval and criticism and this was probably linked with greater tendency to 'fool around' when they were supposed to be working. They also found that these white girls underestimated their attainment in reading and maths. Tizard discusses a range of reasons for this including that put forward by Dweck, drawing on attribution of achievement and learned helplessness, but offers no conclusion about the processes involved. A follow up of this study when the children reached eleven found that children were more accurate in estimating their academic achievements than they were at 7, although white girls still underestimated their achievement (Blatchford, 1992). The researchers' view is that the children became more adept at picking up and reacting to teacher feedback.

Mortimore and colleagues (1988) found differences in feedback among teachers in their London-based Junior School Study although they did not analyze this by gender or ethnic group of the child. Their teachers used positive feedback in the form of praise about work very infrequently, and this got progressively less as the children got older. Most significantly, there were marked variations between teachers in their use of neutral feedback, praise and criticism. Using a generalized measure of self-concept, Mortimore and colleagues found no differences in relation to social class, while girls had a more positive self concepts in relation to school than boys and Asian children rated themselves more positively at the end of the junior third year than other children.

To sum, up many classroom situations involve evaluations of pupils' achievement as success or failure and the causes for this are ascribed by both teachers and pupils. Teachers' causal perceptions are important determinants of their behaviour towards pupils, the relationship between the two being mediated through teacher expectations regarding pupils' future success. In the classroom, teachers' verbal and non-verbal behaviour provides information regarding academic content, classroom events, the pupils themselves, etc. It is this information which affects pupil reactions including their perceptions of success and failure.

Reliability and Validity in Teacher Assessment

In considering the traditional requirements for reliability and validity, Sadler (1989) suggests in view of the purpose of formative assessment that we reverse the polarity of the terms. In summative assessment reliability is presented:

> as a precondition for a consideration of validity. In discussing formative assessment, however, the relation between reliability and validity is more appropriately stated as follows: validity is a sufficient but not necessary condition for reliability. Attention to the validity of judgments about individual pieces of work should take precedence over attention to reliability of grading in any context where the emphasis is on diagnosis and improvement. *Reliability will follow as a corollary.* (p. 122, my emphasis)

The requirement that students improve as a result of feedback can be seen as a consequential validity criterion for formative assessment. In this model the teacher must involve the student in discussion of the evaluation and what is needed to improve, otherwise the student is unlikely to be able to improve her work; the student needs to be involved in this process in order to shift to a process of self-monitoring. Formative assessment thus needs to demonstrate formative validity and in Sadler's definition *must* involve feedback to the pupil; her involvement in and understanding of this feedback is crucial otherwise improvement is unlikely to occur.

We need to consider here the issue of purpose (and fitness for purpose). If assessment is to be used for certification or accountability then it needs an adequate level of reliability for comparability purposes. If however, the assessment is to be used for formative purposes, validity (content, construct *and* consequential aspects) is highly important and reliability is less so. Where teacher assessment is concerned confusion often arises since reliability may be thought to be less important in a generic sense. However, this ignores the interaction with purpose: if teacher assessment is part of an accountability or certificating process, then reliability is important. This is not an insurmountable problem, since various methods of moderation are capable of enhancing reliability in teacher assessment.

Enhancing Reliability in Teacher Assessment Through Moderation

Where students do the 'same' task for internal assessment purposes (for example, a practical maths or science task or an essay with a given title) there are bound to be questions about the comparability of the judgments made by different teachers. Where there is no common task but common assessment criteria or common standards the problem is different but the question the same: can we assume that the assessments are comparable across teachers and institutions?

There are several points at which consistency in teacher assessment can be encouraged: the provision of clear guidelines for any assessment tasks; group moderation of assessment processes; provision of clear marking criteria and schemes; external moderation by visitation or inspection; feedback to the school. These procedures, and points of moderation, are the same for assuring quality in any form of school-based assessment.

The process of group moderation, as described in chapter 4, is one which relies solely on teachers' professional judgment and is essentially concerned with quality assurance and the professional development of teachers.

> The emphasis is on collegial support and the movement toward consensus judgements through social interaction and staff development. (Linn, 1992, p. 25)
> In the use of social moderation, the comparability of scores assigned depends substantially on the development of a consensus among professionals. The process of verification of a sample of student papers or other products at successively higher levels in the system (for example, school, district, state, nation) provides a means of broadening the consensus across the boundaries of individual classrooms or schools. It also serves an audit function that is likely to be an essential element in gaining public acceptance. (*ibid*, p. 26)

It is a form of consensus moderation called by Linn (1992) social moderation. In group moderation examples of work are discussed by groups of teachers, the purpose is to arrive at shared understandings of the criteria in operation and thus both the processes and the products of assessment are considered. Through discussion the assessments assigned to some pieces of work would be changed. The process can be widened to groups of schools within a district or county: samples of graded work can be brought by one or two teachers from each school to be moderated at the district/county level. This would reveal any discrepancies among the various local groups and the same process of discussion and comparison would lead to some assessments being changed in the same way as at the local level meeting. The teachers then take this information back to their own schools and discuss it in order to achieve a broader consensus. This is the procedure used in Queensland where there have been no external examinations for a period of twenty years; all assessment is school-based on a five-point rating scale.

A prerequisite to the process, of course, is a common marking scheme or a shared understanding of assessment criteria (e.g. the SoA in National Curriculum assessment). The provision of exemplars, samples of marked or graded work, is sometimes a part of this process and, whilst not doing away with the need to have discussions about levels of performance, does aid teachers in getting an understanding of the overall standards.

Mislevy (1992), writing from a similar standpoint to Linn's in relation to assessment practice in the USA, suggests that moderation should be viewed as a way to specify the rules of the game, 'It can yield an agreed-upon way of comparing students who differ quantitatively, but it doesn't make information from tests that aren't built to measure the same thing function as if they did' (p. 72). This, of course, is an important point to emphasize: the enhanced validity offered by teacher assessments is gained at a cost to consistency and comparability. Moderation is a process of attempting to *enhance* comparability which in technical terms can never be as great as in highly standardized procedures with all pupils taking the same specified tasks. Interest in moderation in the USA has developed in the wake of the explosion of performance assessment, and an interest in having, not a National Curriculum and national assessment, but national goals or standards to be achieved and assessed in ways which can be determined at district and local level. The question then immediately arises as to whether judgments made of pupils' performance in relation to these goals can be relied upon to be comparable.

Moderation is a key element of teacher, school-based assessment, not only in terms of improving inter-rater reliability, but to support the *process* of assessment too. If we wish to be able to 'warrant assessment-based conclusions' without resorting to highly standardized procedures with all that this implies for poor validity, then we must ensure that teachers have common understandings of the criterion performance and the circumstances and contexts which elicit best performance.

The disadvantage of group moderation is that it is time consuming and costly and this may then be seen to add to any unmanageability in an assessment program. Its great advantage on the other hand lies in its effect on teachers' practice (Linn, 1992). In the UK (Radnor and Shaw 1994) and to a certain extent in the Vermont study (Koretz *et al.*, 1992) it has been found that where teachers come together to discuss performance standards or criteria the moderation process becomes a process of teacher development with wash-back on teaching. It seems that coming together to discuss performance or grading is less personally and professionally threatening than discussing, for example, pedagogy. But discussion of assessment does not end there: issues of production of work follow on and this broadens the scope of discussion and impacts on teaching.

An example of teacher assessment in the UK and the moderation to support it now follows by way of illustration.

Moderation of Teacher Assessment in National Curriculum Assessment at Key Stage 1

In the section on moderation in the TGAT Report (DES, 1988) the authors argue for group moderation as the most appropriate method of moderation for National Curriculum assessment because of its emphasis on communication and its ability to value and enhance teachers' professional judgments. However, the detailed account given of how such group moderation must work (paras. 73 to 77) makes it clear that the process intended by TGAT is much closer to a scaling process using the external SAT results to adjust the distributions of teachers' assessments.

The procedure proposed was as follows: groups of teachers would meet and consider two sets of results for each element of the National Curriculum: their own ratings and the results on the national tests, both expressed in terms of distributions over the levels of the National Curriculum, for example, percentage at Levels 1, 2 and 3. The task of the group would be to explore any lack of match between the two distributions, 'The general aim would be to adjust the overall teacher rating results to match the overall results of the national tests; . . .' (para. 74). The group would then go on to consider any discrepancies for particular schools using samples of work and knowledge of the circumstances of schools. 'The moderation group's aim would here be to arrive at a final distribution for each school or pupil group. In general this would be the distribution on the national tests, with the implication that teachers' ratings would need adjustment, but departures from this could be approved if the group as a whole could be convinced that they were justified in particular cases' (para. 75). While the Report did accept that the process could be carried out without the need for a group meeting at all (by simply adjusting the distribution to agree with those of the national testing) it argued for the opportunity for teachers to discuss mismatches between internal and external assessments in terms of their interpretation of the National Curriculum itself and the national assessment instruments.

Thus what was being suggested here was a group process in which, rather than teachers bringing together pieces of work and agreeing on a common standard on the basis of their own professional judgments, teachers were involved in learning to adjust their ratings in the light of the external test results, which are considered to be the absolute standard (except in very occasional situations). Whilst these 'professional deliberations have a valuable staff development function . . .' (para. 76) it hardly looks like an assessment programme which values the professional judgment of teachers. It is essentially a quality control approach which aims to have a quality assurance role in the longer term.

The reaction from the Schools Examination and Assessment Council to the TGAT approach to moderation was negative for four reasons:

— it would place too many demands on teachers;
— it would take too long;
— for some attainment targets there would be no SAT data;
— moderation in a criterion-referenced system should be focused on individuals' scores, rather than scaling the outcomes of groups of pupils (Daugherty, 1994)

As Daugherty points out, it was less clear what model of moderation should replace the TGAT one. In the event at KS1 a form of moderation by inspection was employed, for Teacher Assessment and SATs. As James and Conner (1993) point out, the SEAC Handbook for moderators emphasized consistency of approach (to conducting the assessments) *and* consistency of standards (inter-rater reliability) which were to be achieved in 1991 and 1992 through the moderation process.

Of major concern in relation to reliability was that the statements of attainment were not sufficiently clear to allow teachers to make unambiguous judgments about performance (see also chapter 6) and the visiting moderator helped in discussions about the meaning of the assessment criteria in some schools (*ibid*).

The process of group moderation, sometimes supported by a visiting moderator, did clearly aid comparability in 1991 and 1992. From 1993, however, the process is to be called 'auditing', the term moderation having been dropped (DFE,1993). The key difference is that rather than offering a system which supports moderation of the process and procedure of the assessments, evidence will be required that results conform to national standards: headteachers will have to ensure that teachers become familiar with national standards and keep evidence of assessment and records for audit when required. It is therefore a process of quality control rather than assurance.

The evaluation of moderation arrangements at KS1 by James and Conner (1993) shows that the moderators (or visiting 'experts') who supported teachers doing the assessments had some concerns over the *validity* of TA, particularly in the areas of speaking and listening. There was evidence that some teachers were assessing, not speaking and listening, but children's enthusiasm and involvement in an activity i.e. personal qualities in relation to motivation and confidence. In this situation, which is not unexpected where teachers have little training in assessing speaking and listening skills, having a visiting moderator or a group moderation process is vital to assuring quality.

A study by Filer (1993) of teacher assessment in KS1 classrooms suggests, further, that quality assurance is deeply problematic since teachers vary in how they construe, for example, writing ability: the construct being evaluated by the teachers when making their assessments may differ, as does what is meant by writing in the classroom (for example, emphasis on imaginative ideas or on structure and organization). This is an issue of validity and Filer claims it means that we can never aim for comparable TA in a skill such as writing or listening and speaking. One might argue, however, that a detailed group moderation process would bring to light such differences in construct and, if successful, allow teachers to reflect on what they value in the writing process and how this relates to the requirements of the National Curriculum which determine the assessment criteria.

Conclusion

Teacher assessment is more professionally rewarding (in terms of enhancing teaching and learning) and valid (because of the range of skills and processes which may be included and the range of contexts in which assessment may take place) than external assessment in which the teacher has little involvement. If, however, such assessment is to be used outside the classroom in reporting to parents or for accountability and certificating purposes, there must be some assurance to those receiving and using the results that there is comparability across teachers, tasks and pupils.

It is possible to ensure this through forms of statistical moderation, inspection of marked work by post and other quality control mechanisms. However, in line with the professional aspect of teacher assessment, forms of moderation which are based on quality assurance and result in teacher development and enhanced understanding of the subject matter and its assessment are more appropriate. Group moderation, which involves discussing criteria as well as pieces of work, what counts as achievement and how such achievement is produced, is the most thorough of the quality assurance approaches. The considerable time (and cost) involved should not be underestimated, but can be seen as a valuable aspect of professional development.

Finally, assuring quality through focusing on the processes of assessment and the assessment tasks will, I believe, lead to quality control of the outcomes of assessment; this together with an emphasis on validity will lead to high quality assessment and confidence in comparability.

Chapter 8

Ethics and Equity

Introduction

Why a chapter on ethics? It should, I hope, be clear by now that assessment is a powerful tool: it can shape curriculum, teaching and learning; it can affect how pupils come to see themselves both as learners and in a more general sense as competent or not; through labelling and sorting pupils (certificating and selecting) it affects how pupils are viewed by others; it controls access to further education and high status careers. As I pointed out on the first page of this book assessment has become increasingly widespread and significant in our education system and shows no sign of going away or losing its power. Given this, a consideration of ethical issues and equity is highly pertinent; indeed the consideration now given to consequential validity in an area that was considered to be largely technical indicates that this issue is now beginning to receive due attention.

Bearing in mind the extent and status of testing and the huge costs involved (see Haney, Madaus and Lyons, 1993; Broadfoot, 1994) it is high time we had an ethical framework for assessment which policy makers, teachers and test developers alike could draw upon. In the USA there is the Code of Fair Testing Practices (JCTP, 1988) which says for example that:

Test developers should help users interpret scores correctly.

Test developers should strive to make tests that are as fair as possible for test takers of different races, gender, ethnic backgrounds, or handicapping conditions.

together with explanations of how this can be done. They are, however, very general and almost superficial. We need to go beyond this sort of check-list and consider a range of other issues.

For example, there is an ethical argument in favour of standards or criterion-referenced assessment (Sadler, 1992b): once the criteria or standards are set they are available to the teachers and pupils which is only fair; this has the potential for providing motivation and a clear sense of direction particularly since all pupils who meet the criteria are eligible to receive recognition for this. By contrast, norm-referenced grading is a 'hidden' process which, if seen as unfair, can be demotivating.

Comparability of standards across institutions for any assessment which is used outside the school, for example, for entry to higher education or for certification, is also an ethical issue, particularly if the stakes are high. Where stakes are high, the assessments must be fair to all the groups:

> The importance of comparability as an issue is directly proportional to the consequences of a wrong or unjust decision. In the present climate of reduced employment opportunities for school leavers, and with the demand for places in tertiary education running at several times the supply, competition is intense. . . . Given these considerations, it is clear that care must be taken to set up and maintain procedures which are soundly based and which foster public confidence. (*ibid*, pp. 10–11)

Sadler is writing here about school-based assessment in Australia, but the same is true of *all* assessment programmes which are used for these purposes.

Consequential Validity

Messick (1989b) in his classic chapter on validity argues that the social consequences of test use and the value implications of test interpretation are integral aspects of validity. As chapter 4 explains, current conceptions of validity have a unitary structure: all aspects of validity including relevance, utility, value implications and social consequences are aspects of, or relevant to, construct validity.

> . . . values are intrinsic to the meaning and outcomes of the testing. For example, information about the utility of scores for a particular purpose is both validity evidence and a value consequence. As opposed to adding values to validity as an adjunct or supplement, the unified view instead exposes the inherent value aspects of score meaning and outcome to open examination

and debate as an integral part of the validation process. This makes explicit what has been latent all along, namely, that validity judgements are value judgments . . . (*ibid*, p. 10)

. . . It is important to recognise, however, that the appraisal of consequences depends not only on their evaluation but on their origins or causes. What matters is not only whether the social consequences of test interpretation and use are positive or negative, but what source and determinants engendered the effect. In particular, it is not that adverse social consequences of test use render the use invalid but, rather, that adverse social consequences should not be attributable to any source of test invalidity such as construct-irrelevant variance. If the adverse social consequences are empirically traceable to sources of test invalidity, such as undue reading comprehension requirements in a purported test of knowledge or of reasoning, then the validity of the test use is jeopardized, especially for less proficient readers. If the social consequences cannot be so traced — or if the validation process can discount sources of test invalidity as the likely determinants, or at least render them less plausible — then the validity of the test use is not overturned. (*ibid*, p. 11)

Messick points out that the test users carry a heavy burden, and that they should be alerted to the dangers of test misuse, whether it be the use of scores invalid for a particular purpose or the mis-use of otherwise valid scores. Test developers therefore have a responsibility to describe not only the constructs assessed by the tests, but also the appropriate uses for test scores and the potential social consequences of alternative test uses. For example, verbal intelligence or verbal reasoning scores for children whose first language is not English should be interpreted in the light of their English language proficiency.

This shift from a purely technical perspective to a test-use perspective — which I would characterize as an ethical perspective — occurred in the USA between 1974 and 1985 when the *Standards for Educational and Psychological Tests* (APA, 1974) became the *Standards for Educational and Psychological Testing* (AERA, 1985). The shift from 'tests' to 'testing', together with a distinction between test developers, test users, test takers, test reviewers, test administrators and test sponsors in the later *Standards* emphasized the importance of test use (Haney and Madaus, 1991).

Madaus (1992b) argues the need in the USA for an independent auditing mechanism for testing, as with other aspects of social life for example consumer protection, protection from incompetent practitioners etc. Consumers of tests, he points out, are essentially unprotected from faulty tests or inappropriate test use. High-stakes tests are necessary, Madaus claims, since they are the most appropriate way of allocating scarce resources and for providing information about the performance of publicly-funded institutions. Test and policy administrators, however, tend to ask the public and pupils to accept their assurance that a particular test is fair, valid and suitable for the purpose intended:

> Pious affirmations by test developers that their products are valid and if used correctly do not hurt people or institutions are no longer enough. They are not a sufficient response to the legitimate question of those adversely affected or to the empirical frequency of mis-classification, particularly of minority candidates. (*ibid*, p. 27)

Test validation is a time-consuming and therefore expensive process which is in tension with commercial test publishers' business interests (and indeed governments with a tight timetable). Not only do construct validity studies take time during the development of a test, but consequential validity studies need to look at test score use *after* the test has been developed.

Madaus' argument is that in the US where test publishing is big business (Haney *et al.*, 1993) documents like the *Standards* and *Code of Fair Testing Practices* are not sufficient to ensure quality control in assessment, and thus a separate audit mechanism is needed. In the UK the situation is different. The School Curriculum and Assessment Authority is the body which in theory could offer a quality control function, as national assessment tests and exams are developed under contract to this central agency or by examination boards which are subject to its authority. In reality however, since there is no equivalent of the *Standards* or the *Code* in the UK, and since political pressure currently is strong to put a comprehensive traditional testing programme in place, evaluations of the national assessment programme have been patchy and there has been a problem with 'delayed publication' where evaluation findings did not suit the political masters (Gipps, 1993b). The other important element in the UK setting is that teachers are themselves involved in assessment and the focus is clearly on assessment in its broadest sense and not just on testing.

In a recent American set of *Criteria for Evaluation of Student Assessment Systems* (NFA, 1992) a number of interesting criteria are put forward. Some, for example, that standards should specify clearly what students should know and be able to do, and that teachers should be involved in the design, use and scoring of assessment tasks are currently routine in the UK. Others are not and are well worth considering, since they are relevant to our definition of educational assessment:

— to ensure fairness, students should have multiple opportunities to meet standards and should be able to met them in different ways

— assessment information should be accompanied by information about access to the curriculum and about opportunities to meet the Standards

— . . . assessment results should be one part of a system of multiple indicators of the quality of education. (*ibid*, p. 32)

Equity Issues[1]

Testing has traditionally been used as a tool of equal opportunities in education, for example the 11+ examination was used to select 'able' pupils for academic secondary schools in England and Wales. The point was to select, impartially, those who regardless of social background who would do well at secondary level. The notion of the standard test as a way of offering impartial assessment is of course a powerful one, though if equality of educational opportunity does not precede the test, then the 'fairness' of this approach is called into question.

The 11+ was in fact amenable to coaching and we know now that this is the same for most tests and examinations; pupils who have very different school experiences are not equally prepared to compete in the same test situation.

As Madaus (1992c) points out

. . . in addressing the equity of alternative assessments in a high-stakes policy-driven exam system policy must be crafted that creates first and foremost a level playing field for students and schools. Only then can the claim be made that a national examination system is an equitable technology for making decisions about individuals, schools or districts. (p. 32)

The same point is also made by Baker and O'Neil (1994). Equity, or fairness, is a complex area in assessment; it is not just to do with the design of tests and assessment material. The traditional psychometric approach to testing operates on the assumption that technical solutions can be found to solve problems of equity with the emphasis on using elaborate techniques to eliminate biased items (Murphy, 1990; Goldstein, 1993). The limitation of this approach is that it does not look at the way in which the subject is defined (i.e. the overall domain from which test items are to be chosen), nor at the initial choice of items from the thus-defined pool, nor does it question what counts as achievement. It simply 'tinkers' with an established selection of items. Focusing on bias in tests, and statistical techniques for eliminating 'biased' items, not only confounds the construct being assessed, but has distracted attention from wider equity issues such as actual equality of access to learning, 'biased' curriculum, and inhibiting classroom practices.

Bias in relation to assessment is generally taken to mean that the assessment is unfair to one particular group or another. This rather simple definition, however, belies the complexity of the underlying situation. Differential performance on a test, i.e. where different groups get different score levels, may not be the result of bias in the assessment; it may be due to real differences in performance among groups which may in turn be due to differing access to learning, or it may be due to real differences in the group's attainment in the topic under consideration. The question of whether a test is biased or whether the group in question has a different underlying level of attainment is actually extremely difficult to answer. Wood (1987) describes these different factors as the opportunity to acquire talent (access issues) and the opportunity to show talent to good effect (fairness in the assessment).

When the existence of group differences in average performance on tests is taken to mean that the tests are biased, the assumption is that one group is *not* inherently less able than the other. However, the two groups may well have been subject to different environmental experiences or unequal access to the curriculum. This difference will be reflected in average test scores, but a test that reflects such unequal opportunity in its scores is not strictly speaking biased, though its use could be invalid.

There is a range of hypotheses which are used to account for group differences (for example between boys and girls) in performance. These are broadly either environmental or biological. Biological hypotheses for differences in group performance suggest that there are underlying psychological differences between groups either genetic, hormonal or due to differences in the structure of the brain. These factors are no longer used to account for differences in performance between ethnic groups, since this approach has been discredited, but are still used to account for differences between the sexes.

Environmental hypotheses include cultural, social and psychological influences (sometimes called psychosocial variables) that affect the development of individuals within specific groups. For example, parents expect different behaviours from boys and girls and consequently they try to provide different types of feedback. Thus boys and girls come to attend to different features of the environment and make sense of the world in different ways. This can affect their learning and performance in school through a variety of processes: different out of school experiences, different within school experiences, perceived male and female domains, differences in attitude, self-image and expectations of success. These, in turn, affect measured performance. In this group of factors for differential performance we must also put equality of opportunity, that is equal access to schooling and curriculum (both formal and actual), for without this there are very likely to be group differences in performance. The environmental hypotheses, though mostly developed in relation to gender differences, are useful in considering differences in performance between ethnic/cultural groups.

Both biological and environmental hypotheses imply that the differences in performance are real. Differential performance, however, may be due to factors in the test itself; in other words groups (or individuals) may have an equal level of knowledge or skill but be unable to show it to the same extent because the test is unfair to one group. This might be because of the language used or artefacts in the illustrations or text which make the task meaningful to one group but less meaningful to another. There is, however, also the possibility that the test itself is not unfair, but something about the administration of the test, produces poor performance in one group of candidates who may have a similar level of knowledge or skill to other groups, but are unable to show it.

As well as formal equality of access to schooling and curriculum there is a second level where covert or hidden differences exist in the curriculum, which result in unequal access to curriculum and learning. As Table 8.1 shows, there are important curricular and assessment questions to be asked in relation to equity. What the questions in the table are getting at is how a subject is defined in the curriculum and how achievement within the curriculum is construed. What constitutes achievement in terms of how it is defined and assessed reflects the value judgments of powerful groups in society. Hence people outside those groups who are subject to different values and experiences will be affected by assessments based on such perspectives. It is not realistic

Table 8.1: *Curriculum and assessment questions in relation to equity*[2]

Curriculum Questions	Assessment Questions
Whose knowledge is taught?	What knowledge is assessed and equated with achievement?
Why is it taught in a particular way to this particular group?	Are the form, content and mode of assessment appropriate for different groups and individuals?
How do we enable the histories and cultures of people of colour, and of women, to be taught in responsible and responsive ways?	Is this range of cultural knowledge reflected in definitions of achievement? How does cultural knowledge mediate individuals' responses to assessments in ways which alter the construct being assessed?

to imagine a time in the future when differential values and power positions will be removed; they will no doubt change but differences in values and barriers to equality will continue. Hence to achieve equity in assessment interpretations of students' performance should be set in the explicit context of what is or is not being valued: an explicit account of the constructs being assessed and of the criteria for assessment will at least make the perspective and values of the test developer open to teachers and pupils. For example, a considerable amount of effort over the years has gone into exploring cognitive deficits in girls in order to explain their poor performance on science tests; it was not until relatively recently that the question was asked whether the reliance on tasks and apparatus associated with middle class white males could possibly have something to do with it. As Goldstein (1993) points out, bias is built into the test developers' construct of the subject and their expectations of differential performance.

Construct validity is the key to developing good quality assessment and we need to look at this not just in relation to the subject but also from the point of view of the pupil being assessed. Moderation among teachers has the potential for focusing on the construct being assessed, initiating discussion about how the meaning of a task is construed by teachers and hopefully by pupils.

As we have seen performance assessment and criterion-referenced assessment cannot be developed using traditional psychometric techniques for analyzing items, because far fewer items are involved and there is no assumed underlying score distribution. This may force a shift towards other ways of reviewing and evaluating items based on qualitative approaches, for example sensitivity review, a consideration of the construct, how the task might interact with experience etc.; such a development is to be welcomed.

Ethical Test Preparation

This is a topic that has received much attention in the USA.

The issue, and this is the same for any country or setting, is what sort of test preparation is appropriate and ethical. Of course, in a high-stakes setting teachers will prepare pupils for tests and exams and the aim is that this preparation will enhance their scores. The hope is that there will be genuine improvement, through this preparation, of the pupils' ability in the domain or skill of interest. The danger is that in teaching too directly to the items and tasks on the test or questions from old exam papers, performance is enhanced narrowly, only on the test items or exam questions. As the chapter on Impact made clear this is inappropriate when we wish to generalize from the test score to the broader domain: '. . . teaching too directly to the items or the specific sample of objectives lowers the validity of the inference' (Mehrens and Kaminski, 1989, p. 14). They suggest that test preparation be viewed as a continuum:

1   general instruction on objectives not determined by looking at the objectives measured on standardized tests;
2   teaching test taking skills;
3   instruction on objectives generated by a commercial organization where the objectives may have been determined by looking at objectives measured by a variety of standardised tests. (The objectives taught may, or may not, contain objectives on teaching test taking skills);
4   instruction based on objectives (skills, subskills) that specifically match those on the standardised test to be administered;
5   instruction on specifically matched objectives (skills, sub-skills) where the practice (instruction) follows the same format as the test questions;
6   practice (instruction) on a published parallel form of the same test; and
7   practice (instruction) on the same test. (*ibid*, p. 16)

with the first as always ethical, the last two always unethical, and the line between ethical and unethical coming somewhere between items 3 and 5.

Smith (1991b) in her qualitative study of the effect of high-stakes testing on teachers (see chapter 3) generated a typology of preparation. Again the focus of interest was the uncertain shift in teacher behaviour from test preparation as good teaching to test preparation as cheating.

What Smith tried to do was to look at test preparation from the teachers' point of view — their meanings-in-action — and from her work produced this typology:

- no special preparation;
- teaching test-taking skills;
- exhortation, for example, getting a good night's sleep and doing 'your very best';
- teaching the content known to be covered by the test;
- teaching to the test, i.e. using materials with the same format and content;
- stress inoculation — this refers to boosting pupils' confidence and feelings of self-efficacy so they can do well on the tests and feel good about themselves '. . . work on test preparation primarily to inoculate their pupils against emotional paralysis in the face of the tests and against feelings of stupidity that the tests seem to engender' (p. 535);
- practising on items of the test itself or parallel forms;
- cheating — the teachers had very precise views about what constituted cheating: giving extra time on tests; providing hints on rephrasing questions; providing correct answers; altering marks on answer sheets; providing hints on rephrasing questions.

Cannell (of the Lake Wobegon report) would describe all but the first two of these as cheating (unethical) because they would result in inflated scores. To take this point of view, Smith (1991) argues, one would have to believe that the standardized test (not taught to) adequately represents the construct (and that teaching to the test results in inflated scores which cannot be generalized to the broader construct). But:

> Preserving the integrity of the inference from indicator to construct may be of primary concern and interest to psychometricians, but it matters much less to school systems or teachers trying to survive in a political world that demands high scores.
>
> To chastise teachers for unethical behaviour or for 'polluting' the inference from the achievement test to the underlying construct of achievement is to miss a critical point: The teachers already view the indicator as polluted. (p. 538)

The teachers were conscious of the test's poor fit with what they taught, the impact of background factors on scores, the many sources of error, the limited scope of the test. Their conclusion was that the test scores were virtually worthless; what is more, due to the high stakes associated with such inadequate measures, they came to believe that testing was a 'game' and they saw test preparation as the only way of exerting some control over the system. In this micropolitical setting only cheating was viewed as unethical.

The importance of Smith's paper is that it puts the teacher's beliefs and concerns at the centre of the debate and looks at the tension they feel in the classic high-stakes testing situation — of course if it were not high-stakes there would be no need to get the 'best' results.

In our study of National Assessment at age 7 in England we found that many of our infant school teachers were including mental arithmetic and emphasizing punctuation and spelling since these were included in the end of key stage assessments. There was no question of this being unethical: it was seen as curriculum alignment rather than enhancing test scores. Indeed curriculum alignment was one of the main intentions of the national assessment programme, so they were 'justified' in doing this, if a little professionally shame-faced since many of them considered the children too young for this type of work. However, they did draw the line at teaching joined-up handwriting, which they considered to be absolutely inappropriate for this age group.

Haladyna, Nolen and Hass (1991) also review ethical and unethical practices in test preparation and arrive at a very similar continuum to that of Mehrens and Kaminski and Smith, however, they add (at the highly unethical end) dismissing low-achieving students on testing day to boost school level scores. They also point out that some activities in an accountability (and therefore comparative) setting will be ethical if all schools do it and not if some do and some do not. Reviewing reports of test preparation practice in Arizona they conclude: 'By any reasonable standard the extensiveness of score-polluting practices revealed in the reports reviewed here is staggering' (p. 5). They point out that unethical test preparation will continue as long as standardized test results are viewed as important indicators of achievement and academic effectiveness of schools in high-stakes settings.

The unethical behaviour of students should also be brought into the frame although it rarely is, in the UK at any rate. In some developing countries where the 'Diploma Disease' is a feature and exams have a life-determining impact quite beyond that in more developed countries, cheating by students is a major issue. In India, for example, a 'minimal malpractice' model is aimed for.

From the evidence reviewed here we can conclude that the higher the stakes, not only the greater the impact on teaching, but also greater the likelihood of cheating and unethical practices.

Will teaching to the test and unethical preparation be the same with 'authentic' assessment? Strong supporters of authentic assessment believe that these tests should be taught towards because they offer genuine intellectual challenge and support good learning experiences (Wiggins, 1989b). The aim with authentic assessment is first to decide what the actual performances are that we want students to be good at, then to design assessment to reflect those performances. Assessment here is seen as a part of students' regular work activity rather than a special one-off prepared-for activity.

Wiggins takes the argument for authentic assessment into the equity arena by claiming that the one-off standardized test that treats all candidates as the same, is inherently inequitable:

> The concept is commonsensical but profound: blank laws and policies (or standardized tests) are inherently unable to encompass the inevitable idiosyncratic cases for which we ought always to make exceptions to the rule. Aristotle put it best: 'The equitable is a correction of the law where it is defective owing to its universality.'
>
> *In the context of testing, equity requires us to insure that human judgment is not overrun or made obsolete by an efficient, mechanical scoring system.* Externally designed and externally mandated tests are dangerously immune to the possibility that a student might legitimately need to have a question rephrased or might deserve the opportunity to defend an unexpected or 'incorrect' answer, even when the test questions are well-structured and the answers are multiple choice. (*ibid*, p. 708, my emphasis)

In support of this argument it is worth pointing out that many British teachers, when trialling active performance-based assessment for 7 and 14-year-olds in National Curriculum assessment felt that, despite the emphasis on language in the tasks, they were a more fair assessment for ethnic minority/E_2L pupils because of their interactive nature (which allowed clarification of the task) and match with classroom activities (which reduced stress levels) (Gipps and Murphy, 1994).

Wiggins also claims that unreliability — the reason usually given for not using teachers' assessments of pupils — is only a problem when teachers operate in private without shared criteria. As chapter 7 makes clear, the process of moderation can enhance the comparability of teachers' judgments. In any case, the focus in authentic assessment on:

...g strengths;

...ng comparisons;

*...*room for student learning styles, aptitudes and interests

...ss and equity, claims Wiggins (1989b). Indeed, authen-*... ...n* Wiggins' model is about as far away from the traditional psychometric model as it is possible to be, which makes a concern with traditional reliability inappropriate.

Conclusions

Teaching directly to the test (whether standardized multiple choice or performance assessment) can be seen as 'unethical' if:

— it improves scores but not performance on the underlying construct;
— in an accountability setting if some schools/teachers do it and others do not.

Where assessment covers a domain more broadly, then teaching to the domain may be in the pupil's interests, professionally acceptable and ethical. The key issue is whether the focused teaching improves learning; of secondary importance is the purpose of assessment: if the focused teaching enhances learning then the fact that the results are to be used for accountability purposes is irrelevant and all teachers should be encouraged to teach to the domain. What must *not* be encouraged is teaching to the task in performance assessment. Given the evidence of lack of generalizability across tasks in this form of assessment (see chapter 6) teaching to the test *directly* is as likely to raise scores without improving achievement on the construct of interest, thus making any inference from the score invalid, as it is in standardized tests and exams.

Pupils do not come to school with identical experiences and they do not have identical experiences at school. We cannot, therefore, expect assessments to have the same meaning for all pupils. What we must aim for, though, is an equitable approach where the concerns, contexts and approaches of one group do not dominate. This, however, is by no means a simple task; for example test developers are told that they should avoid context which may be more familiar to males than females or to the dominant culture. But there are problems inherent in trying to *remove* context effects by doing away with passages that advantage males or females, because it reduces the amount of assessment material available. Decontextualized assessment is anyway not possible, and complex reasoning processes require drawing on complex domain knowledge.

In an assessment which looks for best rather than typical performance the context of the item should be the one which allows the pupil to perform well but this suggests different tasks for different groups which is in itself hugely problematic. However, what we can seek is the use, within any assessment programme, of a range of assessment tasks involving a variety of contexts, a range of modes within the assessment, and a range of response format and style. This broadening of approach is most likely to offer pupils alternative opportunities to demonstrate achievement if they are disadvantaged by any one particular assessment in the programme.

Notes

1   This section draws heavily on Gipps and Murphy, 1994.
2   From Gipps and Murphy 1994 (and after Apple, 1989).

Chapter 9

A Framework for Educational Assessment

To recap on the first pages of this book, a paradigm is a set of interrelated concepts that frames research in a scientific field. The paradigm within which we work determines the way in which we understand and construe what we observe, as well as how we generate the universe of discourse; it constitutes the framework in which observations are made and interpreted, and directs which aspects we attend to.

> 'A paradigm shift redefines what scientists see as problems, and reconstitutes their tool kit for solving them. Previous models and methods remain useful to the extent that certain problems the old paradigm addresses are still meaningful, and the solutions it offers are still satisfactory, but now as viewed from the perspective of the new paradigm'. (Mislevy, 1993, p. 4)

What we are observing in assessment is a shift in practice from psychometrics to educational assessment, from a testing culture to an assessment culture. However, it is not just that we wish to move beyond testing and its technology, but that the shift involves a much deeper set of transformations, hence the paradigm shift: our underlying conceptions of learning, of evaluation and of what counts as achievement are now radically different from those which underpin psychometrics.

The message of this book is that assessment is an important part of education, and that whenever possible it must be of a type suitable to and used for the enhancement of good quality learning. This is not to say that traditional standardized tests and examinations have no role to play in assessment policy, but that we need to design assessment programmes that will have a positive impact on teaching and learning.

What this book proposes is a form of educational assessment which will take up more by way of teacher and pupil time, but if it is true to the principles of educational assessment, it will support the teaching and learning of *important* skills and concepts at both basic and higher levels and the time will be deemed well-spent.

Educational Assessment: A Broader Definition

Having discussed educational assessment in the previous chapters, it is now time to develop the definition:

- Educational assessment recognizes that domains and constructs are multi-dimensional and complex; that assessing achievement is not an exact science; and that the interaction of pupil, task and context is sufficiently complex to make generalization to other tasks and contexts dubious. These issues are well understood in the literature but ignored within much test and examination development because they are inconvenient (Satterly, 1994).

- In educational assessment clear standards are set for performance against which pupils will be assessed; these and assessment processes are shared with pupils (progressively so as they get older); pupils are encouraged to monitor and reflect on their own work/performance (with the positive and constructive help of teachers) so that they become self-monitoring learners in the metacognitive mode. Feedback to pupils, which is a key factor in the assessment process, emphasizes mastery and progress not comparison with other pupils.

- Educational assessment encourages pupils to think rather than tick alternatives or regurgitate facts. (But it is teachers who have to encourage pupils to organize and integrate ideas, to interact with material, to critique and evaluate the logic of an argument.) Good quality assessment needs to have good quality tasks so that pupils are not wasting their time: the tasks need to be anchored in important and relevant subject matter and the nature and mode of the task needs to be based on what we know about equitable and engaging assessment tasks.

- Assessment which elicits an individual's best performance involves tasks that are concrete and within the experience of the pupil (an equal access issue); presented clearly (the pupil must understand what is required of her if she is to perform well); relevant to the current concerns of the pupil (to engender motivation and engagement); and in conditions that are not threatening (to reduce stress and enhance performance) (after Nuttall, 1987).

- Assessment criteria are more holistic than in criterion-referenced assessment as originally conceived, to allow for the assessment of complex skills; this can be supported by having exemplars which allow teachers and others to interpret the criteria/ standards.

- Educational assessment involves grading or scoring by teachers or trained raters; in order to enhance consistency of scoring teachers need to understand the scoring categories and the levels of performance associated with them. This can be achieved through a process of moderation and provision of exemplars. These exemplars and moderation procedures need to be made available to all the teachers involved in any particular assessment scheme. The exemplars and standards can also serve the purpose of explicating to teachers the nature of the skill or concepts being taught and assessed.

- In the culture of testing (Wolf *et al.*, 1991) it is the number of items correct, not the overall quality of response, that determines the score. In educational assessment we move away from the notion of a score, a single statistic, and look at other forms of describing achievement including 'thick' description of achievement and profiles of performance, what Wolf *et al* call 'differentiated portraits of student performance' (p. 62). Aggregation of complex data to produce a simple (simplistic) figure is in many instances misleading and unless strict mastery rules are followed (for example 90 per cent correct) actually may provide 'untrue scores' which do not allow valid inferences about the component skills.

- Teachers' own assessments of pupils are a key component within educational assessment. Such assessment can be interactive in order to engage fully with pupils and to gauge their understanding and misconceptions; it can support or scaffold the learning process and can evaluate performance in a range of contexts. The importance of informal teacher assessment is beginning to be recognized at policy level: it is now time that this recognition is translated into proper preparation and training of teachers in assessment principles and practice, including observation and questioning. Evidence is widespread that teachers are not well trained in assessment; but to get the full benefit out of educational assessment teachers need to be assessment literate.

- Teachers cannot assess well subject matter they do not understand just as they cannot teach it well. Teachers have to understand the constructs which they are assessing (and therefore what sort of tasks to set); they have to know how to get at the pupil's knowledge and understanding (and therefore what sort of questions to ask); and how to elicit the pupil's best performance (which depends on the physical, social and intellectual context in which the assessment takes place).

- Educational assessment is not high stakes: the publication of test data at class and school level distorts the educational process and encourages 'cheating' of various kinds; teachers and pupils cannot avoid this: they are caught in a trap. Using performance based assessment where high stakes external tests are unavoidable, together with teacher assessment, will mitigate the worst effects on teaching but even this, if stakes are too high, will promote assessed activities and therefore teaching to the performance assessment task, rather than to the domain or the higher level skill. When high stakes tests and exams allow a high proportion of pupils to fail there are self-esteem and motivation problems for low-scoring pupils with the concomitant risk of drop-out. Assessment against clear standards, in a low-stakes programme, with constructive feed-back and a focus on the individual's own performance in relation to the standard and to his/her own previous performance, rather than comparison with others, is more likely to maintain the engagement of pupils and retain them in the system.

This account of educational assessment is not academic ivory-towered hyperbole: every statement in this section is supported by the research evidence outlined in previous chapters. Neither is it wishful thinking; we can develop assessment in this way and we must. We have to develop our assessment policy and practice in line with the educational assessment paradigm otherwise our attempts to raise educational standards and get the best out of our education system will be disappointed. The world has moved on: assessment is more pervasive and important than it was twenty years ago and the type of education needed to see us into the next century both as individuals and as a society has changed: basic skills are not enough — the majority of the population, not just the elite, needs to become flexible thinkers, reasoners and intelligent novices, and to believe that they can do so. A pervasive and narrow formal testing and examining system in a high-stakes setting will not allow this to happen.

I will expand on some of the main issues, but first I consider the design of assessment programmes.

Design of Assessment Programmes

The tension between assessment for accountability purposes and to support learning is not restricted to the UK. In a review of assessment for the OECD the two key themes were:

1 Testing national standards, a new political imperative: the use of assessment for monitoring and accountability in national systems, especially in terms of nationwide testing of pupils' achievement in basic skills or core subjects of the curriculum;

2 New approaches to assessment, a paradigm shift towards integrating assessment with learning: continuous assessment using pupils' regular work rather than formal examinations or standardized tests, records of achievement, portfolios, practical tasks, school-based assessment by teachers and self-assessment by pupils, using results as feedback to help define objectives and encourage learners to take responsibility for their own learning.

Theme 1 may be seen as in conflict with Theme 2, the second being favoured by the professionals in education, against pressure for the first from politicians, parents, and administrators. As a result, there is an ideological divide between those who hope to raise standards by more extensive testing and those who hope to improve the quality of learning by changing assessment methods. (Nisbet, 1993, p. 28)

In France, Germany, the Netherlands, Spain, Sweden, the UK and the USA the dilemma was apparent and the same.

Stiggins (1992) gets to the heart of the matter when he points out that centralized assessment for accountability purposes, what he characterizes as trickle-down testing, cannot meet the needs of teachers for assessment information.

Only high-quality classroom assessments developed and conducted under the control of the teacher can serve that teacher's needs well. We will begin to use our assessment resources wisely to the maximum benefit of students when we acknowledge these differences and begin to distribute assessments resources so as to ensure quality in both contexts. (*ibid*, p. 2)

In other words, it is not an either-or issue, but a fitness for purpose issue. The same assessment cannot be used for a range of purposes. Designing assessments with fitness for purpose in mind will mean that a range of assessments is used; the acceptance of a range of types of assessments from traditional formal written examination to teachers' own assessments (via standardized tests, performance assessments, portfolios and RoA) will have valuable spin-offs in terms of fairness (a range of approaches allows pupils who are disadvantaged by one assessment to compensate on another provided that they carry comparable weight) and cost (performance assessment and portfolios are expensive in terms of pupil and teacher time, standardized tests are less so).

We need to move the debate away from false dichotomies: criterion-referenced assessment versus norm-referenced assessment, standardized tests versus performance assessment; they are as unhelpful as the quantitative *versus* qualitative research method argument. What we need is to understand the value of each approach and to follow the fitness for purpose principle; some approaches then, of course, may be seen to have little value. Messick (1992) argues for a realistic mixture of decontextualized structured exercises and contextualized performance-based tasks on the grounds that both basic and higher order skills need assessing. This combination is in any case necessary to ensure full construct representation and to balance the advantages of time-intensive depth of assessment within a domain with broader domain-coverage.

One model for designing assessment programmes is to use teacher assessment and portfolio assessment at the individual child level for formative purposes; APU/NAEP type surveys at the school district and national level for accountability purposes using light sampling and matrix sampling; and a mixture of moderated teacher assessment with optional use of good quality tasks from item banks, carrying national statistics, for school-level accountability purposes and parental/community feedback (Harlen *et al.*, 1992).

Using only a light sample in order to reduce the stakes is possible for national and local district level accountability purposes. It may also be acceptable to light-sample large schools in order to get school level performance and accountability data; but this approach will not work for smaller schools where light sampling does not provide enough pupils for an acceptable sample size. Furthermore, those who advocate light sampling in order to reduce the stakes and costs associated with authentic assessment (for example, Popham, 1993b) ignore the certificating and selecting role of assessment: this cannot be carried out on a sample — it must include all pupils and it will be high stakes. The broader and more performance-based is the assessment for this purpose the 'better' will be the impact on teaching. We are thus back in the conundrum of how performance-based we can afford to make assessment for certification and selection purposes. As chapter 6 shows, given the political will and resources it is possible to have a system wide performance assessment programme for one or two age groups in the system.

Alongside using a variety of approaches it is important to reduce the stakes associated with any single one. It is publication in the (local) press that seems most to influence the stakes as far as teachers are concerned (and the *perception* of the significance of results is what counts). So we need to look for other ways of communicating how well schools are doing than using league tables, for example embedding results within detailed prospectuses.

The original blueprint fo the National Curriculum assessment programme in England and Wales (DES, 1988 — see chapter 6) matched in many ways Frederiksen and Collins' (1989) blueprint for the design of a systemically valid testing system. These include first, a set of tasks that cover the spectrum of knowledge, skills and strategies needed for the activity or domain being tested. Second, a list of 'primary traits' for each task must be made available to teachers and students; the traits should cover knowledge and skills necessary to do well in that activity, for example for expository writing the primary traits might be clarity, persuasiveness, memorability and enticingness. Third, a library of exemplars of all levels of performance of the primary traits with explanation of how they were judged; this would ensure reliability of scoring and help pupils to understand what is required of them. Fourth, there needs to be a training system for scoring the tests reliably; this should be extended to teachers, pupils *and* administrators of the testing system, indeed teachers should encourage pupils to carry out self-assessment. Frederiksen and Collins also discuss fostering improvement on the test through: employing forms of assessment that enhance learning; practice in self-assessment; detailed feedback on performance in relation to the primary traits; and multiple levels of success so that through repeated testing students can strive for higher levels of performance. This blueprint incorporates many of our requirements for an educational assessment programme.

If teacher assessments and performance assessments are used for high-stakes purposes then they must offer comparability of results. It is possible to do this as the GCSE in the UK demonstrates, *but* it is very time and labour intensive and relies on the involvement of teachers. Supporting such a system requires: clear statements of looked-for performance, comprehensive scoring schemes, training of raters, group moderation to ensure comparability across tasks and raters, some form of statistical moderation if appropriate, and an auditing process to check the processes and results. It can be done at one or two points in a school system if there is the political will to support this type of assessment model.

Arguments about the impact of assessment do not by and large apply to the devices used for diagnostic assessment, or to teachers' informal formative assessment in the classroom but to the high-status, high-stakes forms of testing which are used for certification, selection and accountability purposes. This is because tests for these purposes are the ones that have most power within the system and as a result of this power the tests shape the curriculum and teaching. We need to accept that any significant assessment program will have an impact on teachers and pupils so we must put this into the design consideration of a test program.

Ethics and Equity

Raising the stakes enhances the ethical dimension in assessment. The higher the stakes the greater the likelihood of cheating and unethical practices and the more important it is that assessment practice be equitable. There is, however, a confusion over equity within the educational assessment model, in performance assessment in particular. Performance assessment, which is often conflated with educational assessment, is sometimes promoted because it is 'more fair' (but for an alternative view from minority groups, see Baker and O'Neill, 1994); this is a serious misconception of the theoretical rationale underpinning educational assessment. The underlying assumption of most traditional psychometrics is one of fixed abilities and therefore limitation; in educational assessment performance is seen to be dependent on context and motivation and is essentially interactive and elastic. Thus the concept is a positive one with the corollary that in assessment all pupils must be given the opportunity to show what they can do, that it is possible to maximize learning, and that assessment should try to get the best performance out of pupils. But it is still true that some groups may have been better prepared for assessment including performance assessment than others. As an example, Linn *et al.*, (1991) give the use of calculator-based problems: pupil access to calculators may be quite inequitable and if problems using calculators are part of an accountability or certificating assessment then there is an equal access issue.

So, the conception is enabling, but individual assessments may still be inequitable.

The ethics of assessment demand that the constructs and assessment criteria are made available to pupils and teachers, and that a range of tasks and assessments be included in an assessment programme. These requirements are consonant with enhancing construct validity in any case.

We need to be clear about what counts as proper preparation of pupils in any assessment programme. If there are preparation practices which are considered to be unethical then they should be spelled out. The other side of the coin is that teachers and schools have a commitment to teach pupils the material on which they are going to be assessed. To this requirement we should add proper preparation of teachers so that they understand the basic issues in assessment and are equipped to carry out good formative assessment.

The more that teachers are involved in generating or carrying out assessment, through discussing the standards, how to generate best performance, what counts as meeting the criteria, etc., the more teachers will be empowered in the educative process rather than technicians carrying out an imposed curriculum and testing programme.

Given the detailed, and as yet poorly understood, effect of context (Murphy, 1993) on performance, the evidence that girls attend to context in an assessment task more than do boys, and the ability of changes in the context of the task to alter the construct being assessed this is an area of validity which demands detailed study. We certainly need to define the context of an assessment task and the underlying constructs and make sure they reflect what is taught.

Context has a crucial role in both learning and assessment: the learning and performance of a skill interacts with the context in which it takes place. Assessing in a decontextualized way (as in the baldest of multiple-choice questions) is possible but limiting; it is important, however, to strip away irrelevant context from an assessment task since that will cause construct-irrelevance variance. Messick (1992) describes an approach called 'cross-contextual measurement' in which performance on the same skill across contexts is assessed in order to 'develop an aggregate measure of the construct across a variety of item contexts in an effort to balance the effects of different student backgrounds and interests' (*ibid*, p. 25). The findings would also allow one to generalize performance to a broader construct domain. This is essentially what happens in teacher assessment, but is likely to be too time-consuming for external assessment for accountability purposes (which is when one is most likely to generalize).

Paradigm Shift

The most challenging task in developing a theory of educational assessment is that of reconceptualizing reliability. Underlying this challenge is a shift in our world view. The psychometric model carried with it a notion of objectivity — that ability or attainment is a property of the individual which can be reliably (accurately) measured and that the resulting 'score' is unaffected by context or the testing situation. We now know however that performance is very much context bound, affected by motivation and the assessment mode itself. It is also construed according to the perspectives and values of the assessor — whether it is the one who designs the assessment and marking scheme or the one who grades the open-ended performances. We do not therefore see assessment as a scientific, objective, activity, this we now understand to be spurious.

Assessment is not an exact science, and we must stop presenting it as such. This is of course part of the post-modern condition — a suspension of belief in the absolute status of 'scientific' knowledge (Gipps, 1993b; Torrance 1993b). The modernist stance suggests that it is possible to be a disinterested observer, while the post-modernist stance indicates that such detachment is not possible: we are social beings who construe the world according to our values and perceptions. The constructivist paradigm does not accept that reality is fixed and independent of the observer; rather reality is constructed by the observer, thus there are multiple constructions of reality. This paradigm would then deny the existence of such a thing as a 'true score'.

The shift from a psychometric model of assessment to an educational model has a parallel in the experimental versus naturalistic evaluation paradigms. Eisner (1993) elaborates the comparisons between curriculum evaluation and pupil assessment (also called evaluation in the USA) and a similar move towards qualitative approaches in both disciplines which he ascribes to the general dissatisfaction with education and its outcomes and a realization that standards will not be raised by having tough assessment policies. It is improving the quality of teaching and what goes on in schools that will raise standards:

> . . . we find ourselves exploring new routes to excellence, partly because we have recognized that mandates do not work, partly because we have come to realize that the measurement of outcomes on instruments that have little predictive or concurrent validity is not an effective way to improve schools, and partly because we have become aware that unless we can create assess-

ment procedures that have more educational validity than those we have been using, change is unlikely. (*ibid*, p. 224)

Evaluation within the constructivist and naturalistic paradigms rejects the traditional criteria of reliability, validity and generalizability and looks instead for qualities such as trustworthiness and authenticity (Guba and Lincoln, 1989). We need similarly to reconceptualize the concepts of reliability and generalizability in relation to assessment, and the educational evaluation literature is a potential source.

Trustworthiness according to Guba and Lincoln is based on *credibility, transferability* and *dependability. Credibility* comes from prolonged engagement and persistent observation, ie regular on-going assessment in the classroom, and including parents in the dialogue about pupil performance. *Transferability* could replace the notion of generalizability: since performance is context bound the assessor must specify the context in which a particular achievement was demonstrated. Others then judge whether this will be transferable to other contexts; these are referred to as the sending and receiving contexts respectively: the more the sending and receiving contexts are alike the more likely is transfer. It is this description which, through providing extensive information about the sending context, allows judgments about transferability to be made. Dependability replaces traditional reliability, it is related to the process of assessment and the judgments made which must be open to scrutiny. Guba and Lincoln suggest that this be achieved through an audit process — possibly like the quality control process in moderation. *Authenticity* is to do with the extent to which the relevant constructs (and this means all the stakeholders' constructs) are fairly and adequately covered in the assessment. The fairness aspect of authenticity suggests that *all* groups' constructs are included rather than just the test developer's.

Assessment is developing a wider meaning better to represent pupils' broad range of achievement. For example, the descriptions of pupil achievement in RoA are akin to a qualitative form of assessment. Such 'thick description' (Guba and Lincoln, 1989) is a key feature of naturalistic forms of evaluation and one can say is also necessary for a full understanding of what it is pupils know, understand and can do and in what contexts. So we can use profiles of performance in reporting individual attainment for use by parents and teachers. What the qualitative approach to assessment makes difficult, however, is comparison because the detailed description does not easily condense to a single figure, or even a set of figures. But to wish to do this is to confuse the two paradigms and to misunderstand the purpose of newer approaches to assessment.

But first, what can be salvaged, if anything, from the traditional concepts of validity and reliability?

Validity Issues

More has been written about validity in recent years than about any other aspect of assessment practice. Messick's expanded view of validity incorporates evidence of construct validity (which supports test-score interpretation) and social consequences of test use. While Messick's conception has not been seriously challenged, neither is it being adopted in practice probably because it is too complex and all-embracing. While a number of authors (Linn, Baker and Dunbar, 1991; Harnisch and Mabry, 1993) suggest expanding the validity framework what I believe is needed, as Shepard (1993) also points out, is a simplified framework with some priorities identified. To keep expanding the validity framework, whilst accepting the dictum that construct validation is a never-ending process, is to make the validation task so demanding that test and assessment developers cannot (and do not) engage with it.

Shepard (1993) argues that Messick's validity studies when operationalized start 'with a traditional investigation of test score meaning and then adds test relevance, values, and social consequences. Orchestrated this way, typical validity investigations never get to consequences'. Shepard suggests instead that we need to identify which validity questions must be answered to defend a test use and which are less immediate questions. The direct question then is 'What does a testing practice claim to *do*?' (p. 408). An indication of the labyrinthine nature of validity studies is that a test has to be validated for each use: evidence collected to support the interpretations and uses of test scores for individuals does not necessarily support the interpretations and policy uses of the results when aggregated to give data about schools or districts. If a test has not been validated for a particular purpose, then using it for that purpose is highly questionable, particularly if the purpose is high stakes for individuals.

The criticism of Messick's approach is not that his conceptualization is *wrong*, but that it is inappropriate because it is inoperable. The concern is that test developers will simply opt out of the consequential aspect of validity studies because the process is never ending. The danger then is that the responsibility for making judgments about valid test use —

assuming the test developer claims evidence of construct validity — will fall to test users. This is not appropriate since, with the wide-spread publication of test results, virtually every member of the public with an interest in education and schools including parents of school-aged children, and the pupils themselves, is a user of test results.

Most test users cannot carry out validity studies, and so it is the test developer's role to articulate the uses to which a particular test may be put. For this we can pose the question: For what use, and of which construct, is this a valid indicator? Test developers must address this question as a priority in the design of tests and their evaluation of construct validity. This implies an opening up of the test's constructs to users and for test developers to commit themselves to appropriate test use. In assessment programmes designed for accountability purposes, which will in practice be used at a range of levels, independent evaluation of consequences must be carried out; funding of this should be the responsibility of the policy making authority — national or local — which is responsible for commissioning the assessment. The onus must then be on the publisher of results to present them 'fairly', whether it be central government, LEA, local newspaper or school, that is: to state clearly what the results can appropriately be used for and what they cannot, and to contextualize the results when they are used to compare institutions, etc. To summarize:

— the test developer must articulate the constructs assessed and appropriate test use;

— for accountability testing the policy-making authority must commission evaluation of the consequences of test use;

— the 'publisher' of results must present them fairly and with contextual information: of the institution in relation to league tables, of the actual assessment in relation to individuals.

This implies rethinking the partnership between, and responsibilities of, developers, policy-makers and test users. Finally, researchers and evaluators in assessment need to continue to simplify the validity concept so that it becomes manageable.

Studies of consequential validity are particularly important for newer forms of assessment given the promises that are held out for them. In particular in the USA if performance assessment is to do what is hoped for it in terms of broadening teaching, then one thing that needs to be evaluated is whether, in a high-stakes setting, teaching takes place to the task or to the broader domain. Although we have high stakes performance assessment in the UK we have not researched this particular issue.

The pupils' views about the tasks will also be important in order to gauge the impact on pupil motivation and other behavioural effects. This research agenda will, however, require a new focusing of effort: effort is most marked in developing new assessments and setting up new assessment policy. Little or no effort is characteristically put into evaluating the effects of the assessment programme or any adverse impact once it is introduced.

Reliability

Whilst rethinking validity is a question of prioritizing and specifying the responsibility of test developer, policy-maker and user, reliability needs a much more radical approach. Educational assessment does not operate on the assumption of unidimensionality, results are not forced into a normal distribution, fewer items are used, assessment conditions are not fully standardized. Thus many of the statistical approaches used to evaluate reliability in standardized tests are simply not appropriate. In any case we no longer conceive of 'accurate' measurement and 'true scores'. Where traditional reliability measures are not appropriate we need to drop the term reliability and instead use, I suggest, *comparability*, which is based on consistency. The level of comparability demanded for any assessment will be related to its use: for example, if performance assessment is used for accountability purposes then great care will need to be taken to ensure comparability; for teacher assessment for formative purposes comparability is of lesser concern. Consistency leading to comparability is achieved by assessment tasks being presented in the same way to all pupils assessed; assessment criteria being interpreted in the same way by all teachers; and pupil performance being evaluated according to the same rubric and standards by all markers.

This is not as radical a suggestion as it might at first appear. The evidence for high technical reliability in examinations is weak to say the least (Satterley, 1994). Furthermore, the interaction of student with task is such a great source of variation that the relatively small number of tasks assessed even in traditional examinations does not offer results which are robust enough to warrant generalization. Teacher assessment over time and task, if done well, is better equipped to reach a dependable conclusion about students' work. Furthermore, in assessment carried out by teachers and used within the classroom, the importance of comparability may give way to the importance of maximizing the pupil's performance.

Some assessment theorists, for example, Frederiksen and Collins (1989) believe that in educational assessment we must move away from a sampling model of measurement towards a performance model 'where the quality of performance and the fairness of scoring are crucial but where the replicability and generalisability of the performance are not' (Moss, 1992, p. 250). For some forms of assessment we may need to give up on generalizability altogether:

> Rather than attempting to estimate and to predict future per-
> formance on a construct such as mathematics understanding,
> some new assessments simply credit a specific, complex ac-
> complishment in and of itself, without the burden of prediction
> or the constraints of domain generality. (Baker, O'Neil and
> Linn, 1991, p. 14)

Reliability and validity are important dimensions of traditional test development, acting essentially as quality assurance devices and still have a role to play in developing some forms of assessment. But for educational assessment, however, we need other indicators of quality and I will now discuss some of these, before proposing a check-list of alternative criteria for evaluating the quality of assessment.

Alternative Criteria of Quality in Educational Assessment

Curriculum fidelity is a useful alternative criterion for evaluating assessment when that assessment is linked to a specified or National Curriculum: we need to have a broad coverage of the curriculum because of the well-rehearsed problems of assessing only examinable tasks. The concept of curriculum fidelity is particularly useful for teacher assessment (and authentic assessment), because it has the advantage of being easier to specify than construct validity, since curriculum is more apparent than are underlying constructs. The notion of curriculum fidelity is in fact consonant with construct validity: construct underrepresentation is analogous with poor curriculum fidelity.

Dependability is a term which is coming back into use; it attempts to recognize the tension between reliability and validity. Dependability is the 'intersection of reliability and validity' (Wiliam, 1993) in other words an assessment is dependable to the extent that it is both content valid and reliable. Harlen (1994) defines quality in assessment similarly as 'the provision of information of the highest validity and optimum reliability suited to a particular purpose and context' (p. 2). This is useful in that it relates to fitness-for-purpose, but for assessment for which traditional measures of reliability are not suitable we may prefer to define dependability as the highest validity and optimum consistency and comparability for a particular purpose.

In relation to performance assessment and teacher assessment what we must do to assure comparability, and in the name of equity and fairness, is to tie the assessment to criteria, to provide training in observation and questioning, and support group moderation to get consistency across, and indeed within, schools *and* to limit the damaging effects of teacher stereotyping (Gipps and Murphy, 1994).

Public credibility is a criterion (McGaw, 1993) which would be particularly important for high-stakes or accountability testing and is rather different from Guba and Lincoln's concept of credibility. This criterion is important since test users and the general public need to be reassured that results are *consistent* (from one administration to another) and *comparable* (from one school or assessor to another).

Generalization is dubious with performance assessment: not only is performance heavily task and context dependent but the time each task takes means that we are unlikely to be able to get enough tasks to generalize within the domain, never mind outside it. Pupil performance is quite unpredictable; we know that from work in cognitive psychology and learning theory. So to pretend that we can generalize widely is to delude ourselves and others. Instead of generalizability we can focus on *transferability* and this involves much more description of the context in which the assessment took place: since performance is context-bound we must specify the context in which a particular achievement was demonstrated. Performance cannot be generalized beyond the context of assessment although test users often do this. Context description will at least allow for a more informed judgment about possible transferability. With complex constructs and skills it may be more appropriate to credit a specific complex accomplishment in and of itself without the burden of generalizing to, or beyond, the domain as we do at university level with, for example, dissertations.

What we wish good quality assessment to do, therefore, is to elicit quality performance, within a well-defined context; it must then be scored fairly (in a way that the pupil understands) and consistently (across teachers and pupils).

To the definition of educational assessment we can now therefore add a checklist of alternative indicators to assure quality in educational assessment:

- *Curriculum fidelity*: this implies that the construct, domain or curriculum is well specified and there is a broad coverage of the curriculum (if not of each domain) in the assessment.
- *Comparability*: this is achieved through *consistency of approach* to the assessment by teachers; a *common understanding of assessment criteria*; and that performance is evaluated fairly, that is, according to the same rubric by all markers. These can be achieved by a combination of training, moderation and provision of exemplars.
- *Dependability*: this emerges from evidence of curriculum fidelity, consistency and comparability, as will
- *Public credibility*
- *Context description*: this requires that detailed information about context be available so that we may make informed judgments about transferability.
- *Equity*: this requires that a range of indicators be used in an assessment programme to offer pupils multiple opportunities to achieve.

These alternative criteria of quality in educational assessment, and the rethinking of reliability and generalizability, are still relatively untried. The debate has been rumbling in the literature for a number of years, but research in educational assessment is uncoordinated and the technical base is somewhat weak and underconceptualized. The hope is that these chapters, and this framework, will act as an impetus en route to developing good quality educational assessment.

There are those who criticize educational assessment for having no underlying theoretical rationale (for example, Hansen, 1993): it is seen simply as a new bandwagon which criticizes psychometrics without putting anything substantive in its place. What I hope I have shown in this book is that educational assessment, which has the learner at its core, has a theoretical base in theories of learning, motivation and evaluation. That the main area in which development is needed is the 'technical' one, but what is needed is not a technology as such, but a radically different way of conceptualizing purpose, and quality, in assessment.

We must acknowledge the difference between highly standardized testing procedures, performance-based tasks used by teachers or as part of an external testing programme, and teacher assessment. If we move teacher assessment and performance assessment too closely towards standardization in order to satisfy traditional reliability, we are in danger of throwing out the baby with the bath water. The search for objectivity in assessment is not only futile but can be destructive; the alternative criteria proposed will allow us to ensure quality in educational assessment without resorting to highly standardized and narrow testing procedures with all that this implies for teaching and learning.

That some of these criteria are qualitative rather than quantitative is all to the good, since we need to stop supporting the notion of assessment as an objective activity or exact science (see also Broadfoot, 1994). If we wish to continue to include performance assessment and teacher assessment in assessment programmes we must develop these criteria and their use. Otherwise many new developments will be pushed out of formal assessment practice because they fail to meet the traditional criteria of quality. These newer forms of assessment are important because of what they offer by way of impact on teaching and learning practice and broad curriculum coverage.

The message for policy-makers is that assessment programmes, even for accountability purposes, need to include a range of types of assessment to provide manageability in terms of cost and time, construct representation, depth of assessment and broad domain coverage, and in terms of fairness to different groups of pupils.

We need to persuade politicians and policy makers of the importance of lowering the stakes associated with assessment whenever possible, particularly at the level of the teacher and school. With assessment for certification and selection purposes high stakes are unlikely to be reduced and therefore the style and content of assessment tasks is particularly crucial. We also need to persuade policy-makers of their responsibility for evaluation of the educational and social consequences of test use at every level.

The message for assessment developers is that, particularly for assessment for selection and certification, high quality tasks requiring extended responses and a range of modes are important to encourage good impact on teaching and curriculum: we need to design accountability assessment which will provide good quality information about pupils' performance without distorting good teaching practice. These are not impossible demands as earlier chapters show. Furthermore, the constructs assessed and appropriate test use must always be articulated. The development of other forms of assessment which can be used alongside accountability assessment to support learning must also continue as a priority.

Finally, any assessment model, policy or programme will only be as good as the teachers who use it: devalue the role of teachers and deprofessionalize their training and no assessment technology will replace their skill. It is teachers who teach the concepts and skills, prepare pupils for the assessments, feedback to pupils and parents and move learners on in the appropriate direction. To limit the role of teachers in assessment would be the ultimate misconstrual of the process of teaching and learning. To embrace educational assessment, with the professional involvement of well-trained teachers, will be to harness a powerful tool for learning.

References

AIRASIAN, P. (1988a) 'Measurement driven Instruction: A closer look', *Educational Measurement: Issues and Practice*, winter, pp. 6–11.

AIRASIAN, P. (1988b) 'Symbolic validation: The case of state-mandated, high-stakes testing', *Education Evaluation and Policy Analysis*, 10, 4.

ALEXANDER, R., ROSE, J. and WOODHEAD, C. (1992) *Curriculum Organisation and Classroom Practice in Primary Schools*, London, DES.

AMERICAN EDUCATIONAL RESEARCH ASSOCIATION, AMERICAN PSYCHOLOGICAL ASSOCIATION, NATIONAL COUNCIL ON MEASUREMENT IN EDUCATION (1985) *Standards for educational and psychological testing*, Washington, DC, AERA, APA, NCME.

AMERICAN PSYCHOLOGICAL ASSOCIATION (1974) *Standards for Educational and Psychological Tests*, Washington, DC, APA.

AMERICAN PSYCHOLOGICAL ASSOCIATION (1985) *Joint Technical Standards for Educational and Psychological Testing*, Washington, DC, APA.

APPLE, M.W. (1989) 'How equality has been redefined in the Conservative restoration', in SECADA, W. (Ed) *Equity and Education*, New York, Falmer Press.

ATKINS, M., BEATTIE, J. and DOCKRELL, B. (1992) *Assessment Issues in Higher Education*, Newcastle School of Education, University of Newcastle.

BAKER, E. (1992) *The Role of Domain Specifications in Improving the Technical Quality of Performance Assessment*, CRESST/UCLA.

BAKER, E. and O'NEIL, H. (1994) 'Performance assessment and equity: A view from the USA', *Assessment in Education*, 1, 1.

BAKER, E., O'NEIL, H. and LINN, R. (1991) '*Policy and validity prospects for performance-based assessment*', paper presented at APA annual meeting, August.

BENNETT, S.N. (1982) 'Time to teach: Teaching-learning processes in primary schools', in WILKINSON, W.J. and GEORGE, N.J. (Eds) *Pupil Behaviour and Performance: Recent Theory and Research*, Hull, University of Hull.

BENNETT, S.N. and DESFORGES, C. (1985) 'Recent advances in classroom research', *British Journal of Educational Psychology Monograph Series No 2*, Scottish Academic Press.

BENNETT, S.N., DESFORGES, C., COCKBURN, A. and WILKINSON, B. (1984) *The Quality of Pupil Learning Experiences*, London, Lawrence Erlbaum Associates.

BENNETT, N. and KELL, J. (1989) *A Good Start? Four Year Olds in Infant Schools*, Oxford, Blackwell.

BEREITER, C. and SCARDAMALIA, M. (1989) 'Intentional learning as a goal of instruction', in RESNICK, L. (1989) (Ed.) *Knowing, Learning and Instruction. Essays in honour of R Glaser*, New Jersey, Lawrence Erlbaum Associates.

BERLAK, H., NEWMANN, F., ADAMS, E., ARCHBALD, D., BURGESS, T., RAVEN, J. and ROMBERG, T. (1992) *Towards a New Science of Educational Testing and Assessment*, New York, State University of New York Press.

BLACK, P. (1993a) 'The shifting scenery of the National Curriculum', in CHITTY, C. and SIMON, B. (Eds) *Education Answers Back*, London, Lawrence Wishart.

BLACK, P.J. (1993b) 'Formative and summative assessment by teachers', *Studies in Science Education*, 21, pp. 49–97.

BLATCHFORD, P. (1992) 'Academic self-assessment at 7 and 11 years: Its accuracy and association with ethnic group and sex', *British Journal of Educational Psychology*, 63, pp. 35–44.

BLOOM, B.S. (1976) *Human Characteristics and School Learning*, New York, McGraw-Hill.

BROADFOOT, P. (1993) *'Performance assessment in perspective: Some international insights'*, paper presented at the AERA Conference, Atlanta.

BROADFOOT, P. (1994) *Educational Assessment: The Myth of Measurement*, Inaugural Lecture, University of Bristol.

BROADFOOT, P., JAMES, M., MCMEEKING, S., NUTTALL, D. and STIERER, S. (1988) *Records of Achievement: Report of the National Evaluation of Pilot Schemes* (PRAISE), London, HMSO.

BROWN, A., ASH, D., RUTHERFORD, M., NAKAGAWA, K., GORDON, A. and CAMPIONE, J. (1993) 'Distributed expertise in the classroom', in SALOMON, G. (Ed) *Distributed Cognitions*, New York, Cambridge University Press.

BROWN, A., CAMPIONE, J., WEBBER, L. and McGILLY, K. (1992) 'Interactive learning environments: A new look at assessment and instruction' in GIFFORD, B. and O'CONNOR, M. (Eds) *Changing Assessments: Alternative Views of Aptitude, Achievement and Instruction*, Boston, Kluwer Academic.

BROWN, M. (1988) 'Issues in formulating and organising attainment targets in relation to their assessment', in TORRANCE, H. (Ed) *National Assessment and Testing: A Research Response*, London, British Educational Research Association.

BROWN, M. (1991) 'Problematic issues in national assessment', *Cambridge Journal of Education*, 21, 2.

BROWN, M. (1992) 'Elaborate nonsense? The muddled tale of SATs in mathematics at KS 3', in GIPPS, C. (Ed) *Developing Assessment for the National Curriculum*, London, ULIE/Kogan Page.

BUTKOWSKY, I.S. and WILLOWS, D.M. (1980) 'Cognitive-motivational characteristics of children varying in reading ability: Evidence of learned helplessness in poor readers', *Journal of Educational Psychology*, 72, pp. 408–22.

CANNELL, J.J. (1987) *Nationally Normed Elementary Achievement Testing in America's Public Schools: How all 50 States are above the National Average*, WV Daniels, Friends for Education.

CANNELL, J.J. (1988) 'Nationally normed elementary achievement testing in America's public schools: How all 50 states are above the national average', *Educational Measurement: Issues and Practice*, 7, 2, pp. 5–9.

CANNELL, J.J. (1989) *The Lake Wobegon Report: How Public Educators Cheat on Standardised Achievement Tests*, Albuquerque, NM, Friends for Education.

CHAPMAN, J.W. (1988) 'Learning disabled children's self-concepts', *Review of Educational Research*, 58, 3, pp. 347–71.

CHITTY, C. and SIMON, B. (Eds) (1993) *Education Answers Back*, London, Lawrence Wishart.

CLARK, J.L. (1993) '*Targets and target-related assessment: Hong Kong's curriculum and assessment project*', paper presented at IAEA Conference, Mauritius.

COLE, N. and MOSS, P. (1989) 'Bias in test use', in LINN, R. (Ed) (3rd edn) *Educational Measurement*, AERA/NCME, Macmillan.

COOPERSMITH, S. (1967) *The Antecedents of Self-Esteem*, San Francisco, CA, WH Freeman.

CORBETT, D. and WILSON, B. (1988) 'Raising the stakes in state-wide minimum competency testing', *Politics of Education Association Yearbook*, pp. 27–39.

CORBETT, D. and WILSON, B. (1990) '*Unintended and unwelcome: The local impact of state testing*', paper presented at the AERA Conference, April, Boston.

CRASKE, M.L. (1988) 'Learned helplessness, self-worth motivation and attribution retraining for primary school children', *British Journal of Educational Psychology*, 58, pp. 152–64.

CROCKER, A.C. and CHEESEMAN, R.G. (1988a) 'The ability of young children to rank themselves for academic ability', *Educational Studies*, 14, 1, pp. 105–10.

CROCKER, A.C. and CHEESEMAN, R.G. (1988b) 'Infant teachers have a major impact on children's self-awareness', *Children and Society*, 2, pp. 3–8.

CRONBACH, L. (1988) 'Five perspectives on validity argument', in WEINER, H. and BRAUN, H. (Eds) Princeton, NJ, *Test Validity*, Erlbaum.

CRONBACH, L.J. (1980) 'Validity on parole: How can we go straight?', *New Directions for Testing and Measurement: Measuring Achievement over a Decade*, proceedings of the 1979 ETS Invitational Conference, San Francisco, CA, Jossey-Bass.

CROOKS, T.J. (1988) 'The impact of classroom evaluation practices on students', *Review of Educational Research*, 58, 4.

DAUGHERTY, R. (1994) *National Curriculum Assessment: A Review of Policy 1987–1993*, London, Falmer Press (in Press).

DEPARTMENT OF EDUCATION, N.Z. (1989) *Assessment for Better Learning: A Public Discussion Document*, Wellington, NZ, Government Printer.

DES (1986) *Education in the Federal Republic of Germany: Aspects of Curriculum and Assessment*, an HMI Report, London, HMSO.

DES (1987a) *The National Curriculum 5–16: A Consultation Document*, London, DES/WO. (the TGAT Report)

DES (1987b) *'Improving the basis for awarding GCSE grades'*, unpublished paper, September (made available to TGAT).

DES (1988) *National Curriculum Task Group on Assessment and Testing: A Report*, London, DES/WO. (the TGAT Report)

DFE (1993) *The Education (Assessment Arrangements for the Core Subjects) (Key Stage 1) Order 1993* (Circular 11/93), London, DFE.

DREVER, E. (1988) 'Criterion-referencing and grade-related criteria: The experience of standard grade', in BROWN, S. (Ed) *Assessment: A Changing Practice*, Edinburgh, Scottish Academic Press.

DUNBAR, S., KORETZ, D. and HOOVER, H.D. (1991) 'Quality control in the development and use of performance assessments', *Applied Measurement in Education*, 4, 4, pp. 289–303.

DWECK, C.S. (1986) 'Motivational processes affecting learning', *American Psychologist*, 41, pp. 1040–8.

DWECK, C.S., DAVIDSON, W., NELSON, S. and ENNA, B. (1978) 'Sex differences in learned helplessness: II The contingencies of evaluative feedback in the classroom and III, An experimental analysis', *Developmental Psychology*, 14, 3, pp. 268–76.

DWECK, C.S. and GILLIARD, D. (1975) 'Expectancy statements as determinants of reactions to failure: Sex differences in persistence and expectancy change', *Journal of Personal and Social Psychology*, 32, pp. 1077–84.

EDUCATIONAL TESTING SERVICE (1986) *ETS Standards for Quality and Fairness*, Princeton, NJ, ETS.

EDWARDS, D. and MERCER, N. (1989) *Common Knowledge*, London, Routledge.

EISNER, E. (1993) 'Reshaping assessment in education: Some criteria in search of practice', *Journal Curriculum Studies*, 25, 3, pp. 219–33.

ENTWISTLE, N. (1992) *The Impact of Teaching on Learning Outcomes in Higher Education*, Sheffield, CVCP, Staff Development Unit.

FILER, A. (1993) 'Contexts of assessment in a primary classroom', *British Educational Research Journal*, 19, 1.

FRECHTLING, J. (1991) 'Performance assessment: Moonstruck or the real thing?', *Educational Measurement: Issues and Practice*, winter.

FREDERIKSEN, J. and COLLINS, A. (1989) 'A systems approach to educational testing', *Educational Researcher*, 18, 9, pp. 27–32.

FREDERIKSEN, N. (1984) 'The real test bias: Influences of testing on teaching and learning', *American Psychologist*, 39, 3, March, pp. 193–202.

GIPPS, C. (1990) *Assessment: A Teachers' Guide to the Issues*, London, Hodder and Stoughton.

GIPPS, C. (1991) unpublished report of ULIE visit to Academy of Pedagogical Science, Moscow, March.

GIPPS, C. (1992a) *'National testing at seven: What can it tell us?'*, paper presented at the AERA conference, April, San Francisco.

GIPPS, C. (1992b) *What We Know About Effective Primary Teaching*, London File, Tufnell Press.

GIPPS, C. (1993a) *'Reliability validity and manageability in large scale performance assessment'*, paper presented at the AERA conference, April, Atlanta.

GIPPS, C. (1993b) 'The profession of educational research', BERA Presidential Address, *British Educational Research Journal*, 19, 1, pp. 3–16.

GIPPS, C. and GOLDSTEIN, H. (1983) *Monitoring Children: An Evaluation of the Assessment of Performance Unit*, London, Heinemann Educational Books.

GIPPS, C., McCALLUM, B., McALISTER, S. and BROWN, M. (1992) 'National assessment at seven: Some emerging themes', in GIPPS,

C. (Ed) *Developing Assessment for the National Curriculum*, London, Bedford Way Series, ULIE/Kogan Page.

GIPPS, C. and STOBART, G. (1993) *Assessment: A Teachers' Guide to the Issues* (2nd edn), London, Hodder and Stoughton.

GIPPS, C. and MURPHY, P. (1994) *A Fair Test? Assessment, Achievement and Equity*, Milton Keynes, Open University Press.

GIPPS, C., STEADMAN, S., STIERER, B. and BLACKSTONE, T. (1983) *Testing Children, Standardised Testing in Schools and LEAs*, London, Heinemann Educational Books.

GIPPS, C., BROADFOOT, P., DOCKRELL, B., HARLEN, W. and NUTTALL, D. (1993) 'Problems in national assessment: A research critique', in BROADFOOT, P., DOCKRELL, B., GIPPS, C., HARLEN, W. and NUTTALL, D. (Eds) *Policy Issues in National Assessment*, BERA Dialogues 7, Multilingual Matters.

GLASER, R. (1963) 'Instructional technology and the measurement of learning outcomes: Some questions', *American Psychologist*, 18, pp. 519–21.

GLASER, R. (1990) 'Toward new models for assessment', *International Journal of Educational Research*, 14, 5, pp. 475–83.

GODDARD-SPEAR, M. (1983) *Sex Bias in Science Teachers' Ratings of Work*, Contribution to the Second GASAT Conference, Oslo, Norway.

GOLDSTEIN, H. (1992) *Recontextualising Mental Measurement*, London, ICRA Research Working Paper, ULIE. [Published in *Educational Mreasurement: Issues and Practice* 1994, Vol. 13, 1]

GOLDSTEIN, H. (1993) 'Assessing group differences', *Oxford Review of Education*, 19, 2, pp. 141–50.

GOLDSTEIN, H. and WOOD, R. (1989) 'Five decades of item response modelling', *British Journal of Mathematical and Statistical Psychology*, 42, pp. 139–67.

GROSVENOR, R.W. (1993) '*Developing a new certification programme incorporating internal and external criterion-based assessment*', paper presented at the IAEA Conference, Mauritius.

GUBA, E. and LINCOLN, Y. (1989) *Fourth Generation Evaluation*, London Sage.

GUION, R.M. (1980) 'On trinitarian doctrines of validity', *Professional Psychology*, 11, pp. 385–98.

GURNEY, P. (1987) 'Self-esteem enhancement in children: A review of research findings', *Educational Research*, 29, 2, pp. 130–6.

GURNEY, P. (1988) *Self Esteem in Children with Special Educational Needs*, London, Routledge.

HAERTEL, E. (1991) 'New forms of teacher assessment', *Review of Research in Education*, 17, pp. 3–29.

HAERTEL, E. (1992) 'Performance measurement', in ALKIN, M. (Ed) *Encyclopedia of Educational Research* (6th edn), London, Macmillan Publishing.

HAERTEL, E. (1993) *'Evolving conceptions of the generalisability of perform-ance assessments'*, paper presented at the AERA conference, April, Atlanta.

HALADYNA, T., NOLEN, S. and HAAS, N. (1991) 'Raising standardised achievement test scores and the origins of test score pollution', *Educational Researcher*, 20, 5, pp. 2–7.

HAMBLETON, R.K. and ROGERS, H.J. (1991) 'Advances in criterion-referenced measurement', in HAMBLETON, R.K. and ZAAL, J.N. (Eds) *Advances in Educational and Psychological Testing: Theory and Applications*, London, Kluwer Academic Publishers.

HANEY, W. and MADAUS, G. (1989) 'Searching for alternatives to standardised tests: The whats, whys and whithers', *Phi Delta Kappa*, 70, 9, pp. 683–7.

HANEY, W. and MADAUS, G. (1991) 'The evolution of ethical and tech-nical standards for testing', in HAMBLETON, R.K. and ZAAL, J.N. (Eds) *Advances in Educational and Psychological Testing: Theory and Applications*, London, Kluwer Academic Publishers.

HANEY, W., MADAUS, G. and LYONS, R. (1993) *The Fractured Mar-ketplace for Standardized Testing*, London, Kluwer Academic Publishers.

HANSEN, J. (1993) *'Assessment in the year 2001: The darkness and the light'*, paper presented at the NCME Conference, April, Atlanta.

HARGREAVES, A. (1986) 'Record breakers?' in BROADFOOT, P. (Ed) *Profiles and Records of Achievement*, London, Holt, Rinehart and Winston.

HARGREAVES, A. and REYNOLDS, D. (1988) 'The crisis of motivation and assessment' in *Education Policies: Controversies and Critiques*, London, Falmer Press.

HARLEN, W. (Ed) (1994) *Enhancing Quality in Assessment*, BERA Policy Task Group on Assessment, Paul Chapman Publishers.

HARLEN, W., GIPPS, C., BROADFOOT, P. and NUTTALL, D. (1992) 'Assessment and the improvement of education', *The Curriculum Journal*, 3, 3.

HARNISCH, D. and MABRY, L. (1993) 'Issues in the development and evaluation of alternative assessments', *Journal of Curriculum Studies*, 25, 2, pp. 179–87.

HMI (1979) *Aspects of Secondary Education in England*, London, HMSO.

HMI (1988) *The Introduction of the GCSE in Schools 1986–1988*, Lon-don, HMSO.

HOLMES, E. (1911) *What Is and What Might Be*, London, Constable and Co Ltd.

IVIC, I. (1991) '*Theories of mental development and the problem of education outcomes*', paper presented at the General Assembly of the ANES Project September, Switzerland, CERI/OECD.

JAMES, M. and CONNER, C. (1993) 'Are reliability and validity achievable in National Curriculum assessment? Some observations on moderation at Key Stage One in 1992', *The Curriculum Journal*, 4, 1.

JENSEN, M. (1985) 'Development of a pre-school self-concept scale', *Early Child Development and Care*, 22, pp. 89–107.

JESSUP, G. (1991) *Outcomes: NVQs and the Emerging Model of Education and Training*, London, Falmer Press.

JOHNSON, C. and BLINKHORN, S. (1992) *Validating NVQ Assessment*, Technical Report No 7, Employment Department Methods Strategies Unit.

JOINT COMMITTEE ON TESTING PRACTICES (1988) *Code of Fair Testing Practices in Education*, Washington, DC, JCTP.

KELLAGHAN, T. and MADAUS, G. (1993) '*Using public examinations to improve motivation*', paper prese nted at the AERA conference, April, Atlanta.

KELLAGHAN, T., MADAUS, G. and AIRASIAN, P. (1982) *The Effects of Standardised Testing*, Boston, MA, Klumer Nijhoff Publishing.

KINGDON, M. and STOBART, G. (1987) *The Draft Grade Criteria: A Review of LEAG Research*, LEAG Discussion Paper.

KORETZ, D. (1988) 'Arriving in Lake Wobegon: Are standardised tests exaggerating achievement and distorting instruction?', *American Educator*, 12, 2.

KORETZ, D., LINN, R., DUNBAR, S. and SHEPARD, L. (1991) '*The effects of high stakes testing on achievement: Preliminary findings about generalization across tests*', paper presented to the AERA/NCME, April, Chicago.

KORETZ, D., McCAFFREY, D., KLEIN, S., BELL, R. and STECHER, B. (1993) *The Reliability of Scores from the Vermont Portfolio Assessment Program*, CSE Technical Report 355, CRESST, UCLA.

KORETZ, D., STECHER, B. and DIEBERT, E. (1992) *The Vermont Portfolio Assessment Program: Interim Report*, CRESST, February.

KUHN, T.S. (1970) *The Structure of Scientific Revolutions*, Chicago, IL, University of Chicago Press.

KULHAVEY, R.W. (1977) 'Feedback in written instruction', *Review of Educational Research*, 47, 1, pp. 211–32.

KULIK, J.A., KULIK, C-L.C. and BANGERT-DROWNS, R.L. (1990) 'Effectiveness of mastery learning programs: A meta-analysis', *Review of Educational Research*, 60, pp. 265–300.

LANE, S., STONE, C., ANKENMAUM, R. and LIU, M. (1992) *'Empirical evidence for the reliability and validity of performance assessments'*, paper presented at the AERA conference, San Francisco.

LAWRENCE, D. (1988) *Enhancing Self-Esteem in the Classroom*, London, Chapman.

LE UNES, A.K., NATION, J.R. and TURLEY, N.M. (1980) 'Male-female performance in learned helplessness', *Journal of Psychology*, 104, pp. 255–8.

LINDQUIST, E.F. (1951) 'Preliminary considerations in objective text construction', in LINDQUIST, E.F. (Ed) *Educational Measurement*, American Council on Education, Washington, Macmillan. pp. 119–184.

LINN, M.C. (1992) 'Gender differences in educational achievement' in Educational Testing Service *Sex Equity in Educational Opportunity, Achievement and Testing*, Princeton, NJ, E.T.S.

LINN, R.L. (1980) 'Issues of validity for criterion-referenced measures', *Applied Psychological Measurement*, 4, 4, Fall.

LINN, R.L. (1981) *'Curricular validity: Convincing the courts that it was taught without precluding the possibility of measuring it'*, paper presented at the Ford Foundation conference, October, Boston College, MA.

LINN, R.L. (Ed) (1989) *Educational Measurement* (3rd edn), American Council on Education, Washington Macmillan.

LINN, R.L. (1992) *'Linking results of distinct assessments'*, unpublished, August.

LINN, R.L. (1993a) 'Educational assessment: Expanded expectations and challenges', *Educational Evaluation and Policy Analysis*, 15, 1.

LINN, R.L. (1993b) *'Criterion-referenced measurement: A celebrated and frequently elaborated concept needed for the 21st century*, paper presented at the AERA conference, April, Atlanta.

LINN, R.L., BAKER, E. and DUNBAR, S. (1991) 'Complex, performance-based assessment: Expectations and validation criteria', *Educational Researcher*, 20, 8, pp. 15–21.

LINN, R.L., GRAVE, E. and SANDERS, N. (1990) 'Comparing state and district test results to national norms: The validity of the claim that "everyone is above average" ', *Educational Measurement: Issues and Practice*, 5, 14, Fall.

McCALLUM, B., McALISTER, S., BROWN, M. and GIPPS, C. (1993) 'Teacher assessment at Key Stage One', *Research Papers in Education*, 8, 3, pp. 305–27.

McGAW, B. (1993) *Presidential Address*, IAEA Conference, May, Mauritius.

McIntyre, D. and Brown, S. (1978) 'The conceptualisation of attainment', *British Educational Research Journal*, 4, 2, pp. 41–50.

Madaus, G. (1988) 'The influence of testing on the curriculum' in Tanner (Ed) *Critical Issues in Curriculum*, 87th Yearbook of NSSE Part 1, Chicago, IL, University of Chicago Press.

Madaus, G. (1992a) *'Educational measurement in America: What's right, what's wrong? A proper-use perspective'*, paper presented at the AERA conference, April, San Francisco.

Madaus, G. (1992b) 'An independent auditing mechanism for testing', *Educational Measurement: Issues and Practice*, Spring, pp. 26–31.

Madaus, G. (1992c) *'A technological and historical consideration of equity issues associated with proposals to change the nation's testing policy'*, paper presented at the symposium on Equity and Educational Testing and Assessment, March, Washington, DC.

Mehrens, W. (1992) 'Using performance assessment for accountability purposes', *Educational Measurement: Issues and Practice*, spring, pp. 3–20.

Mehrens, W. and Kaminski, J. (1989) 'Methods for improving standardised test scores: Fruitful, fruitless or fraudulent?', *Educational Measurement: Issues and Practice*, Spring, pp. 14–22.

Messick, S. (1981) 'Constructs and their vicissitudes in educational and psychological measurement', *Psychological Bulletin*, 89, pp. 575–88.

Messick, S. (1984) 'The psychology of educational measurement', *Journal of Educational Measurement*, 21, pp. 215–38.

Messick, S. (1989a) 'Validity', in Linn, R. (Ed) *Educational Measurement* (3rd edn) American Council on Education, Washington, Macmillan.

Messick, S. (1989b) 'Meaning and values in test validation: The science and ethics of assessment', *Educational Researcher*, 18, 2, pp. 5–11.

Messick, S. (1992) *The Interplay of Evidence and Consequences in the Validation of Performance Assessments*, Research Report ETS, July.

Meyer, C.A. (1992) 'What's the difference between authentic and performance assessment?', *Educational Leadership*, 49, 8.

Miller, D. and Seraphine, A. (1992) *'Teaching to the test with alternative assessment'*, paper presented at the NCME conference, April, San Francisco.

Mislevy, R.J. (1992) *Linking Educational Assessments. Concepts, Issues, Methods and Prospects*, Princeton, NJ, ETS.

Mislevy, R.J. (1993) *'Test theory reconceived'*, paper presented at the NCME conference, April, Atlanta.

Mitchell, R. and Kane, M. (1992) *Evaluating Educational Reform:*

Assessment of Student Performance, Draft Report Pelavin Associates Inc. Washington, DC.

MORTIMORE, P., SAMMONS, P., STOLL, L., LEWIS, D. and ECOB, R. (1988) *School Matters: The Junior Years*, Wells, Open Books.

MOSS, P.A. (1992) 'Shifting conceptions of validity in educational measurement: Implications for performance assessment', *Review of Educational Research*, 62, 3, pp. 229–58.

MURPHY, P. (1993) '*Some teacher dilemmas in practising authentic assessment*', paper presented to the AERA Conference, April, Atlanta.

MURPHY, R. (1982) 'A further report of investigations into the reliability of marking of GCE examinations', *BJEP*, 52, pp. 58–63.

MURPHY, R. (1986) 'The emperor has no clothes: Grade criteria and the GCSE' in GIPPS, C. (Ed) *The GCSE: An Uncommon Exam* London, ULIE, Bedford Way Paper No 29.

MURPHY, R. (1990) 'National assessment proposals: Analysing the debate' in FLUDE, M. and HAMMER, M. (Eds) *The Education Reform Act 1988*, London, Falmer Press.

NATIONAL FORUM ON ASSESSMENT (1992) 'Criteria for evaluation of student assessment systems', *Educational Measurement: Issues and Practice*, Spring, p. 32.

NEEDS (1990) *GCSE Coursework and its Management*, The NEEDS project, London, ULEAC.

NFER/BGC (1991) *An Evaluation of National Curriculum Assessment: Report 3*, June.

NFER/BGC (1992) *An Evaluation of the 1992 National Curriculum Assessment at KS1*, September.

NISBET, J. (1993) 'Introduction' in *Curriculum Reform: Assessment in Question* Paris, OECD.

NISEAC (1991) *Pupil Assessment in Northern Ireland*, Advice to Lord Belstead, Paymaster General, January.

NORRIS, S.P. (1989) 'Can we test validly for critical thinking?', *Educational Researcher*, 18, 9, pp. 21–6.

NUTTALL, D. (1987) 'The validity of assessments', *European Journal of Psychology of Education*, 11, 2, pp. 109–18.

NUTTALL, D. (1992) 'Performance assessment: The message from England', *Educational Leadership*, 49, 8.

NUTTALL, D., BACKHOUSE, G. and WILLMOTT, A. (1974) *Comparability of Standards Between Subjects*, Schools Council Bulletin 29, Methuen.

OAKES, J. (1991) 'The many-sided dilemmas of testing' in *Voices from the Field: 30 Expert Opinions on America 2000, the Bush Administration Strategy to 'Reinvent' America's Schools*, William T Grant Foundation Commission.

OERI (1992) *Hard Work and High Expectations: Motivating Students to Learn?* Washington, D.C., OERI.

ORR, L. and NUTTALL, D. (1983) *Determining standards in the proposed system of examining at 16+*, Comparability in Examinations Occasional Paper 2, London, Schools Council.

PHILLIPS, D. (1991) 'Assessment in German schools', *Journal of Curriculum Studies*, 23, 6.

PHILLIPS, G. (1990) 'The Lake Wobegon effect', *Educational Measurement: Issues and Practice*, Fall, p. 3 and 14.

PILLINER, A.E.G. (1979) 'Norm-referenced and criterion-referenced tests — An evaluation' in *Issues in Educational Assessment*, Edinburgh, Scottish Education Department, HMSO.

PINTRICH, P.R. and BLUMENFELD, P.C. (1985) 'Classroom experience and children's self-perceptions of ability, effort and conduct', *Journal of Educational Psychology*, 77, 6, pp. 646–57.

PIPHO, C. (1985) 'Tracking the reforms, Part 5: Testing — can it measure the success of the reform movement?', *Education Week*, 22 May, p. 19, quoted in HANEY, W. and MADAUS, G. (1989).

POLLARD, A. (1985) *The Social World of the Primary School*, London, Holt, Rinehart and Winston.

POLLARD, A. (1990) 'Toward a sociology of learning in primary school', *British Journal of Sociology of Education*, 11, 3.

POPHAM, J. (1984) 'Specifying the domain of content or behaviours', in BERK, R.A. (Ed) *A Guide to Criterion-Referenced Test Construction*, Baltimore, MD, John Hopkins University Press.

POPHAM, J. (1987a) 'The merits of measurement-driven instruction', *Phi Delta Kappa*, May, pp. 679–82.

POPHAM, J. (1987b) 'Two-plus decades of educational objectives', *International Journal of Educational Research*, 11, 1.

POPHAM, J. (1992) *Educational testing in America: What's right, what's wrong?*, paper presented at the AERA conference, April, San Francisco.

POPHAM, J. (1993a) *The instructional consequences of criterion-referenced clarity*, paper presented at the AERA conference, April, Atlanta.

POPHAM, J. (1993b) 'Circumventing the high costs of authentic assessment', *Phi Delta Kappan*, February.

RADNOR, H. and SHAW, K. (1994) 'Developing a colaborative approach to moderation: The moderation and assessment project-southwest', in TORRANCE, H. (Ed) *Evaluating Authentic Assessment*, Buckingham, Open University Press.

RESNICK, L. (1989) 'Introduction' in RESNICK, L. (Ed) (1989) Knowing, Learning and Instruction. Essays in honour of R Glaser, New Jersey Lawrence Erlbaum Associates.

RESNICK, L.B. and RESNICK, D.P. (1992) 'Assessing the thinking curriculum: New tools for educational reform', in GIFFORD, B. and O'CONNOR, M. (Eds) *Changing Assessments: Alternative Views of Aptitude, Achievement and Instruction*, London, Kluwer Academic Publishers.

SADLER, R. (1987) 'Specifying and promulgating achievement standards', *Oxford Review of Education*, 13, 2.

SADLER, R. (1989) 'Formative assessment and the design of instructional systems', *Instructional Science*, 18, pp. 119–44.

SADLER, R. (1992a) 'Scaled school assessments: The effect of measurement errors in the scaling test', *Australian Journal of Education*, 36, 1, pp. 30–7.

SADLER, R. (1992b) '*Standards-based assessment in the secondary school: The Queensland experience*', paper presented at the conference 'Qualifications for the 21st Century', January, Wellington, New Zealand Qualifications Authority.

SALMON-COX, L. (1981) 'Teachers and standardised achievement tests: What's really happening?', *Phi Delta Kappa*, May.

SATTERLY, D. (1994) 'The quality of external assessment', in HARLEN, W. (Ed) *Enhancing Quality in Assessment*, Paul Chapman Publishers.

SCHAGEN, I. and HUTCHISON, D. (1991) *Reliability and Allied Measurements for Criterion-Referenced Assessment*, Final Report to ESRC, December, Windsor, NFER.

SEAC (1989) *Progress Report on the GCSE*, July.

SEAC (1991) *National Curriculum Assessment at Key Stage 3: A Review of the 1991 Pilots with Implications for 1992*, EMU, SEAC.

SEAC (1992) 'National Curriculum assessment: Assessment arrangements for core and other foundation subjects', *A Moderator's Handbook 1991/2*, London, SEAC.

SEAC (1993) *School Assessment Folder*, London, SEAC.

SEC (1984) *The Development of Grade-Related Criteria for the GCSE: A briefing Paper for Working Parties*, London, SEC.

SEC (1985) *Differentiated Assessment in GCSE*, Working Paper One, London, SEC.

SENIOR SECONDARY ASSESSMENT BOARD OF SOUTH AUSTRALIA (1988) *Assessment and Moderation Policy*, Information Booklet No 2.

SHAVELSON, R., BAXTER, G. and PINE, J. (1992) 'Performance assessments: Political rhetoric and measurement reality', *Educational Researcher*, 21, 4.

SHEPARD, L. (1990) 'Inflated test score gains: Is the problem old norms or teaching to the test?', *Educational Measurement: Issues and Practice*, Fall, pp. 15–22.

SHEPARD, L. (1991) 'Psychometricians' beliefs about learning', *Educational Researcher*, 20, 7.

SHEPARD, L. (1992a) 'What policy makers who mandate tests should know about the new psychology of intellectual ability and learning', in GIFFORD, B. and O'CONNOR, M. (Eds) *Changing Assessments: Alternative Views of Aptitude, Achievement and Instruction* London, Kluwer Academic Publishers.

SHEPARD, L. (1992b) *Will National Tests Improve Student Learning?*, CSE Technical Report 342, CRESST, University of Colorado, Boulder.

SHEPARD, L. (1993) 'Evaluating test validity', *Review of Research in Education*, 19, pp. 405–50.

SHORROCKS, D., DANIELS, S., FROBISHER, L., NELSON, N., WATERSON, A. and BELL, J. (1992) *ENCA 1 Project Report*, London, SEAC.

SMITH, M.L. (1991a) 'Put to the test: The effects of external testing on teachers', *Educational Researcher*, 20, 5, June-July, pp. 8–11.

SMITH, M.L. (1991b) 'Meanings of test preparation', *American Educational Research Journal*, 28, 3.

STERNBERG, R.J. (1981) 'Testing and cognitive psychology', *American Psychologist*, 36, pp. 1181–9.

STIGGINS, R.J. (1992) 'Two disciplines of educational assessment', paper presented at ECS Assessment Conference June 1992, Boulder, Colorado. In Press: *Measurement and Evaluation in Counseling and Development*.

STIGGINS, R. and BRIDGEFORD, N. (1982) '*The role of performance assessment in day to day classroom assessment and evaluation*', paper presented at the NCME conference, March, New York.

SWAIN, M. (1990) 'Second language testing and second language acquisition: Is there a conflict with traditional psychometrics?', in *Georgetown University Round Table on Languages and Linguistics*, Washington, DC, Georgetown University Press.

TITTLE, C.K. (1989) 'Validity: Whose construction is it in the teaching and learning context?', *Educational Measurement: Issues and Practice*, 8, 1, Spring.

TIZARD, B., BLATCHFORD, P., BURKE, J., FARQUHAR, C. and PLEWIS, I. (1988) *Young Children at School in the Inner City*, Hove, Lawrence Erlbaum Associates.

TORRANCE, H. (1991) 'Records of achievement and formative assessment: Some complexities of practice', in STAKE, R. (Ed) *Advances in Program Evaluation*, 1, Part A, London, JAI Press.

TORRANCE, H. (1993a) 'Formative assessment — Some theoretical problems and empirical questions', *Cambridge Journal of Education*, 23, 3.

TORRANCE, H. (1993b) *'Assessment, curriculum and theories of learning: Some thoughts on assessment and postmodernism'*, paper presented to ESRC/BERA Seminar, June Liverpool.

VAN OUDENHOVEN, J.P. and SIERO, F. (1985) 'Evaluative feedback as a determinant of the Pygmalion effect', *Psychological Reports*, 57, pp. 755–61.

WALKERDINE, V. (1984) 'Developmental psychology and the child centred pedagogy' in HENRIQUES, J. *et al.* (Eds) *Changing the Subject: Psychology, Social Regulation and Subjectivity*, London, Methuen.

WHITE, R.T. (1992) 'Implications of recent research on learning for curriculum and assessment', *Journal of Curriculum Studies*, 24, 2, pp. 153–64.

WIGGINS, G. (1989a) 'A true test: Toward more authentic and equitable assessment' *Phi Delta Kappa*, 70, pp. 703–13.

WIGGINS, G. (1989b) 'Teaching to the (authentic) test', *Educational Leadership*, 46, 7, pp. 41–7.

WIGGINS, G. (1992) 'Creating tests worth taking', *Educational Leadership*, 49, 8.

WILIAM, D. (1992) 'Some technical issues in assessment: A user's guide, *British Journal of Curriculum and Assessment*, 2, 3, pp. 11–20.

WILIAM, D. (1993) *'Reconceptualising validity, dependability and reliability for National Curriculum assessment*, paper given to BERA Conference, Liverpool.

WILLIS, D. (1992a) 'Educational assessment and accountability: A New Zealand case study', *Journal of Education Policy*, 7, 2.

WILLIS, D. (1992b) *'Learning and assessment: Exposing the inconsistencies of theory and practice'*, paper presented at ULIE, March.

WILSON, M. (1992) 'Educational leverage from a political necessity: Implications of new perspectives on student assessment for chapter I evaluation', *Educational Evaluation and Policy Analysis*, 14, 2, pp. 123–44.

WITTROCK, M.C. and BAKER, E.L. (1991) *Testing and Cognition*, Englewood Cliffs, NJ, Prentice Hall.

WOLF, A. (1993) *Assessment Issues and Problems in a Criterion-Based System*, FEU Occasional Paper.

WOLF, A., KELSON, M. and SILVER, R. (1990) *Learning in Context: Patterns of Skills Transfer and Training Implications*, Sheffield, The Training Agency.

WOLF, D., BIXBY, J., GLENN, J. and GARDNER, H. (1991) 'To use their minds well: Investigating new forms of student assessment', *Review of Research in Education*, 17, pp. 31–74.

WOOD, R. (1986) 'The agenda for educational measurement', in NUTTALL, D. (Ed) *Assessing Educational Achievement*, London, Falmer Press.

WOOD, R. (1987) *Measurement and Assessment in Education and Psychology*, London, Falmer Press.

WOOD, R. (1991) *Assessment and Testing. A Survey of Research*, Cambridge, Cambridge University Press.

Index